Sacred Power, Sacred Space

An Introduction to Christian Architecture and Worship

JEANNE HALGREN KILDE

D1563860

OXFORD
UNIVERSITY PRESS

2008

OXFORD
UNIVERSITY PRESS

Oxford University Press, Inc., publishes works that further
Oxford University's objective of excellence
in research, scholarship, and education.

Oxford   New York
Auckland   Cape Town   Dar es Salaam   Hong Kong   Karachi
Kuala Lumpur   Madrid   Melbourne   Mexico City   Nairobi
New Delhi   Shanghai   Taipei   Toronto

With offices in
Argentina   Austria   Brazil   Chile   Czech Republic   France   Greece
Guatemala   Hungary   Italy   Japan   Poland   Portugal   Singapore
South Korea   Switzerland   Thailand   Turkey   Ukraine   Vietnam

Published by Oxford University Press, Inc.
198 Madison Avenue, New York, New York 10016

www.oup.com

Oxford is a registered trademark of Oxford University Press

Library of Congress Cataloging-in-Publication Data
Kilde, Jeanne Halgren, 1957–
Sacred power, sacred space : an introduction to Christian architecture and worship /
Jeanne Halgren Kilde.
  p. cm.
Includes bibliographical references and index.
ISBN 978-0-19-531469-4; 978-0-19-533606-1 (pbk.)
1. Liturgy and architecture—History.   2. Church architecture—History.   I. Title.
NA4605.K48 2008
246'.909—dc22   2007040449

9 8 7 6 5 4 3 2 1

Printed in the United States of America
on acid-free paper

For Paul R. Kilde, Jr.

Acknowledgments

Among the many debts of gratitude I have incurred along the way in writing this book, I most want to recognize the generous and expert suggestions made by several friends and colleagues who read early drafts of various chapters, provided helpful suggestions, and offered encouragement: Peter Williams, Marilyn Chiat, Gretchen Buggeln, Michael Driscoll, the anonymous reviewer for Oxford University Press, Jeanne Barker-Nunn, Calvin Roetzel, and Susan Graham. Numerous people stepped up to provide illustrations, and they, too, have my enduring gratitude. Also, I want to note that this synthetic survey rests upon the meticulous scholarship of many gifted researchers to whom I owe a great debt of gratitude. Finally, I dedicate this book to my husband, Paul Kilde, who convinced me that this would be a useful project and provided aid and encouragement every step of the way.

Contents

Illustrations

Sacred Power, Sacred Space

I

A Method for Thinking about Power Dynamics in Christian Space

Religious space is dynamic space. Religious spaces house religious ritual, of course, but they do far more than simply provide the setting within which ritual takes place. They contribute in important ways to the very meaning of ritual practices and to the shape and content of religious systems themselves. Consider Christian churches, for instance. Church buildings influence worship practices, facilitating some activities and impeding others. They focus the attention of believers on the divine, and they frequently mediate the relationship between the individual and God. They change with religious activities over time. They contribute to the formation and maintenance of internal relationships within congregations. They designate hierarchy and they demarcate community, serving a multiplicity of users with a host of objectives. They teach insiders and outsiders about Christianity, and they convey messages about the religious group housed in the building to the community at large. Indeed, church buildings are dynamic agents in the construction, development, and persistence of Christianity itself.

This dynamic character renders religious space a particularly complex subject. The diversity among types of church buildings; their multiple functions and various users; their embedded layers of religious, social, and cultural meaning; and their tendency to change dramatically over time create real challenges for those who wish to augment their understanding of Christianity with a knowledge of the architecture of worship. The purpose of this book is to provide a method for sorting through this dynamism, a set of questions and categories that can guide a systematic analysis of space. Although we will be focusing on Christian architecture, this method can also be applied to other traditions and thus provides a foundation for comparative work across religions.

The following chapters will demonstrate this method with a brief tour through the historical development of Christian church buildings, beginning with the earliest Christian worship spaces described in Christian scriptures and proceeding chronologically through history to the present day. In each period under discussion in this admittedly rapid survey, we will examine some of the fundamental features of churches, with an eye toward unpacking the meanings within them. Along the way, we will trace the general patterns of change in Christian church space and worship practices over the past two millennia. By the end of the book, readers will have seen a specific set of categories and accompanying questions applied to a variety of buildings existing within a host of social, cultural, political, and religious circumstances. Having completed this introduction, readers will be well equipped to think critically about the dynamism of Christian space and to pursue much more detailed analyses of not only the spaces and buildings of Christians, but those of other religious groups as well.

Three Types of Power in Religious Space

Religious space is powerful space. Within it the awesome power of the divine is often understood to dwell. Proximity to this power is deemed to yield authority and spiritual empowerment to individuals. The power of religious leaders is made manifest within religious space, their authority indicated in various ways. Similarly, the relative influence of ordinary believers is embedded in religious space as are profound personal experiences of the divine. Power, then, comes in three different categories: (1) divine or supernatural power, or that attributed to God; (2) social power, or that pertaining to a variety of social, particularly clerical, hierarchies; and (3) personal power, or the various feelings of spiritual empowerment that individuals derive from an experience of the divine. This categorization of power, which will provide the methodological foundation of our study of Christian space, draws upon almost three generations of scholarly work on religious space.

The most familiar way of thinking about religious space was elaborated by noted history of religions scholar Mircea Eliade in his landmark book, *The Sacred and the Profane*. In this book, Eliade explores how cultures sense and respond to the presence of divine power within certain spaces. For Eliade, "every sacred space implies a hierophany" or an "irruption of the sacred."[1] Places are deemed sacred precisely because a divine or supernatural power dwells in them. These powerful places help to center the community, orienting its members to the rest of the nonsacred, or profane, world. These holy centers orient individuals and groups "vertically," creating a spatial link between heavenly power above and the more problematic, even evil, power of the underworld below. They also orient groups "horizontally," dividing the landscape into sacred centers and profane fringes, imprinting a hierarchy of meaning onto the very earth itself. The presence of the divine, this *axis mundi*, or world center, broadcasts spiritual meanings that provide context for all other spaces and knowledge.[2]

Eliade's view is termed *substantive* because it emphasizes the substance of the supernatural or divine presence and views certain spaces as being inherently sacred due to that supernatural presence within them. This perspective, of course, is how believers have looked upon the sacred spaces of their cultures for eons. From indigenous peoples of the world to the ancient Greeks to the early Jews to many present-day Christians, many religious groups have believed and do believe that particular gods or powers exist or reside within certain places. Frequently, groups mark those places with buildings. A *temple* is the quintessential building created to house a god. Hindu temples shelter stone or bronze sculptures (called *murti*), which the deities have been invited to inhabit. Within Hindu temples, priests perform numerous rituals, including the daily waking, bathing, and feeding of those deities, as well as the offering of prayers and praise. Worshippers bring offerings of food and materials for the god and perform other acts of worship called *puja*. Similarly, ancient Greek temples such as the Parthenon housed mammoth statues of gods—Athena, for instance, in the Parthenon—which were also understood to be inhabited by their divine presences. The Jewish Temple of Solomon can also be included in this category as it was constructed to house both the Ark of the Lord, the symbol of the covenant between the people and its G-d, as well as the divine presence, or Shekhinah. In contemporary times, similar perspectives remain central to the beliefs of many groups. Many Native American groups, for instance, base moral and legal claims to certain lands upon a substantive understanding of an indwelling spiritual essence within them. Similarly, Latter-day Saints, or Mormons, invest their temples with the belief that the divine is particularly present within.

Although many religious groups firmly believe in the physical presence of the divine within certain spaces, others have viewed the supernatural "presence" within sacred spaces as metaphorical—although there is often a very fine line between "real" presence and metaphorical presence. In Christianity, the language of "real presence," of course, echoes language used to describe Jesus's presence in the elements of the Eucharist, and, in many ways, the situations parallel one another. For instance, Roman Catholics, who believe in the real (substantive) presence of the Lord in the consecrated bread and wine of the Eucharist meal, similarly tend to believe in a real divine presence within their churches. One feels close to God, many Catholics feel, within a shrine, church, or cathedral. Many believe that the grotto at Lourdes, for instance, commemorating the three appearances of the Virgin Mary to St. Bernadette beginning in 1858, is infused with the healing power of her continued, holy presence through the water that flows from the spring within it. In contrast, many Protestants, although seeing churches as places of great spiritual importance, view neither the buildings nor the bread and wine of the communion service as necessarily filled with a real presence of God. Buildings shelter the worshipping community but are not necessarily infused with the divine. As we shall see, there are many perspectives on this question of the presence of divine elements within churches.

Although Eliade linked sacred space to the presence of the divine, others have suggested that such a view is too narrow to account for the many human understandings of religious space. Scholar of religion Jonathan Z. Smith discusses a variety of attributes of Christian sacred space in his book *To Take Place*, an exploration of ancient Jewish and early Christian understandings of religious spaces. Smith points out that various types of sacred space carried various meanings. For early Christians, the idea of space being imbued with holiness, or the presence of the divine, is illustrated in attempts in the fourth century to memorialize places important in the life of Jesus, including his birthplace and his tomb, venerated in the Church of the Nativity in Bethlehem and the Church of the Holy Sepulcher in Jerusalem, respectively. Early Christians believed that these places, linked closely with crucial events in the life of Christ, were permeated with divine power.[3] Nevertheless, Smith argues, these memorials also demonstrate the opposite idea that societies *create* their sacred spaces, ascribing sacred meanings to spaces and places that previously had no such meanings ascribed to them. To illustrate this, he traces the processes through which such places were identified as important in the life of Jesus centuries after his death. We should keep in mind, then, that although the idea of an indwelling sacred presence appeals to insiders, or believers, within a religious tradition, those on the outside of traditions tend to be more aware of how people within traditions work to establish and then maintain the sacred meanings they generate and connect to places, that is, how they work to *sacralize* certain places.

Along these lines of the human production of sacred space, a variety of processes and dynamics can be seen to contribute to the sacralization of certain places. For instance, Smith argues that the distinctive ways in which religious sites organize or arrange the people who use them constitute an important component of the perceived holiness of a place. Using the instructions for building a temple that appear in the book of Ezekiel as his example, Smith shows that the spaces of the temple were organized hierarchically along the longitudinal axis that ran from the exterior spaces of the building through the interior rooms to the *holy of holies,* the place where the godhead was believed may dwell. The social hierarchy was mapped onto these spaces from the least sacred outer areas that were open to nonbelievers, through the more important semi-exterior spaces reserved for lay believers, to the interior spaces reserved for different levels of the priesthood, to the holy of holies reserved exclusively for the High Priest.[4] Following a similar logic, historian and archaeologist Peter Richardson has used archaeological evidence to discuss the hierarchy of spaces associated with the Second Temple in Jerusalem, outlining a similar ranking of space based upon proximity to the holy of holies.[5] In these cases precise differentiation of space articulated the ranked authority of the several groups. In turn, the very sacredness ascribed to each space rested in part upon its function in defining those ranks, its holiness varying with the ranks themselves.

The relative position of different groups within religious spaces, then, and the power and influence those positions signify, constitute an important defining feature of religious spaces. Indeed, unlike the differing views on whether the presence of the divine is a necessary characteristic of sacred space, the spatial organization of *people* in specific ways is a characteristic shared by all sacred and religious spaces. How people organize themselves and behave within specific places imbue those places with sacred importance. In this view, space is sacralized by human action and behavior, and certain spaces become sacred because people treat them differently from ordinary spaces.

Thus, Smith's analysis of the importance of relational placement points to a significant conclusion: that places are sacred because they are made so by human beings. Places are not inherently holy in Smith's view; sacredness is *situational,* or dependent upon the situation or treatment, not on a substantive indwelling of the supernatural. Groups of believers create holy places by investing certain places or spaces with religious meanings and then acting upon those meanings. Just as many Protestant Christians do not believe that Jesus physically exists within the Eucharist elements, though they still ascribe strong religious meaning to ordinary bread and wine under certain circumstances and through certain actions (e.g., the communal celebration of the Lord's Supper), places, in this view, are similarly redefined under certain circumstances and through certain actions. In effect, people sacralized certain places, thereby literally creating sacred space.

This view significantly challenges the Eliadian perspective of an indwelling divinity as the key feature of sacred space. Although in many cases believers within a religious system do, indeed, reflect the Eliadian interpretation, believing the supernatural to be present in certain places, nonbelievers or outsiders looking in do not see an indwelling supernatural force but rather human behaviors that heighten the meaning of certain spaces, behaviors that, in effect, sacralize space. As students of religious space, part of our challenge will be to negotiate between these perspectives, retaining the analytical character of the situational view while remaining cognizant of the power of the substantive view.

Locating the creation of sacred space within the realm of human activity helps us focus on those behaviors that sacralize certain places. As Smith's analysis of the hierarchical placement of specific groups within relative proximity to the holy of holies in Ezekiel's Temple suggests, much of this behavior has to do with acknowledging and expressing reverence for different types of power. Certainly, a temple constructed to house a god and the ritual activities performed there acknowledge and reverence the divine or supernatural power of the god him- or herself. Many societies have believed that expressing proper reverence toward supernatural power brings positive outcomes whereas the absence of such reverence courts disaster.

But in addition to supernatural power, other types of power are also acknowledged and reverenced as believers sacralize certain spaces. As we have already seen in Smith's and Richardson's work on the Jewish temples, acknowledging and reverencing the power of individual people or special groups of people—that is, the formation of social power—is accomplished through rules pertaining to the proper location of believers vis-à-vis the location of perceived supernatural power. In the Second Temple, only the High Priest was allowed into the holy of holies (the *devir*) and only on the Day of Atonement (Yom Kippur), and his occupation of that space both announced and helped to maintain his religious authority. Ritual actions performed before entering the holy space, such as washing and purifying the body and donning special clothing, further underscored the social power of the highest priestly office. Lay believers and neophytes, allowed only in the courtyard, easily understood the messages about power articulated symbolically by such actions and such spaces. Similar patterns are found in other temple traditions. The assigned locations and actions indicate, maintain, and ultimately help to naturalize hierarchical systems of human rank. Those with higher rank wield greater power over not only religious matters but also, frequently, social and civic ones as well. Thus, the demarking of social power among the clergy, patrons, and ordinary people is frequently part of the sacralization process.

Just as with the variety of understandings of supernatural power, Christianity also exhibits a wide variety of articulations of social power within religious buildings. Some groups rigidly demark spaces. For example, Orthodox Christians allow only clergy or other religious leaders to enter their church sanctuaries, which are fully or partially screened from the eyes of ordinary worshippers by an iconostasis, whose doors are opened only at certain points in the service, allowing a restricted view of the altar and actions of the priest. On the other end of the spectrum, many contemporary Quaker meetinghouses make no distinctions among worshippers, identifying no leaders, and placing all who gather for worship in undifferentiated space and on the same level vis-à-vis social power. Church buildings indicate social power, then, as a means of articulating and lending legitimacy to the organizational structures of the religious group. The isolated chancel or sanctuary indicates the special knowledge and power of the priest. The elevated pulpit indicates the special knowledge and power of the preacher. By indicating the importance of these and other religious offices, churches are created and treated as "special," or sacred, places.

In addition to these ideas of the relational placement of groups, historians David Chidester and Edward Linenthal, following Smith, have noted a number of means by which groups sacralized space situationally. For them, one of the most important catalysts for the sacralization of space is conflict, or in their terminology, "contestation."[6] Sacred space is not placid; it often exists at the heart of tumultuous controversies. An example is the Dome of the Rock, the sacred mosque erected in Jerusalem in the seventh century on the ruins of the Jewish Second Temple. For Jews, this place, as the site of both Solomon's and Herod's temples is the holiest place in the world. For Christians, the site figures in the life of Jesus and particularly in his crucifixion. For Muslims, the site is the third most holy place in the world, following Mecca and Medina. Struggle among these groups over this meaningful place has heightened its importance and sacredness. In these ways, then, social power—evident in hierarchies and in relations among different groups—informs religious spaces.

Lastly, in addition to supernatural power and social power, we must also keep in mind the very individual, personal empowerment that is frequently associated with church buildings and sacred spaces. Individuals connect profound spiritual meanings to specific places, including buildings and landscapes, and personal feelings of spiritual empowerment often result from connection to those spaces. From a substantive perspective, a pilgrimage to a holy site such as the Lourdes grotto empowers believers with grace through the presence of the Virgin. A situational view might focus attention on the way in which the ritual of the pilgrimage journey draws the believer's attention to the spiritual and thus empowers him or her through active participation in and expression of his or her understanding of the divine.[7] Upon arrival at the site, an individual's status as a pilgrim locates him or her within both human and divine hierarchies and defines a set of traditional behaviors or activities for the pilgrim. Threat or contest may also function to sacralize this space in ways that empower individuals. For instance Lourdes, a healing site, is fraught with misery even amidst hope for cures. Here the threat is internal, as ill health and physical suffering challenge individuals' faith. The hope believers place in the grotto and its healing water, as well as their sacralization of the grotto through their various activities, are direct results of personal claims to power in the face of adversity.

Such places make the connection between human life and the divine concrete, tangible, palpable. Most believers rarely stop to reflect on just how these connections are made, how personal empowerment is achieved, but this category of personal empowerment will be brought to bear in our study of church spaces in order to remind us of the power that church spaces afford the faithful. Throughout this book, then, attention to divine, social, and personal power will guide our questions as we consider Christian spaces. Awareness of the various means through which individuals and groups attribute meanings to specific spaces and thus participate in the sacralization of them will also inform the following pages.

Sacred space, then, including the Christian churches that are the focus of this book, should be understood as powerful space. The following chapters explore how power works within churches in an effort to illuminate the meanings of Christian buildings through the centuries. To accomplish this, the book closely examines the relationship between specific spaces and the religious practices and behaviors that invest them with meaning. We will be examining the function of power within the various aspects of Christian life, specifically with respect to Christian thought or *creed*, Christian ethics or *code*, and Christian practice or *cultus*. As a result, this study is as much about Christianity as it is about buildings. Indeed, one of the goals of the book and of the method presented is to use buildings and spaces to shed light upon Christianity itself.

This book, then, is an extended essay on the form, function, and meaning of Christian worship spaces, how they have changed over time, and what we can learn about Christianity by looking at the places in which it has been practiced. As a brief survey, however, it can only scratch the surface of the many extraordinary buildings and groups discussed here. But it can provide readers with a set of categories and questions that they can employ as they look more deeply into the buildings and meanings that interest them.[8] By offering a look across the sweep of two millennia of Christian architecture, it exposes several patterns and meanings that are inherent in Christianity, but which have often been neglected precisely because they are so deeply embedded in architecture and space.

2

Early Christian Meeting Space in the Roman Empire

Were we able to go back in time to walk through a city of the Roman Empire during the first three centuries of the Common Era,[1] we would undoubtedly be struck by the diverse religious meanings carried by the built landscape. From Rome to Antioch to Carthage, the largest public buildings were temples dedicated to a panoply of gods and governmental buildings erected on behalf of the emperor, himself a godlike figure. Jerusalem, for instance, housed both the Temple of the Jews and temples dedicated to Roman gods. On the Greek island of Delos, sanctuaries constructed by the Hermaists (Roman devotees of Hermes) and Herakleiasts (devotees of Hera) from Tyre were located near meeting places of the Samaritans and the Jews.[2] In the ancient town of Dura-Europos in Eastern Syria, we would find a synagogue, a Mithrian temple, and a house used for Christian meetings located close together. Religious diversity was imprinted on the ancient world through its buildings, just as it is in the cities and towns of today.

We would also notice another familiar sight: buildings being torn down and new ones being erected in their place. Then as now, the destruction and reconstruction of city landscapes was a continuous process. Houses, temples, government buildings, apartments, and shops were razed by design and accident (fire and building collapse being frequent occurrences) and new buildings were erected in their place. Change, like diversity, helped to create dynamic cities and cityscapes.

Diversity and change will be important themes as we examine the early development of Christian meetings and buildings during the first three centuries of the Common Era. Dozens of Christian groups organized during this period across the Mediterranean region, from Antioch to Rome, Palestine to North Africa, and their worship practices varied with their various cultural contexts. The spaces these Christians used also varied significantly. This diversity, present within Christianity from its earliest years, reminds us that there is no single Christian architecture. Looking at the various spaces early Christians used for their meetings, however, can tell us a great deal about their lives, their conception of this new religion, and the worship practices they created to express the profound meanings of faith and belief in Jesus Christ. This chapter, then, presents some of the key features of early Christian spaces and worship and important transformations that took place in both as Christianity became formalized and institutionalized over the course of the first three centuries of the Common Era.

Worship and Religious Space in the Ancient World

The cultural context of the Mediterranean world and the Roman Empire provided much of the raw material that the followers of Jesus shaped into a new religion over the course of the first and second centuries. Given the wide cultural diversity that marked the empire, its citizens practiced several different religions and carried out many different types of worship in many types of places. As we would expect, the early followers of Jesus were strongly influenced by the types of worship practices and spaces with which they were already familiar.

The most public of religious gatherings in the Roman Empire were large celebrations and festivals held in the public temples. Worshippers believed that proximity to the divine within a temple—that is, the relative distance between oneself and the image or venerated artifact of the divine housed within the building—imbued the individual with power. The closer one could approach the god, they believed, the stronger and more auspicious the connection. Not surprisingly, access to the space nearest the manifestation of the god was restricted to only a few individuals, priests who had been properly educated and initiated in the meanings and practices required of them by tradition in such a holy place. Access to the temple was also decreed by tradition and closely regulated by law. The longitudinal axis of the Jewish temple, for instance, ran through a series of partitions and other demarcations that designated spaces reserved for specific groups—at the outer edge of the space, Gentiles were allowed; then, closer in, Jewish women and children; closer still, Jewish men; and finally, the priests.[3] Similar distinctions were made in the temples devoted to other gods, although the specific form of those distinctions varied widely.[4] Temple worship was based on direct interaction between humans and the divine. In the Roman and Jewish traditions, this interaction was facilitated or mediated by worshippers' performance of tribute, including the sacrifice of animals and the offering of food, goods, and prayers. These and other rituals were carried out by priests who had undergone years of study and initiation in the secrets of the divine practice.

Religious practice during this period was not limited to temples, however. Smaller meetings often took place in chapels and sanctuaries, as well as in rented rooms. For instance, at the same time that the followers of Jesus began coming together, the worshippers of the god Mithras were also growing in number and by the third century were meeting in small sanctuaries called *mithraeums*, rooms designed to suggest a cave or the underworld. In these oblong spaces, benches lined the two long walls and a small shrine or altar was placed at the end of the room. The ceilings were frequently vaulted and decorated with stars to suggest the heavens. In this intimate setting, initiated worshippers occupied the same space as the shrine and participated in communal worship.[5] Similarly, by the second century, Jews had organized synagogues and prayer halls in formerly private houses converted for the purpose. One early example, at Delos, had been created through the destruction of a wall between two adjacent rooms, resulting in a single large room. Benches lined the walls of this assembly room, and a carved marble chair occupying one wall provided a focal point. No Torah shrine was found in this room, although Torah niches have been found in other early synagogues, including that at Priene, where another house renovated sometime in the second century was found.[6] Within these spaces, worship practices were diverse, consisting of a variety of prayers and liturgies.[7]

Worshippers of various faiths also used private houses for religious observances. These house meetings were generally organized not by a priest but by the patron who lent his or her home for the use of the group. This patron, whether a man or a woman, might lead the service (in the case of acknowledged religious teachers or leaders) or arrange for qualified leaders and speakers to address the gathering. Such house gatherings consisted of shared meals along with the veneration of images, prayer, and other rituals.

As members of the Roman Empire began to follow the Jesus cult, they adapted these familiar practices and spaces for their new purposes, infusing them with new meanings. As we will see, space and the use of space served an integral role in the development of the new religion.

Types of Early Christian Worship

It was in this context of diverse religious practices and spaces that Jesus and his followers spread his message and in which those followers gathered together to carry on that message after his crucifixion. The Gospel texts give us some understanding of the very earliest meetings and indicate that Jesus himself preached in a variety of places: in synagogues, in the open air as in the sermon delivered on the Mount of Olives, near the shore of the Dead Sea, and, as a boy, on the steps of the Temple itself. More frequently, however, Jesus is said to have presided at gatherings (of the sick, of disciples, of Pharisees) in individual homes.

As significant as Jesus's gatherings were, however, they do not bring us near the church itself, for there was no organized Christian church until quite some time after his crucifixion. In fact, through the next two centuries, the followers of Jesus would continue to come together in an array of such groups, all claiming to carry on the work of the man they called Lord. Even if their numbers and resources had allowed it, the construction of large public temples was not a possibility during this period, because Christianity was not an officially recognized religion in the Roman Empire. As neither the early worship practices nor the numbers of Jesus's followers required large gathering spaces, the spaces of homes and the outdoors served them well, just as they had Jesus.

The meetings of the followers of Jesus in the first few generations after his death were of three major types, all adaptations of the practices of other religious groups, particularly those of the Jews, for indeed the followers were Jewish, as well as other Roman and Greek religions. Most of these meetings involved a shared meal, actual or symbolic, for in the Greco-Roman world, extending hospitality by sharing a meal was a fundamental form of social interaction. These communal meals brought Christians together to learn about their faith, to worship, and to share experiences, but they also functioned to create cohesion within the new community of Christians. As historian L. Michael White points out, communal meals formed "the center of fellowship (*koinonia*)" by indicating that a social relationship existed among those gathered and thus "served to define the worshipping community, the church (*ekklesia*) in household assembly."[8]

Of these meeting types, the *agape* meal, or love feast, was most important, and although it drew upon Greco-Roman practice in many ways, it replaced the drinking and carousing that traditionally followed Roman feasts with teaching and worship. Those who gathered at a Christian meal would bring some food item with them as an offering for the meal—usually bread, wine, or fish—just as many people do today in what is commonly known as the potluck supper. Upon arriving, the participants would share the kiss of peace and, following Greco-Roman practice, would usually eat immediately. Eating too quickly upon arrival, however, might result in insufficient food for those who arrived later, and thus Paul admonished the Corinthians that "when you come together to eat, wait for one another," urging those who could not wait to eat to do so at home before they came (I Cor. 11:33–34).[9] Such advice, which counters common Roman practice, indicates that the emerging Christian practice was still relatively informal and flexible, with new etiquette or rules slowly being incorporated into the meetings. After the meal, those gathered would share a ceremonial breaking and eating of bread, followed by a blessing and sharing of a cup of wine, commemorating Jesus's dictum for his remembrance at the Last Supper.[10] After this, they participated in a variety of learning and worship activities, which, according to historians Carolyn Osiek and David L. Balch, included "singing, teaching, prophesying, and glossolalia (with translations)."[11]

In addition to the agape meal, early Christians also held funerary meetings to honor deceased figures in the Jesus movement, including leaders and martyrs. This second type of meeting, which also consisted of a shared meal and prayer, took place at the burial site on the yearly anniversaries of the death of the individual being memorialized. Early Christian funerary practices paralleled those of other religious traditions of the period, in which those gathered often shared their food with the deceased through offerings left on a sarcophagus or near the wall in which the deceased was interred.

A third type of gathering was the Eucharistic meeting, in which the shared meal was transformed into a symbolic ritual focused exclusively on bread and wine as tropes for the flesh and blood of Christ. Although the development of the agape and funerary meals, which did include a sharing of bread and wine in remembrance of Jesus Christ, likely preceded the emergence of Eucharistic practices, just when and how the purely Eucharistic gathering emerged is unclear. Like the agape meals, these Eucharist meals took place in private homes, but over the second and third centuries significant changes in services indicate they were becoming increasingly formalized both in leadership and in activities. Justin, in the second century, refers to the person leading the service as the *presider* or the *president,* but by the third century, the organizational structures of the Christian movement developed into an *episcopos,* a Greek term meaning "overseer" or, in modern parlance, a bishop; the term *priest* also became popular. The service itself was changing as well, described by Justin and his contemporary Ignatius, the bishop of Antioch, as symbolic or representational, a celebration of Christ's sacrifice of his own flesh and blood.[12] By the third century, as we will see below, the growing popularity of these

representational services would require a special space that would accommodate them, leading to the creation of formal assembly rooms.[13]

A fourth type of early Christian meeting took place out of doors, such as
the meeting of the followers of Jesus on the Mount of Olives shortly after his
death, a story related in *The Letter of Peter to Philip*, which was found among
other Gnostic texts at Nag Hammadi in Upper Egypt.[14] Little is known,
however, about such outdoor meetings, in part because they seem to have been
used mostly by Gnostic groups, whose beliefs and practices challenged those
of the emerging orthodoxy and were consequently stricken from orthodox culture and documents. Outdoor worship thus became associated with heretical
groups and fell out of favor. Roman Catholicism, for instance, would continue
to eschew outdoor celebration of the Mass well into the twentieth century,
deeming such services too similar to transgressive Greco-Roman (i.e. "pagan")
and early Gnostic practices.[15]

What must be kept in mind, however, is that despite the differences
among these early types of worship, early Christian worship spaces and practices were highly diverse. No single, original, pure Christian practice ever existed.[16] From the earliest period, Christian groups expressed their ideas about
Jesus and God in different ways, and those ideas, ranging from the eventual
orthodoxy of the major episcopacies in Rome, Antioch, and Carthage to the
Gnostic views of the Marcionites, Donatists, and Montanists, were highly diverse. Early Christians expressed their religious ideas through a variety of religious practices ways, just as contemporary Christians do.

The Setting and Practice of Early Christian Meetings

Biblical scholars, classicists, and archaeologists agree that the meeting of
Christians, like those of other religious groups, generally took place in the
homes of patrons, that is, in Greco-Roman houses. The phrase "meeting from
house to house," found repeatedly in the Gospel texts, well characterized the
practice of early Christians. The physical realities of those spaces, and the
homes in particular, along with the cultural customs of the period, strongly
influenced emerging Christian practice. To understand how, it helps to have
some knowledge of the physical characteristics of those homes.

Architectural and textual evidence of Greco-Roman houses in the first and
second centuries indicate that several varieties existed. Given the long, hot
summers of the Mediterranean region, the houses of the wealthiest home-
owners literally turned in on themselves, offering a stark, bare façade to the
street but opening into a series of rooms arranged around an oasis-like open

space that brought air and light into the house. Entry into the house was gained through a vestibule or hallway. In a Greek house, this led to a room in which the household patron conducted business, and beyond this was the heart of the house: the *peristyle,* or courtyard, which was roofless but lined by columns that supported an overhead latticework that would be covered with vegetation to protect the occupants from the sun. In a Roman or Latin house, the vestibule off the street generally led right into an *atrium,* or open courtyard, which would be open to the sky and contain an *impluvium,* a shallow pool that gathered rainwater (fig. 2.1).[17] Ringing the peristyle or atrium were the private spaces of the home, several closed rooms reserved for the members of the household. These would include an *oecus* (roughly the equivalent of a family room), a *triclinium* or dining room, bedrooms, slave quarters, and women's rooms.

Unlike the interiors of contemporary homes, which are considered private space, the central portions of ancient houses—the vestibules, atria, and peristyles—were considered much more public in character. Such houses, particularly those in which the business of the wealthy was routinely carried out, welcomed the entry of people from the street. Many homes included a shop run by the household on the street side, where customers and strangers could enter the houses. Similarly, the head of the household might conduct his or her

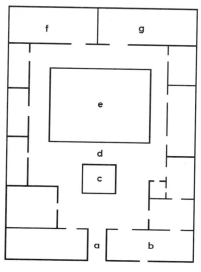

FIGURE 2.1. Generic Roman house. Key: a. entry, b. shop, c. impluvium, d. atrium, e. peristyle, f. oecus, g. triclinium. Line drawing by Paul Kilde, after Deborah Wells in Osiek and Balch (8).

business in an office near the front entrance and would use the atrium as a reception area for those seeking interviews.

Although the public could readily enter the central portion of the houses, the side and back rooms of these homes were restricted to household members. The largest of those household rooms, the *triclinium* or dining room, was most likely the usual site of many early Christian meetings. The Greco-Roman triclinium was a specialized space designed to accommodate the then-common practice of reclining during meals. The room was lined on three sides with couches that were either freestanding pieces of wooden furniture or constructed of stone and built into the walls. A table typically occupied the center of the room. Servants or slaves would serve the meals, their labor accommodating the diners. Men, particularly men of status, would recline on their left arm and eat with their right hand. Women, however, generally did not recline as it was considered inappropriate for them to do so, particularly in mixed-sex gatherings (though there is some evidence that at least some women did). Some houses contained two triclinia, perhaps to accommodate sex-segregated meals. During meals at which men and women ate together, the women would typically sit in chairs placed next to the couches.[18] These dining rooms, like many other rooms in the homes of the wealthy, were highly decorated with mosaics or murals covering the floor and walls. Not surprisingly, images of eating and drinking were prominent in these artworks, including mosaics and paintings of fish, bread, or meat. In some cases, floor mosaics even depicted the stripped bones of fish or fowl, mimicking the real ones that diners would toss on the floor during meals.[19]

In thinking about these houses as locations for the meetings of the early followers of Jesus, we must keep in mind their semipublic character. Although one ancient commentator, the architect Vitruvius, stated that the triclinium was considered off-limits to strangers who might otherwise be welcomed into the atrium of a house, the Gospel writers mention without comment that a women "who knew Jesus was reclining in [a] house" (that is, knew he was eating a meal there) apparently entered and anointed him without invitation (Luke 7:36–50; Mark 14:3–9; Matt. 26:6–13; John 12:1–8). Such entry of strangers into homes was probably not uncommon given the multipurpose use of houses and the general understanding of private and public space during the period.[20]

Families and households of lesser economic means during this period occupied a variety of dwellings. Common were multiple-storied apartment houses called *insulae*, which typically consisted of a few rooms. In areas of high population density and poverty, these could be squalid tenements, but in more affluent areas, they would be comfortable dwellings with windows, an atrium, and mosaic ornamentation.[21] Although housing plans varied throughout the

Roman world and local preferences are discernable in a variety of places, the types of rooms and their uses were relatively constant.

The meetings that took place in these homes were deeply embedded in the cultural practices that shaped them. Hospitality emerged as an important virtue in Christian life, fostered not only by the sociable character of the culture but also by the itinerate character of church leaders. Apostles, including Paul, and other preachers would travel from town to town, meeting with Christian groups.[22] A patron or patroness who welcomed the Christian guests into his or her home would provide food and lodging for these wanderers, and invite others to an agape meal at which the honored guest would speak. The patron/patroness might also wash the feet of the guests and share the kiss of peace, following the model of Jesus (particularly his reversal of social rank).

The term *tituli* or "house church" has been applied to such homes that were regularly used for Christian assembly. A "tituli," literally, was a stone placed near the door of a house and inscribed with the name of the owner; thus Christians would say, for instance, *Tituli Prisca* to refer to Prisca's home, used for Christian meetings.[23] Various texts name many individuals who opened their homes to meetings. Prisca and her husband Aquila, whom Paul calls coworkers in Christ (Rom. 16:3), opened the various homes they occupied in Corinth, Ephesus, and Rome to Christian meetings. Titus Justus, Stephanas, Crispus, and Gaius also hosted Paul and his meetings in their homes. Chloe also seems to have hosted regular meetings, as Paul mentions her "people" as distinct group (I Cor. 1:11). Phoebe, a *diakonos* or minister (Rom. 16:1), was a principle benefactor to Paul, opening her household at Cenchreae near Corinth to him.[24] Paul also mentions the work of Junia, whom he calls an apostle, although it is unclear whether she provided meeting space for Christians. Writers among the next generation of Christians also mention the importance of houses used to host religious travelers and meetings. Ignatius of Antioch, for instance, mentions the hospitality of Tavia in Smyrna, a Christian woman whose apparently non-Christian husband practiced religious toleration.[25] *The Martyrdom of Justin* indicates that Justin taught Christianity out of his second-story apartment home in Rome and used the public baths below for baptisms.[26] Given the public character of Roman houses, gatherings in homes for religious purposes were likely not private in the same sense as we use the term today. People who knew about the meetings could readily attend, invited or not—a situation that disputes the modern perception that the meetings of Early Christians were always secret in character, carried on surreptitiously because of a disparaging or hostile public.

Just how homes and apartments were used during Christian meetings remains somewhat obscure. Over the course of the twentieth century, scholars have debated just what rooms were used. Although earlier scholars suggested that the atrium, a larger "public" space within the house, was the primary meeting room for Christian groups, recent scholarship has identified the triclinium as the more likely site of Christian meetings in houses. The earlier theory rested on the assumption that early Christian worship consisted exclusively of a symbolic Eucharist celebration, which could attract relatively large numbers of people and require a large space, but recent scholarship has argued that most early gatherings were likely to have been agape meals, with the ritualized Eucharist observance only slowly emerging and separating from the communal meal. Given that the centrality of a communal meal to Christian gatherings paralleled practices of other religious groups in the Roman Empire, where shared meals were a significant component of religious practice across communities, it is likely that the emerging Christians similarly located their meals in the dining areas of the homes in which they met.

In addition, given the widespread significance of the communal meal, it is likely that common protocols and etiquette would have been closely adhered to as it was served. For instance, it would have been natural for those participating in the meal to recline during it, as this was the common practice of the period (irrespective of Leonardo da Vinci's popular depiction of the Last Supper, created centuries later). Yet chairs might also have been brought into the room to accommodate larger numbers than the regular couches could hold. Large gatherings, presumably, might spill out of the dining room and into other spaces of the house.[27]

Just what occurred in these spaces during meetings has been difficult to ascertain. Documentary evidence indicates to some extent *what* generally occurred during services but not exactly *how* it occurred within specific spaces.[28] For instance, the description of the incident at Troas, in which Paul resurrected a young man who fell from a window sill during a late-night meeting (Acts 20: 5–21), offers only the faintest clues about the meeting space and how it was being used. The text explains only that "there were many lights in the upper chamber" in which the meeting was held. Although architectural historian Richard Krautheimer has speculated that the room may have been crowded and overheated, which is certainly plausible, the story might also suggest that a certain level of informality existed in the meeting, in which people seem to have accommodated themselves around the room as best they could, even perching on windowsills.[29]

Despite such informality it is unlikely that participants relaxed commonly accepted rules of decorum during agape meals. In particular, seating (reclining) assignments around the main couches would likely have been carefully determined, with the places of honor reserved for the host and/or hostess and the featured guest, perhaps a traveling bishop or a teacher such as Paul himself. By Roman custom, as Krautheimer points out, "the main couch opposite the entrance was presumably reserved for the elder, the host, the speaker as honored guest."[30] Anyone entering such a meeting room could likely identify the relative importance of those attending by their place at the table, if not by other cues like clothing or language.

Transformation of the House Church into the Domus Ecclesiae

Given this use of residences for the earliest meetings, the house churches of the first- and second-century meetings should be considered "Christian architecture" only in the broadest sense of the term. They were simply the homes of believers or Jesus followers that were opened for meetings. Despite a lack of documentary or archeological evidence of these house meetings or of the specific houses within which they occurred, we can assume that their primary function and character most likely remained residential.[31] By the third century, however, some believers were remodeling their homes for the specific purpose of accommodating Christian meetings, and archeological examples of a few of these do exist. The oldest known of these buildings, located at Dura-Europos in modern-day Syria, dates from sometime between 232 C.E. and 256 C.E., when it was partially destroyed along with the rest of the town, the ruins laying buried until 1928.[32] Unlike the house churches whose rooms performed double duty, servicing both Christian meetings and everyday family needs, the building at Dura-Europos had originally been a house but at some point had been renovated to primarily or exclusively serve religious meetings.[33] This extraordinary residence-cum-church retained its domestic exterior character, masking the unique character of its renovated interior.

The term *domus ecclesiae* has been applied to this and similar buildings that, though domestic in exterior appearance, were clearly used exclusively for Christian assemblies. Renovation of a house or a house church into a domus ecclesiae was very likely a response to a variety of shifting social, liturgical, and ecclesiastical circumstances. As Christian groups grew in size, the triclinium and/or atrium spaces of most homes would have proven too small to accommodate all who wished to gather for services. (Having followers falling out of upper story windows was not good for the strength of the religious community.) Thus, larger spaces were increasingly required.[34]

Even given these larger spaces, however, maintaining the centrality of the communal meal in Christian practice would have proved difficult. As mentioned above, the general pattern of services began to shift away from the shared meal and toward symbolic, ritualized, and formal practices in which large groups of people could participate more readily. Although praying, scripture reading, and psalm singing remained important in the increasingly formalized services, the most significant change in the meetings was the separation of the agape meal from the commemorative sharing of bread and wine that commenced and terminated each gathering. During the second century, services gradually eliminated the actual meal, favoring the symbolic use of bread and wine over the communal sharing of food. As White explains, "As the meal became less practical . . . it was possible to stylize the meal elements into symbolic forms, resulting in the liturgical pattern seen in Justin and Tertullian in the latter half of the second century. Ritual forms then came to replace the casual elements of house church dining though they attempted to preserve it through symbolism."[35] Eliminating the meal brought other changes as well, among them the elimination of the need for food contributions. This earlier practice also became translated into a symbolic act, the offertory, which now took the form of alms.[36]

As communal meals became unwieldy and the ritualization of the Eucharist gradually became the centerpiece of Christian gatherings, a new type of worship space was needed. In the Christian house at Dura-Europos, it appears that two rooms on the south side of the house, the triclinium and a small adjacent room, were combined to create a long, rectangular assembly room measuring approximately forty-two by seventeen feet (fig. 2.2), which could accommodate sixty-five to seventy-five people.[37] Little decoration is evident in this room. The whitewashed walls seem spare, although a section of a Bacchic plaster frieze, probably left over from the original house, remains. Decorated with satyrs, panpipes, cymbals, and animals, this improbable reference to the Roman god Bacchus seems odd in a room renovated for Christian use, but it may well indicate a certain tolerance for other religious views or a level of comfort with the syncretistic blending of symbols from different religious perspectives.[38] Another distinctive feature that appears in this room is a *bema* or platform, measuring approximately three by five feet and raised eight inches off the floor, at the east end of the oblong assembly hall. This dais accommodated the bishop or priest who led the service, while the remainder of the room accommodated worshippers.[39]

The bema and the separation it created between the clergy and the ordinary worshippers indicate that Christianity was becoming increasingly institutionalized. The new clergy, presiding over the symbolic Eucharist services that were becoming the centerpiece of Christian worship, played a very powerful role, in effect mediating between the gathered assembly and the god they worshipped. The offices of the clergy took on symbolic meaning as, in what

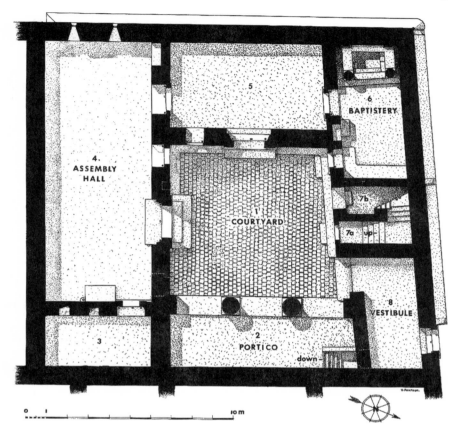

FIGURE 2.2. Isometric drawing of the Christian building at Dura-Europos. Courtesy Yale University Art Gallery, Dura-Europos Collection.

became the orthodox model, bishops, priests, and deacons held power through what was seen as their spiritual descent from the original apostles called by Christ. These notions of divine calling and spiritual descent legitimated and cemented hierarchical episcopal power.[40] Thus this new spatial arrangement attests to the growing formalization of Christian services and to the distinction between clergy and laity. Meetings in this room would have been presided over not by the patron or patroness who owned the building but by a clergy member, a priest or bishop whose role was legitimated on these new institutional grounds.

The arrangement of these new spaces, with their designated areas for each group, also indicates that an increasing formality characterized the services. Although in the previous triclinium meetings, worshippers could gather around and near the service leaders by reclining or sitting at the same table or perching around the room in whatever space was available, designated boundaries existed in the new worship spaces of domus ecclesiae. Whether penalties existed for violating those boundaries is unknown, but their very existence implied a new type of reverence on the part of the assembled people and a greater control over the people and their behavior by clerical leaders.

Thus, new spatial relationships in this new building type underscored and helped to maintain distinctions among Christian participants in services. Those distinctions rested specifically upon the creation of a clerical class, which wielded greater power and influence within the group by right of their ordination. Although some distinctions in power had certainly existed in earlier Christian gatherings—particularly among patrons, honored teachers, and ordinary guests—it was not until the emergence of the domus ecclesiae that they were fully inscribed into the spatial arrangement of the religious space itself. Thus, with the domus ecclesiae, Christian space began to function to delineate and maintain distinctions of power and influence among Christians and became a crucial factor in the institutionalization of and maintenance of these new religious offices. By the middle of the third century, ordination, a process through which an individual took on the knowledge, role, and power of the clergy, became closely associated with the space reserved for the clergy. When Cyprian, bishop of Carthage, referred to the clerical dais as a *tribunal,* "the sacred and venerated congestum of the clergy," stating that to "ascend the platform" indicated ordination, the place itself had become a metonym for the power and authority of the clergy.[41]

But this was not the only important hierarchical message embedded in the domus ecclesiae. Status distinctions existed among the laity as well, and these had their own spatial counterparts in the buildings. The major distinction among believers was between baptized Christians and *catechumens,* or novices who were in the process of learning about the religion in preparation for baptism. Services in the third century began with the Mass of the Catechumens, in which novices and the baptized either vied for standing room in the worship hall or gravitated to specific areas designated by custom. After this service, the catechumens were required to retire to an adjacent room, situated so that they could hear but not see the centerpiece of the service, the Mass of the Faithful (including the Eucharist service), which was attended only by the baptized. In the domus ecclesiae at Dura-Europos, this separation was accommodated by an auxiliary room adjacent to the main meeting hall; catechumens moved into this room during the Mass of the Faithful.[42] This spatial segregation publicly announced individuals' progress toward full initiation even as it underscored the greater importance and influence of baptized members.

By spatially distinguishing among specific groups, the domus ecclesiae •
building type advanced the institutionalization of Christianity during the late
second and early third centuries. As the earlier distinctions made for elders,
preachers, hosts, and hostesses developed into the hierarchical ecclesiastical
structure of clerical offices, renovated domus ecclesiae reflected those distinctions by formalizing them within architectural space. The physical location
of service leaders, elevated on a bema or tribunal at one end of a rectilinear
room, rendered the distinctions visible and helped to maintain them. The physical placement of neophytes in a separate room during the Mass of the Faithful
both indicated their lesser status and underscored the great significance of the
Mass from which they were excluded.

Diversity in seating arrangements also seems to have been common. In
Rome, "seating" (more precisely, standing room) during services was often
based on gender, with men and women separated on either side of the room.
Age was also a criterion for location during services in some areas. For instance, a Syrian religious order placed children nearest the tribunal, with men
behind them and women behind the men.[43] Such variations suggest what
these Christian groups considered were appropriate relationships among the
various groups of members as well as their relative rank vis-à-vis their proximity to the tribunal.

•The creation of a distinct space for the baptismal service also underscored
the formalization of Christian ritual. A separate room within the domus ecclesiae at Dura-Europos accommodated baptisms, a rite undertaken only by
adults in this period. This small room featured an alcove at one end, which
housed a tiled pool raised a few steps above the level of the floor and covered by
a vaulted canopy supported by columns. Unlike the assembly hall with its
minimal decoration (and that referring to Bacchic religion), this room featured
lavish decoration of a distinctly Christian character (fig. 2.3). The ceiling of the
alcove and the room resembled the night sky, painted dark blue and dotted
with stars. Murals painted on the walls of the room depicted scenes from the
Hebrew Bible and the life of Christ, including the Good Shepherd, Adam and
Eve, the Woman at the Well, David and Goliath, Jesus healing the Paralytic,
Peter and Jesus walking on water, and the Women at the Tomb of Jesus.[44] The
lavishness of this ornament suggests that this room was of special significance
to the community; undoubtedly, it indicates the importance ascribed to baptism. To undergo baptism in such a room was not simply to be familiar with
the stories and miracles illustrated on the walls, but to have absorbed their
deep significance and embraced them as the foundation of faith.

The baptistery pool itself was the visual focal point of the room, occupying
a short wall and covered by a round arch supported on columns. This same

FIGURE 2.3. Reconstruction of the Christian baptistery at Dura-Europos. Courtesy Yale University Art Gallery, Dura-Europos Collection.

architectural feature is also used in the synagogue of the same period found on the Dura site, but there it shelters the Torah scrolls, the symbol of the Jewish covenant with God. In each case, a highly articulated architectural element, a canopy, signals a place in which the human relationship with the divine is made manifest. In the synagogue that manifestation is in the Torah; in the baptistery it occurs during baptism, the ritual transformation of the individual into a member of the Christian community.[45] The Jewish and Christian canopies also share iconography, with bunches of grapes and clusters of three pomegranates decorating both arches and emphasizing the close relationship between the two religious perspectives. Although the meaning of these particular symbols is unclear, scholars speculate that the use of such fruits may have pointed to a heavenly banquet and suggested immortality.

In addition to the assembly room, the catechumen's room, and the baptistery, two other distinctive spaces have been found in the archaeological and documentary remains of early Christian buildings. These include libraries with cupboards and storage rooms for offerings of alms. White reports that a search of the Christian building at Cirta, Numidia, discovered similar rooms, including a storeroom that held a great deal of clothing, likely intended for the poor. Indeed, White surmises, the room was most likely "the charitable store of the Christian community" and suggests that such storerooms and their contents give further evidence of the formalizing of Christian practices, in this case almsgiving and distribution.[46]

The Formalization of Space and Worship in the Domus Ecclesiae

Although the use of homes and the development of the domus ecclesiae overlapped one another for perhaps a century or more, the relatively informal space of residences must have proven increasingly inappropriate and unsuitable as more formalized liturgical and social practices became common. Meanings associated with homes may have allowed for greater leeway in behavior—youths dozing on windowsills, and men and women reclining together. Everyday settings likely allowed everyday meanings to intrude; the furnishings and the spaces themselves suggest an ordinariness that might easily contradict the growing extraordinariness of religious observance. Thus we might expect that as the Eucharist meal became ritualized and formalized, the space necessarily did as well, becoming in effect sacralized.

Sacralized, or sacred, space functions differently from ordinary space. A primary function of sacred or sacralized space, as Jonathan Z. Smith notes, is to focus the mind on spiritual matters. The formalized spaces of the domus ecclesiae would have achieved this much more effectively than the everyday spaces of ordinary residences. Meeting places devoted exclusively to worship, containing artifacts that carried exclusively Christian meanings, would have helped minimize the intrusions of everyday concerns and thoughts. Decorations and ornamentation in these rooms, such as the murals in the Dura-Europos baptistery, featured Christian symbols and scriptures, which would have helped to concentrate viewers' attention on Christ and worship. With the shift from multiuse ordinary homes to the domus ecclesiae, the followers of Jesus would no longer take their behavioral cues from the familiar domestic territory of the triclinium; in the domus ecclesiae, Christians learned to play out their varied roles as clergy, as catechumens, as the baptized faithful. Thus despite the term *domus ecclesiae*, the interior of the new building type was hardly domestic or household-like at all, although it was enclosed in a residential form. The term *domus ecclesiae*, translated generally as "house of the church," or, more literally, the "house of the assembly," with its emphasis on the "house," does not fully indicate the radical nature of the renovated interior spaces and their role in the formalization of Christian offices and liturgies. Although its exterior remained domestic in character, interiors may well have retained only superficial connections with the original domestic spaces. Some of the walls may have remained, but the function and, more importantly, the meaning of the spaces were dramatically redefined.

The shift from meetings centered on the relative if not full equality of Christian fellowship and the agape meal to the distinctive and hierarchical roles imposed by the spatial distinctions within the domus ecclesiae is a considerable one. And we can read this shift in the very term *domus ecclesiae,* which points up the tension between the traditional exteriors and the institutional changes taking place inside the building. For if *domus* characterizes the familiar residential exterior, the pull of change is indicated by the term's reference to the ever-growing assemblies or *ecclesiae,* increasingly requiring a more formal space.

Surely such changes were slow and marked by a remarkable diversity among these "houses of the church." For instance, an inventory of a house used for Christian meetings in 303 C.E. stated that the house still contained a triclinium (along with other domestic rooms such as a library), suggesting perhaps that communal meals continued among the group that used the building.[47] Scholars have posited several intermediary architectural stages in the gradual development from the use of houses to the domus ecclesiae and eventually to churches themselves, including what White terms the *aula ecclesiae,* or hall church, an intermediate building type that emerged between the renovation of houses into the domus ecclesiae and the creation of the Christian basilica, described in the next chapter.[48] In White's view, the aula ecclesiae resulted from a "conscious plan to redesign [an] entire edifice for religious functions" and standardized "the rectangular hall plan for assembly and cluster[ed] ancillary rooms, annexes, or dependencies around it."[49] At this point in the history of Christian worship spaces, renovation would no longer do; now a full redesign of a building was necessary. The interior of an aula ecclesiae retained no references to previous domestic use. The triclinium was gone, and the oblong space was given over entirely to a single meeting hall with a bema at one end. In aula ecclesiae, there would be no chance of mixed signals from the former domestic function of the building. Although the exterior of these buildings did continue to mimic domestic architecture to some extent, some differences must have been apparent, given that some sources likened them to temples.[50] White, however, makes a distinction, if a fine one, between the temple-like yet still somewhat domestic exterior appearance of the aula ecclesiae and the public façades of the churches that would follow it. The exteriors of this intermediate form may well have combined or mixed visual cues— mimicking residential exteriors in some ways, perhaps in use of materials or in scale, while also incorporating some elements of more public buildings (i.e., temples), perhaps in the exterior shape or ornamentation. So although the tension between the domestic and the public was resolved in the interior hall (*aula*) plan of this building type, it remained somewhat visible on the exteriors.[51]

The shifting meanings associated with these worship spaces—from domestic space associated with household operations and a certain level of informality to a formal ecclesiastical space—over a period of at least a century also had certain social ramifications. For instance, this transformation may mark women's declining power within the Christian community as meetings moved from domestic space in which women held some authority to a formal and hierarchal setting that separated them from positions of power. Among the many scholars who have examined the roles of women and their relative power in the early church, Osiek and Balch argue that the early growth of Christianity paralleled the increasing social power and visibility of women, particularly in areas most strongly influenced by Rome.[52] Such expansion of women's functions within society helps to explain the many women whose support and public roles helped to establish Christianity during the first century after Jesus's death. Naturally, a woman hosting a Christian meeting in her home would be highly honored, as both a patron and a leader. Paul's mention of "Chloe's people" in Corinth, for instance, suggests that she served as an important religious leader as well as patron among Christians. This rise in women's social power, however, met with resistance. For instance, the Pastoral Epistles (1 and 2 Timothy and Titus) severely limit women's activities in the church. Written not by Paul but by a second-generation imitator, the letters proscribe women's speaking, teaching, and wielding of authority over men—activities that Paul himself had praised on the part of a number of women with whom he had worked.[53] Whatever the motivation behind these proscriptions, they are clearly aimed at contemporary practices that the author considered contemptible. Change was afoot. As Christianity institutionalized, it did in fact suppress women's religious power, eliminating them from the clergy despite the fact that prior to the establishment of institutionalized offices, women were found in the highest leadership positions.[54] By the fourth century, and the construction of monumental Christian buildings, women in some localities would be relegated to galleries above the aisle, isolated from the powerful main floor, tribunal, and altar.[55]

The shift toward exclusively ecclesiastical buildings also suggests increasing participation in Christianity by the wealthy. As Christian meeting spaces shifted from homes to remodeled buildings to entirely new edifices, the investment needed to provide worship facilities increased dramatically. Only with the full recognition of Christianity by the empire in the fourth century would sufficient funds be available to create monumental Christian architecture.

Personal Empowerment within Early Christian Buildings

In these ways, the process of spatial development not only accompanied but also contributed to the early institutionalization of Christianity and to the shifting power relations that accompanied the process. The new domus ecclesiae reflected and contributed to significant transformations in social power among Christians, helping to establish and maintain distinctions of rank. But, as pointed out in the previous chapter, social power is only one type of power within religious spaces. How, we might ask, did personal power function within these spaces? Did Christians feel closer to God within their buildings? Did the building contribute to Christians' spiritual lives?

Christianity of the first two centuries was a waiting game. Jesus had said he would return. The miracle of his resurrection demonstrated that he had the power to depart—and therefore return—at will, and so it was just a matter of time until he would be back to save his flock and establish divine justice. Empowerment lay in one's connection to Jesus, and connection to Jesus came in the form of the gathered community sharing *koinonia* or fellowship, the agape meal, and offerings for the poor. Remembrance was the key to connection with the divine. Insofar as the rooms of the early house churches brought together Christian communities, then, they supported personal connection to the divine. This was not a period of strong individuals. Spiritual power rested as much with the group as with the individual.

Within a few generations, however, as the house churches were developing into the more formal domus ecclesiae, Christians found it necessary to find new ways to pass along and maintain knowledge of Jesus, which in turn would provide new means of empowerment. Teaching and ordination accomplished this for the clergy. Architecturally, the use of ornament aided in transmitting information about Jesus to the broader Christian community. As mentioned above, among the many interesting features of the domus ecclesiae at Dura-Europos is the rich artwork in the baptistery, especially as compared to the lack of ornament in the assembly room, a distinction which may suggest how early Christians perceived individualism and personal spiritual power in this period.

The iconography in the baptistery, which clearly served a didactic or educational purpose, also provided a means through which believers could experience a personal connection with Jesus. Baptism was the key ritual of the individual's relation to the faith, the point at which he or she made a personal and public commitment to Christianity and was accepted into the promise of salvation. The depictions of Jesus's miracles in the baptistery signal the significance of this intimate and highly charged setting by emphasizing Jesus's power, his closeness, and the salvation he offered the individual. In the baptistery, where attention was focused on the individual believer, death (symbolized by submersion in water) and eternal life come together, and the iconography provided a reminder of incidents in which Jesus overcame death. Through baptism, the individual joined Jesus in the death-rebirth cycle. The baptistery, then, was most likely the site of the greatest individual empowerment.

The assembly hall, on the other hand, signaling the authority of the clergy, offered fewer avenues to personal empowerment. As mentioned above, the only ornament found by archaeologists in the assembly hall was the portion of a Bacchic frieze. There could be a number of reasons for this lack of ornament and retention of the non-Christian images. Perhaps the room, being somewhat more public than the baptistery, was subject to search by authorities, and the lack of overtly Christian elements provided a "cover" for an underground group. This hypothesis, however, seems unlikely, as no evidence of Christian persecution in this small town has been found, and, in fact, the presence of several other religious sites suggests that its residents practiced religious diversity and toleration. More likely ornament was considered inappropriate in the hall, or of less importance there than in the baptistery. In the hall, where individuals focused on the shared experience of worship and not on their individual musings, remembrance came in the form of preaching and the shared Eucharist. In the baptistery, remembrance took on a more personal character, which was fostered by the images of Christ. Or it could be that the Christian community at Dura-Europos had simply not gotten around to decorating the assembly hall. Perceiving the baptistery as the more significant, more holy space, perhaps they worked on the ornamentation there before turning their attention to the assembly hall. With the siege and sacking of the town in 256 C.E., further work in the church was abruptly halted.

In any event, the presence of the murals suggests that the religious experience that a believer had in the baptistery was quite different from that which would be experienced in the assembly room. That difference stemmed not only from different rituals, but also from the distinctly different settings: the baptistery focused on the individual experience of the divine, and the assembly room focused on the fellowship of the Christian community. The baptistery was the site of individual empowerment, the assembly hall the site of social power.

The Development of the Christian Martyrium

Another distinct building type played a role in the process of developing an architectural expression of the institutionalizing faith. At the same time that the domus and aula ecclesiae encompassed rectangular spaces oriented lon-gitudinally, another early Christian building type, the centrally planned build-ing, followed a different but equally distinctive architectural plan. Centrally planned space radiates from a center point as in a circular or polygonal shape or in a Greek cross shape with arms of equal length. Whatever the shape, centrally planned buildings are quite distinct from the axial orientation of longitudinal plans. During the early Christian period, buildings with circular, polygonal, and Greek cross plans were devoted to two highly specialized prac-tices, baptism and funerary rituals, and remained intimately linked to these functions until the late fourth century. Centrally planned buildings and spaces were typically quite small. Neither baptism nor funerary rituals, such as com-muning with the dead or worshipping a martyr, required a large assembly space. In these small, centrally planned rooms, the center of attention—the font, sarcophagus, or relic—occupied the center of the space. In the case of baptisteries, many were often small rooms within or attachments to larger buildings (as in the case of the baptistery in the domus ecclesiae in Dura-Europos).

The Christian use of central plans grew out of the cults of the "special" dead, or those who were perceived as holy in some way, practiced widely within the Roman Empire. Cults of the special dead, evident in Greek, Roman, and Early Christian practices, conceived of a direct link between human society and supernatural power. These cults shared the belief that the spirit of a spe-cial person inhabited his or her gravesite and had special powers to which the living could appeal for aid. Thus veneration of the dead brought these communities—including Christians—into direct relation with the spiritual realm. At the graves of martyrs, teachers, and other leaders, early Christians, according to archeologist Graydon Snyder, "celebrated their kinship with the Christian special dead and with each other."[56] There they shared a communal meal, sometimes inserting food into the sarcophagus, and prayed, petitioning the special dead on behalf of living individuals.

The spaces used for these rituals varied. Some scholars have suggested that catacombs, underground communal burial sites excavated in the early third century, were used for these meetings. Several pre-Constantinian cata-combs still exist, including those of Rome, which comprise of a network of several dozen miles and house thousands of burials. The graves themselves, called loculi, were often highly decorated, covered with marble and ornamented with frescoes of Christian images and stories. Given the cramped quarters within the catacombs, however, it seems unlikely that these burial sites were used for ritual observances. Instead, cubicula, or large underground rooms located on tunnels near gravesites, may have been so used.[57] Yet space was limited even in these cubicula, allowing for only very small memorial services to be conducted within them. Thus, by the mid-third century, when open-air cemeteries appeared, dedicated funerary buildings called *martyria* were constructed.

Martyria shared similarities with pagan *mausolea,* although differences did exist. The Christian structures ranged in form from simple walled-in courtyards terminating in an apse or curved area surrounding the tomb of the martyr to elaborately porticoed courtyards with multiple apses and tombs to two-storied, round, square, polygonal, and cross-shaped vaulted buildings.[58] Although central plans predominated in martyria design, other types, most notably the longitudinal transept or T-shaped form exemplified by St. Peter's in Rome, are also evident. In situations in which a large meeting area was required, a basilica (a long assembly hall with an apse at one end) and/or an atrium might be attached to the martyrium to produce a dual-function building: the martyrium devoted to the cult of the martyr and the assembly hall used for the rite of the Mass.

Examples of martyria abound, particularly from the late third and fourth centuries. The Church of the Nativity in Bethlehem (circa 333), commissioned by Constantine, is an example. Constantine also ordered the construction of the first freestanding Christian centralized martyrium, the Anastasis Rotunda (circa 335), erected over the site where Jesus Christ was said to have been entombed and from which he arose. The round Anastasis, 110 feet in diameter with a surrounding ambulatory, was large enough to accommodate many worshippers and performed the dual function of martyrium and church (fig. 2.4). Although it was later attached to an atrium and a basilica, called the Church of the Holy Sepulcher, this large, freestanding martyrium set the stage, as Krautheimer has argued, for the continuing "absorption of the martyrium plan as a regular church." By the fourth and fifth centuries, the centrally planned building type commonly became self-sufficient, standing on its own without a nave, and its function expanded from sheltering a tomb or a relic and accommodating small numbers of worshippers to serving as a church in its own right.[59]

Martyria not only housed the special dead and ritual ceremonies, but also provided space for the burial of ordinary people. Nevertheless, whether providing space for sharing a meal with, praying to, or being interred near the special dead, martyria accommodated and regulated proximity to supernatural power. Sharing a meal with a deceased loved one or with a renowned and holy spirit connected believers with divine power in a profoundly personal way. The small scale of martyrium spaces mirrored the closeness of the relationship to the special dead, enhancing the personal spiritual experience in a way that the

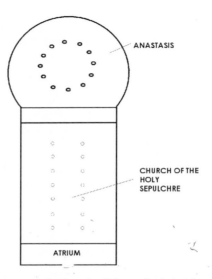

FIGURE 2.4. Anastasis and Church of the Holy Sepulcher, Jerusalem. Line
drawing by Paul R. Kilde.

increasingly large churches could not.[60] The centralized spaces of martyria
encircled the gravesite or tomb, and people arranged themselves in relation to
it and the power that emanated from it. Given the personal, familial nature of
the rituals performed within these martyria, it is unlikely that strong spatial
distinctions among worshippers were made within them. The modest size of
the buildings, some less than twenty meters in diameter, and the proportion
of space devoted to the sarcophagus and an occasional altar would likely have
precluded the kinds of spatial distinctions possible in a domus ecclesiae or aula
ecclesiae. Although conventions regarding the physical arrangement of worshippers around the tomb are impossible to ascertain from archeological remains, it is likely that they involved proximity to some part of the sarcophagus
or to the altar, as do the seating arrangements at funerals today, with clergy and
family closest to the deceased.

The intimacy of the space underscored a strong message about power:
to be inside the martyrium was to be in the presence of a supernatural and
spiritual power that pervaded every centimeter of the space. To illustrate the
spiritual power associated with martyria, historian Peter Brown quotes a sixth-
century layman: "When I find that I am in a place where there are relics of the
holy martyrs, I am obsessed by the need to go in and venerate them. Every time
I pass in front of them, I feel I should bow my head."[61] Unlike the assembly
rooms of the domus ecclesiae and the aula ecclesiae, the entire atmosphere of
the martyrium was perceived as infused with divine power. Although the

assembly rooms may have been sacralized by the depiction of sacred stories of their walls and by the performance of sacred rituals within them, the martyrium was a sacred site much more akin to a temple—here the divine, or at least the dead who had a strong connection to the divine, permeated the building. This view, similar to Eliade's substantive understanding of sacred space, would come to lend a powerful legitimacy to the construction of many other ecclesiastical buildings in the fourth century. As we will see, under the Roman emperor Constantine the centrally planned martyrium would play an important role in the expression of imperial power, as well as in the development of formalized Christian spaces.

In summary, then, as early Christians came together in groups in remembrance of Jesus, their practices and the spaces they used laid the groundwork for the next two centuries of Christian worship. As their worship, which shifted from sharing the actual agape meal to the symbolic celebration of the Eucharistic sacrifice, slowly became institutionalized and performed by an ordained clergy, the spaces that necessarily grew to accommodate the increasing numbers also took on greater symbolic meaning. The multiuse triclinium of the Roman house gave way to larger, more formal assembly rooms and baptisteries, some of which announced their special character through ornamentation, including images of Christ and his life. Though the institutionalization of Christian space was set in motion during this period, it would not be fully achieved until the fourth century, when the still relatively new religion would be granted official status in the Roman world.

3

Imperial Power in Constantinian and Byzantine Churches

Though he would be baptized only on his deathbed in 337, Roman Emperor Constantine embraced Christianity in 312, when he came to believe that the sign of Christ, appearing to him in a dream, aided his army in battle. With the Edict of Milan a year later, Constantine gave Christianity official status in the empire.[1] Constantine's embrace of Christianity was no ordinary conversion, for in the Roman tradition, the emperor himself was considered akin to a god, a personage who ruled through divine imprimatur. Constantine not only believed he was guided by God but that he ruled over the earthly Christian empire as God ruled in Heaven. This commingling of state power (that of the empire) with supernatural power (that of the divine god) propagated *caesaropapism,* a term coined by historian Deno John Geanakoplos to indicate the "unity of the empire—one church, one state, both under the rule of God's representative or viceregent on earth, the *Basileus* [Emperor]."[2] In other words, God and state came together in the figure of Constantine to form a powerful alliance. Thus Constantine's conversion and granting of official status to Christianity imbued the religion with a new sociopolitical legitimacy and the emperor himself with a new religious legitimacy.

Constantine demonstrated this correspondence between supernatural power and the state to his people in a number of ways, among them the launching of what would come to be a building program of immense proportions. Though the exact number of churches Constantine had a hand in creating is unknown, he was involved in the construction of many of the most influential of their day, including the Basilica Salvatoris at the Laterani palace near Rome (a church now known as St. John Lateran), the Church of the Holy Sepulchre in Jerusalem, and the Church of the Nativity in Bethlehem. It was with these and the many other churches of the Roman Empire that a public Christian architecture came into its own. This new Christian architecture was radically different from the modest vernacular buildings of earlier Christians, for the now-state-sponsored religion demanded an architectural expression commensurate with its new social, political, and spiritual prestige.

The purpose of the new Christian buildings was not simply to house worship rituals but to demonstrate the power of the emperor and of Christianity—in other words, these buildings were informed by clear social, political, and religious agendas. Constantine's churches were symbols of both religious and imperial power. Consequently, under Constantine and his successors, Christian buildings shed the inconspicuous domestic façades that had previously marked the religion as a private cult. The new buildings flaunted their important public locations and their great size as badges of the new public legitimacy of Christianity. Changes occurred inside the buildings, as well, as Christian worship was transformed through the integration of the forms and formality of the imperial court into both liturgy and architecture. Thus the churches of Constantine transformed not only Christian architecture but Christianity itself.

The Power of Location

Among the most profound changes Constantine wrought on Christian worship space was the redefining of its purpose to embrace political and spiritual functions. This was accomplished in part by the careful selection of the locations for new churches. No longer would Christian churches be inconspicuously nestled on residential streets or in tenement buildings. Under Constantine, the locations of churches themselves would play important political and religious roles, underscoring the fusion of religious and imperial power.

The city of Rome was over 500 years old when Constantine began building churches, and as in most cities, the best opportunities for building were on the outskirts, in suburban areas rather than in the long-since-overbuilt city center. Constantine's earliest churches were thus located in the outer precincts of Rome rather than at its heart. In deciding where to locate them, however, he typically chose sites in close proximity to preexisting episcopates (locations of Christian bishops) or imperial properties. The Lateran basilica, for instance, begun around 313, was designed to adjoin the Laterani palace, which stood at the edge of the city and would come to house the bishop of Rome in appropriate state.[3] The palace had come into Constantine's control through his wife Fausta, by whose name the new church would sometimes be known: Domus Faustae. Though the exact features of the original Lateran church are unknown (the building was destroyed in an earthquake in 896), it was likely a moderate-sized *basilica*—that is, a longitudinally oriented, rectangular building with an apse at the far end—and may have been a conversion of an existing building, rather than a new construction. Befitting Constantine's debt to what he perceived as Christ's help in battle, the new church was dedicated to Christ the Savior, as the Basilica Salvatoris, and would become the center of Christianity in the Rome. By ordering his first Christian building efforts to take place at the Lateran palace, Constantine, this new convert to Christianity, likely curried favor with the bishop, the most influential Christian figure in the region, and reassured the powerful religious figure of his sincerity, if not his deference.[4] The location of the Lateran basilica demonstrated the new coupling of state power with the social power of the clergy that was already developing within Christianity.

In other instances, Constantine's careful selection of location demonstrated his willingness to use perceived supernatural power to legitimate both his religious and imperial agendas. This is particularly evident in his creation of memorials to commemorate key events in the life of Jesus Christ. The memorial he erected over the supposed site of Jesus's entombment and resurrection, for instance, demonstrates a savvy use of a religious building to advance specific agendas. By the early fourth century, the site that was assumed to be the tomb of Jesus was occupied by a temple to Aphrodite, which the Romans may well have constructed over the tomb precisely in order to suppress the upstart religious group. Constantine ordered the temple destroyed and all evidence of it dispersed. According to Eusebius, Constantine's biographer and an ardent Christian, far beneath the surface of the site, a cave assumed to be Jesus's tomb, the "holy of holies," was revealed, which Constantine vowed to make "a center of attraction and venerable to all."[5] Justified by the discovery of the cave, Constantine went ahead with his plan to transform the site into a memorial. He had the cave excavated into a cone-shaped pile and around it erected a peristyle supported by columns. Then he ordered the construction of a monumental new church, the Church of the Holy Sepulchre. As the church went up on the site, it proudly announced the triumph of Christianity over the older Roman religion.

But this is only one version of the story. In another, commonly told in the latter part of the fourth century and elaborated by Rufinus around 400, it is not Constantine but his mother, Helena, who is the main actor. Learning that remnants of the cross upon which Jesus was crucified lay under the Aphrodite temple, she ordered the temple destroyed. Pieces of three crosses were subsequently found and tested to ascertain which was that on which Jesus died. One piece passed the test by performing a healing miracle, and Helena ordered a church to be built on the place where it was found.

In both versions of the story about how the location of this memorial building was chosen, social and supernatural power are intermingled. For Eusebius, intent upon demonstrating Constantine's role as God's vice-regent, the emperor's discovery and memorializing of the site of Christ's resurrection elevated him to a patron of divinity. The emperor saved this holy site from oblivion and erected a magnificent shrine and pilgrimage site for God and for the people. Importantly, the emperor's power was required to re-ignite the sacred meaning of the place. In Rufinus's version, the story of Helena also demonstrated how divine guidance had led her to the site. Here again, the sacred place was dependent upon imperial patronage to expose its true meaning.[6] Further, in both these versions the construction of the Christian building, which required the destruction of the Temple of Aphrodite, is characterized as a strategy in an ongoing ideological battle between religious perspectives. The temple, according to Constantinian and later sources, had been deliberately erected to obliterate the importance of the site as Christian, and the new church in turn deliberately obliterated the temple. In this scenario, the Christian God triumphed over Aphrodite, and the new building purified the site and heralded Christianity's superiority. It may have been a form of atonement as well, for the destruction of the previous temple.[7] As historian Peter Richardson argues, however, "the notion of rivalry [among religions] is largely a Christian (and perhaps Jewish and Muslim) construct."[8] Monotheism lies at the heart of religious rivalry. In the Roman Empire, in which multiple religions and gods coexisted, the political ramifications of the reuse of spaces and buildings—including the destruction and replacement of existing buildings and the taking over of an existing building by a new group—are difficult to ascertain. Sites and buildings were sold to or otherwise obtained by new groups quite peaceably. The Constantinian and Helena legends are aimed at demonstrating the supernatural power of Christianity and its superiority over the Aphrodite cult. From this perspective, rivalry is assumed, and contestation serves to heighten the importance and sacredness of the site. Yet the accusation that the temple had been purposely built over the site of Jesus's tomb is simply that—an accusation, which remains unsubstantiated. In any case, the stories well illustrate the point that church building is a process that frequently involves meanings and goals in the social and political realms as well as religious ones.

These are not the only political meanings embedded in this church location, however. In addition to these messages regarding the faith and power of the imperial family, this location, supposedly the very spot on which the resurrection of Christ took place, physically supported one side in a centuries-old theological debate. This debate focused on the character of Jesus's resurrection, which had stirred disagreement among his followers since its occurrence. Many, like second-century author Tertullian, believed that the resurrection was a miraculous physical resurrection of the flesh that expressed Jesus's divinity. This view of Jesus's divine nature evolved into discussions of the relationship of the divinity of God and that of Jesus, which ultimately developed into the doctrine of the Trinity. In contrast, other early Christians emphasized the humanity of Jesus and viewed the resurrection as a spiritual release and transport of the soul rather than a physical event revealing the divinity of the body. This position was articulated in early Gnostic texts, including the *Gospel of Mary* and the *Gospel of Philip*, which indicate that some of the apostles believed that Jesus had come to them in dreams and visions rather than in the flesh. This spirit or soul resurrection, they felt, was no less profound than a physical resurrection and assured them of Christ's continuing ministry. This Gnostic interpretation of the event was held by a number of groups during Constantine's day, including the Arians, followers of Arius, who adhered to this centuries-old belief.[9]

At the time that Constantine affirmed the legal status of Christianity, just which type of Christianity, among its multiform manifestations, would be acknowledged as correct or orthodox had not yet been decided. Constantine himself seems to have generally sided with those who believed that the divine body of Christ had been resurrected—the miraculous resurrection of the flesh proving his divinity—and in the next several years his actions generally supported those who wished to suppress Gnostic or Arian views. For instance, in 352 he hosted the Council of Nicaea, a gathering of Christian leaders, which resulted in the still-used Nicene Creed, which strongly affirms the divinity of Jesus and went a long way to establish the orthodoxy of this view.[10] The emperor's earlier memorial to Jesus, the Church of the Holy Sepulchre, had also reified this theological view (that is, presented the abstract idea as a material, concrete thing) by commemorating the tomb of Jesus, the physical site of his supernatural resurrection. This building, essentially a martyrium, focused Christian attention on the miraculous event: here it happened, here Jesus's lifeless flesh was reinvigorated with divine breath. This was the exact spot of a miraculous *hierophany*, a site where divinity broke through and touched human experience.[11] Evidencing the singular importance of this event, the impressive Church of the Holy Sepulchre not only memorialized it but contributed significantly to the establishment of the orthodoxy of Jesus's divinity. Whether or not this was part of Constantine's intention in constructing the building, the memorial was certainly meant to remind all Christians of Jesus's death, entombment, and physical resurrection, all critical elements in what would become the orthodox Christian position.

Helena similarly advanced this position. Again according to Eusebius, Helena, during a pilgrimage to Palestine undertaken quite late in her life, directed churches to be built at the site of Jesus's birth in Bethlehem (the Church of the Nativity) and at the site of his ascension, the Mount of Olives (the Church of the Ascension). In particular, Helena's patronage of the construction of the Church of the Ascension, built sometime before 392, memorialized what she believed was the exact spot at which Christ's divinity was ultimately revealed to humanity.[12] Drawing upon the imperial coffers, Helena endowed these buildings with wealth unprecedented in Christian experience, creating large churches (that of the Nativity is some seventy-five meters in length) highly ornamented with precious metals, mosaics, and sculptures.[13]

These and other churches provided powerful statements in the debates over the nature of Jesus and the developing Christology, serving as symbols of his miraculous existence and divine character. For instance, the Church of St. Pudenziana in Rome, completed around 400, contains a *tympanum* mosaic depicting Christ enthroned as holy judge, surrounded by devotees, including Peter and Paul and St. Pudenziana and her sister, St. Praxedes (Prassede; fig. 3.1).[14] Above these the conventional symbols of the four evangelists hover on wings: the man for Matthew, the lion for Mark, the ox for Luke, and the eagle for John. In the background are images of the Church of the Nativity on the left, the cross of Golgotha rising in the middle, and the Church of the Holy Sepulchre on the right. In this image, the buildings and their sites point to the divinity of Jesus.

Yet, the tympanum image does not go as far in presenting him as a supernatural being as would later depictions. Its depiction of Christ himself, in "majesty" or sitting in judgment, is tempered. In his role as eschatological judge, Jesus wears the judicial robes of a human judge, a choice that links him with the human institution and signals his humanity. His location in the picture midway between the heavens and the human characters also suggests some moderation in its interpretation of Jesus's nature, for he is physically located closer to the row of people than to the roiling heavens. He also holds an inscription identifying the human patron of the work. Composed around 400, the image suggests that there remained a commitment to maintain some understanding of Jesus's humanity. Nevertheless, the figure's halo (borrowed from non-Christian Greek sources) and elevation attest to his fundamentally

FIGURE 3.1. Tympanum, Church of St. Pudenziana, Rome. Photo by Marilyn Chiat, Ph.D.

supernatural character. This image of a somewhat human risen Christ, combined with the buildings memorializing the sites of his birth, death, and miraculous resurrection, is a significant indication of the orthodox position. Jesus lived as a human being, but his physical resurrection attested to his divinity, which at least some of the faithful had intuited all along.

At the same time that these churches played an important role in the theological debates of the Byzantine period, they also played a role in linking the state to the religious realm. Whether or not, after nearly three centuries, the precise locations of these events in the life of Jesus had been identified correctly (and there is serious doubt among contemporary scholars that they were[15]), the desire and power of the state to memorialize certain places emerged as a defining factor in church location. We can see, then, that in Constantine's churches, efforts to mark imperial, social, religious, and supernatural power were mutually reinforcing, supporting each other and often becoming so inextricably linked as to be indistinguishable as separate agendas. As the new buildings conveyed power and grandeur through both scale and rich decor, they not only articulated the new official standing of Christianity during Constantine's reign, but also served to maintain Christianity's public presence and symbolic significance to this day.

This blending of political, social, and religious agendas requires us to think critically about sacred space itself—how it is created, how we might define it. As Mircea Eliade contends, from the standpoint of believers, the power of a sacred location lies in the perception of the indwelling power of the divine within it. For nearly two millennia, many Christian devotees have resolutely believed that holiness and divine power permeate these sites. Jonathan Z. Smith, taking a more anthropological view, would argue that the presence of an indwelling divinity in the locations is not something that scholars can ascertain, but the very erection of churches, the development of pilgrimages to the sites, and the reverence with which believers treat the sites have in effect sacralized the churches, imbuing them with sacred meaning that remains powerful to this day. As we continue throughout this book to consider the relationships between articulations of divine, social, and supernatural power, these two perspectives will help us negotiate the gray areas between understanding buildings from the point of view of the faithful and from that of scholars.

The Basilica Form

The churches constructed during this period exhibit two primary plans. The first, the centrally planned church, developed directly from the centrally planned martyria discussed in the previous chapter. As we shall see, centrally planned religious buildings continued to serve memorial functions in the Constantinian period while also providing worshippers a focal point for devotions and a place for pilgrimage. Most churches, however, featured a different form, the rectangular plan characteristic of a building type known as the basilica. The use of this plan and building type signaled both the imperial and the religious significance of these buildings.

In the Roman era, the term *basilica* was used to designate any large hall used for public assemblies and generally pointed to the function of the building rather than its plan or architectural characteristics. Thus, wide variation in the use of the term existed, and it was applied to a variety of buildings. Nevertheless, its strong connection to the *basileus,* or emperor, remained clear.[16] Constantine's program of church building became closely associated with one particular variation: an oblong or rectangular building, oriented on a longitudinal axis running from the entry through the *narthex,* or vestibule, and *nave,* or main assembly area, to a terminating *apse,* or semicircular area (fig. 3.2). The nave was flanked by side *aisles* formed by columns that typically supported a timbered ceiling, although basilica churches also sometimes had vaulted

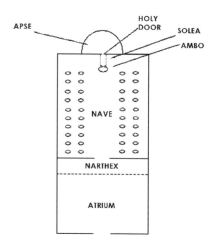

FIGURE 3.2. Generic basilica church. Line drawing by Paul R. Kilde.

ceilings. The semicircular apse, often covered by a semidome, was the focal point of the room and contained a platform or *dais* upon which various dignitaries sat and performed their duties. Used in public halls in Rome and in throne rooms in imperial palaces throughout the empire, this building type and spatial plan was not only closely associated with imperial power but also functioned to reify that power. These buildings, with their high, coffered ceilings, rich décor, and formal arrangements, were designed to impress. It is this particular building type that has come to be called a basilica in modern parlance.

Constantine adopted this space not only in the Lateran basilica, his first Christian church, but also in many later churches in Rome and Constantinople and throughout the empire. In fact, having rapidly achieved the status of an official template, the Christian basilica would be further repeated in buildings under Constantine's successor Constantinius II and later Christian rulers. Indeed, it remains popular to the present day.

Much of the basilica's appeal derives from its flexibility and ready absorption of symbolic meaning. Oriented on an east-west axis, with the apse in the east end, basilica churches mirrored those of other religions in heralding the direction of the rising sun, though in Western Christian signification, the direction came to indicate Jerusalem. Basilica space can be easily altered, widened by adding more aisles along the sides of the nave or lengthened by extending the nave. Constantine's Church of the Holy Sepulchre, for instance, constructed in 335, featured double aisles on each side of the nave. The apse, in which the altar was placed on the dais, was made more accommodating to service requirements by the addition of a *synthronon,* a curved bank of benches lining the back wall, used by various clergy and other participants in the service. Additional apses could be added to increase the size of the sanctuary space as well. *Clerestory* windows, intended to bring in light, were often included above the aisles, and galleries above the aisles could accommodate large audiences. In some instances, *transepts,* rectangular spaces crossing at right angles to the nave, were also added, either across the east end to form a *headed transept,* as in the original St. Peter's basilica in Rome, or partway up the nave to from a *cruciform,* or Latin cross, plan.

A dual set of meanings saturated the fourth-century Christian basilicas. The first group of meanings sprang from the basilica's imperial derivation. As mentioned above, the extent to which people of the Roman Empire associated this architectural form with the emperor and buildings of state was the extent to which its use in religious buildings marked Christianity with the stamp of imperial approval.[17] Like these new churches' monumentality, their basilica plan visually proclaimed the imperial significance of Christianity to the surrounding community. Large and lavishly ornamented, the Christian basilicas of the Constantinian period served, in art historian Richard Krautheimer's words, as "political-architectural propaganda" that reflected "the splendor of the Empire and its divine ruler."[18]

In addition to the splendor of its treatment as an imperial art form, the visual power of the basilica also stemmed from the oblong plan itself and the capacity of the resulting space to make manifest the importance of physical elements in religious experience. Upon entering a Christian basilica, one's eye is led down the long nave toward the point of significance, the altar, located some distance away on the dais in the apse. The colonnaded nave itself extends an invitation to approach the dais. The approach or journey toward the dais constitutes the raison d'être of the basilica. Some people, particularly members of the episcopate and imperial court, would approach with confidence, sailing down the nave in a grand ceremonial procession. Others, however, including the bulk of worshippers, would walk the long nave slowly, approaching the dais, the center of social and divine power, with humility, awe, and even fear.

The basilica is an architectural form designed to bring the worshipper to the sanctuary, the Christian equivalent of the "holy of holies," not immediately upon entering the building, but after a significant journey. Its entire design emphasizes this approach. The journey down the long nave encourages worshippers to think about the significance of their approach to the chancel, to consider their spiritual situation as the physical distance decreases. What does it mean to approach the altar? In what state of mind should one do so? How should one prepare one's self before and during this approach?[19] The physical emphasis on the approach achieved by the basilica emerged as the perfect architectural metonym or metaphor for the Christian life, a long journey toward God.

Liturgy and Hierarchical Power in the Basilica

A strict hierarchical arrangement characterized the interior spaces of these churches. This arrangement, borrowed from the imperial court, underscored the hierarchical character of the episcopacy, which was well established by the fourth century. In Roman basilicas, the organization of space proceeded hierarchically along the longitudinal axis, which began outside of the church itself. The axis ran from the street through a vestibule to an open-air atrium and then through a covered plaza just outside the west end of the church. Inside the church, the axis ran from the narthex up the nave to the sanctuary at the eastern end, which housed the altar and, behind it, the synthronon, an impressive curved seating area reserved for members of the episcopate, created by the addition of an apse to the eastern end of the building. The hierarchy could be read, from top to bottom, in this axis. At the far eastern end of the sanctuary, the celebrant, frequently the bishop, occupied the top step of the synthronon. The lower steps seated other priests, deacons, and presbyters. The nave housed worshippers, with the most politically, economically, and socially powerful nearest the sanctuary at the front.

Worship services during the period commenced with an elaborate procession that followed this hierarchical path from the exterior to the holiest place in the interior. Gathering outside the church in the expansive atrium, lay worshippers watched as the bishop and the emperor met in the porch or narthex and prepared for the First Entrance into the church. Entering the church together, the bishop and emperor were followed by a deacon carrying the Gospel, then by the celebrant, other clergy, the emperor's guards, and the empress and her attendants.[20] The procession continued up the nave to the sanctuary. This route was in some cases elaborated further with the addition of an *ambo,* a large raised lectern approached on either side by stairs and placed in the center of the nave, and, by the sixth century, a *solea,* a raised pathway from the ambo to the sanctuary lined with low parapets (fig. 3.2). This architectural path led to the Holy Door of the *sanctuary,* the area immediately surrounding the altar upon which the Eucharist would be prepared. The sanctuary was typically enclosed with some type of balustrade or colonnade, and in some regions shielded from view with veils, curtains, or even walls. The bishop stepped up into the sanctuary followed by the emperor, who placed a gift on the altar and immediately exited and moved to his *loge,* or imperial platform, in the right aisle. The bishop and clergy proceeded through the sanctuary into the apse, where they took seats on the steps of the semicircular synthronon. Lay worshippers then followed these official processors into the church and took up locations in the aisles and nave, as near the sanctuary, ambo, and solea as was deemed appropriate.[21]

The basilica plan effectively staged this religious performance in a way that underscored the interplay between supernatural and sociopolitical power. The long nave not only accommodated but profoundly encouraged the stately procession of clergy and emperor through the space. Culminating in the sanctuary, such processionals indicated both the power of those participating in it and the significance of the terminus. Processionals focused attention upon the sanctuary. Like a moving arrow, the procession gathered the attention of the worshippers and directed it toward the "holy of holies." The sanctuary was sacralized as the holiest of spaces in the church through a number of other strategies as well: through the exclusion of the laity from the space, through the limiting of imperial access, through the accommodations made for the consecrated altar, and through its central role in the sacred Eucharist ritual performed in it. The performance of the Eucharistic ritual, with its invoking of the holy presence of Christ, defined the sanctuary as a locus of divine power.

The architectural elements of the basilica placed various groups in hierarchical relation to one another, rigidly separating them along status lines. Proximity to the sanctuary indicated a connection to divine power that legitimated rank and sociopolitical power and also provided a sense of personal empowerment. Only those who were ordained at the highest levels could enter the sanctuary—the emperor himself could occupy it only briefly.[22] The borders of the sanctuary were clearly marked architecturally with an arch or a raised dais or separated with an altar rail, a feature borrowed directly from secular basilicas in which a low banister marked the boundary between the dais reserved for officials and the areas open to the public. In some churches the low separation was replaced with a tall, chancel screen of columns (*colonnades*) topped by an ornate molding (*architrave*). In Syrian churches, curtains were commonly used between the columns of the colonnade to conceal the mysteries of the sanctuary from the eyes of laypeople. In some churches the altar was sheltered under a *ciborium* or canopy, or under a vaulted *baldacchino* supported on columns. These would be draped with curtains to exclude all but the most privileged from viewing the powerful site.

The emperor occupied the *loge* in the aisle to the north (or right, given the typical east-west orientation), accessible to the sanctuary through a door but not actually within the holy space. The loge contained a dais and throne to indicate the elevated rank of the emperor. From the emperor's perspective, the loge offered a good view of the sanctuary as well as the crowds gathered in the nave. From the lay worshipper's perspective, it offered a focal point that rivaled the sanctuary.[23] The various court dignitaries and guards who occupied the loge with the emperor further underscored its role as a powerful space. Yet in religious terms, its power did not exceed that of the sanctuary, though a visual tension between the two may well have existed.[24]

The basilica plan readily accommodated large numbers of lay worshippers. In the Constantinian and early Byzantine churches, worshippers scattered themselves throughout the nave and aisles of the church, vying for the best position they could find. This spatial openness and relative freedom strongly contrasted with Syrian churches in which curtains were used to keep lay worshippers in the aisles and to conceal the nave itself from them. The galleries in Constantinian and Byzantine churches accommodated women as well as the catechumens who were required to withdraw from the building at the commencement of the Liturgy of the Faithful.[25] Accordingly, time was also an important ranking factor in these churches. Catechumens were allowed to witness only a portion of the full service, just as in services two centuries earlier, and, as we have seen, the emperor himself was allowed to stay within the sanctuary only briefly.

These spaces, highly rational and easily read by visitors, created rigid distinctions among the various participants in worship. At the same time, they emphasized the close physical and ideological kinship or propinquity between the emperor and the episcopate. These imperial basilicas physically demonstrated the localizing of both supernatural and social power within the body of the emperor and the body of the episcopate—and, ultimately, the body of Christ. In this regard, Krautheimer argues that the basilicas of Constantine were, in effect, "audience halls for the Lord," a god who was increasingly perceived as an imperial "Emperor of Heaven" rather than "primarily the god of the humble, the miracle-worker and savior."[26] Though Jesus himself was mockingly called a king in his day, Constantine reconstructed his image as a real king, and this imperial view of the King of Heaven would grow increasingly influential in the coming centuries.

Christian services, now focused on this new imperial view of God, adopted several features from imperial court ritual, including its performative character. The liturgy, according to Krautheimer, "became a ceremonial performed before the Lord or before his representative, the bishop, just as rigidly adhered to as the ceremonial performed before the emperor or his magistrate."[27]

Indeed, the religious liturgy borrowed many of its features from the imperial court, including the processional entry into the church, the vestments of high magistrates, ritual gestures such as bowing and kissing the ring, the use of candles, the accommodation for the bishop on an elaborate throne, all of which were commonly used when approaching the emperor and all were transferred to the episcopate. Such continuity in setting, ritual, material elements, and symbols constituted and underscored the caesaropapism of the Christianity of the time, emphasizing the congruence between divine and earthly political power and using the ceremonial pomp of the state to demonstrate the legitimacy of Christianity.

These churches also served as pseudo-audience halls for the emperor. Social and supernatural power intertwined in the basilica. The church space not only designated both religious and sociopolitical rank, but, as these meanings were associated with it, the space also helped to maintain these ranks. Furthermore, as physical expressions of hierarchy, church spaces also naturalized these relationships. While the imperial function was clearly compatible with congregations' need for increasingly large meeting spaces, its spatial symbolic power far outstripped the previous symbolism of a Christian community of near-equals meeting in koinonia fellowship. Thus, not only did the ritual itself define and express sociopolitical power in relation to divine power, but that expression was also inscribed on the very spaces within which it occurred.[28]

Although some critics of this imperial commingling of divine and social power have unfavorably compared the Constantinian period of Christianity to an earlier pre-Constantinian period assumed to be characterized by social and spiritual equals, we would do well to carefully examine such conclusions. As we have seen, rank and hierarchy were apparent in the earliest Christian meetings, though clearly not on this scale. Moreover, personal power plays an important role in Christian basilicas. Lay audiences participated in the procession, entering the church after the dignitaries. Indeed, it was the entrance of the laity that, in effect, transformed the building into a "church": the assembly of the gathered faithful created the symbolic *ecclesiae*.[29] As Thomas Mathews has argued, the liturgical procession that the basilica architecture so readily accommodated and encouraged constituted for the average layperson "a very real symbolic action which for him was entrance into divine life."[30] To enter the west doors was to enter a distinctive, sacred world in which one's own place was clear. By enhancing this mystical event, Constantinian and Byzantine churches linked the supernatural and the personal in a way that inspired great devotion.

Experimentation and Centrally Planned Churches

The popularity of the basilica plan described above was rivaled only by the centrally planned church, which developed out of the funerary mausoleums of Roman culture. In the fourth and fifth centuries, this building type was increasingly adapted for general worship, although it remained closely associated with venerated sites. Among the most influential of these Christian churches was the Anastasis, a circular building or *rotunda* erected over the purported site of Jesus's tomb sometime after the completion of Constantine's basilica of the Holy Sepulchre, located near the tomb.

Constantine, as we have seen, had earlier excavated the cave that constituted the tomb into a cone-shaped pile and decorated it with a colonnade and *baldacchino* that allowed one to look down through a gaping hole into the tomb itself. Around 350, the decision was made to enhance the memorial, and the Anastasis was erected over the tomb itself. The floor plan of the Anastasis rotunda measured over fifty-five feet in diameter. At its center was the tomb, still surrounded by colonnade and baldacchino, encircled by a walkway, or *ambulatory*, with a gallery for worshippers. Surmounting the room was a huge dome.[31]

Given the importance of the Anastasis as the martyrium of Christ, it is not surprising that it was widely imitated in the coming centuries. The building itself was rebuilt several times, and its image was used as a powerful symbol within Christianity during the Byzantine and medieval periods. With the Anastasis and its imitators, the centrally planned building type was employed well beyond its funerary origins. Round churches, like the one dedicated to Saints Karpos and Polykarpos in Constantinople, were increasingly erected primarily to accommodate worship, although by being dedicated to martyred saints, they retained a reminder of the original funerary purpose.[32]

Centrally planned buildings were particularly suited to their original purpose of drawing attention to the significance of the martyred individual, in that the space allowed the placement of the sarcophagus at its very center. As centralized plans were adopted into worship space requiring a sanctuary and accommodation for clergy, the results were often a less natural use of space. Whereas a centrally planned space emphasizes the center, placing the sanctuary in the center of the space would be unacceptable, for to do so would be to invite worshippers to wander around the sanctuary as in the Anastasis ambulatory. The hierarchical and exclusive character of the sanctuary, however, required that access be limited and that the adjacent space for the episcopate be similarly exclusive. Thus, a sanctuary in a centrally planned church is necessarily placed to one side, disrupting the balanced centrality of the space itself. Typically, an apse extends the plan to accommodate the sanctuary, compromising the centrality of the plan. But this strategy works more effectively in some plans than in others. For instance, in a Greek cross plan with equivalent arms, the placement of the sanctuary within one arm (frequently spilling out into the crossing) effectively works with the space rather than against it.

Despite this potential for awkwardness at the ground level, centralized spaces did allow room for great experimentation with vertical elements. Centered domes, resting on *drums* and *pendentives* atop massive piers, gave these rooms a vertical thrust lacking in the basilica, drawing the eye upward in contrast to the horizontal or linear focus on the sanctuary encouraged by the basilica. Niches called *exedra* between the piers supported half domes that together created complex, undulating coverings that also drew the eye upward. Though domes were most successfully used to enclose centralized space, by the sixth century they were also used in series to cover basilica space. The Church of St. John at Ephesus, for instance, featured a Latin cross plan with two small domes over the nave and one over the apse along with three larger domes covering the crossing and the north and south transepts. In such a building, the verticality created by the domed ceiling tempered the linearity of the nave.

The Byzantine Church

Experimentation with domed space reached a peak several generations later with the construction of Hagia Sophia, completed in Constantinople in 537 under Justinian I. This building, too, combined what Rowland Mainstone calls "the centrality of the dome with the axiality typical of a normal basilica,"[33] but did so in a way that counterposed the two to create an extraordinarily complex space. Within the rather squat rectangular plan of the building, four massive piers inscribe a square. Colonnades between these piers on the north and south sides suggest a basilica-type space leading to the sanctuary, which is defined by an apse, projecting beyond the outer rectangle of the plan. Exedra supporting half-domes between the piers and the outer walls create an undulating effect in the overall rectangular plan of the nave. The massive piers themselves support pendentives, upon which rests a drum pierced by many closely spaced windows. Above this hovers the large, though shallow, dome.

It is the vertical thrust of the dome that dominates this building, despite the blending of verticality and axial orientations. Upon entering Hagia Sophia, one's eye is drawn immediately upward (fig 3.3). Four levels of vertical space

FIGURE 3.3. Hagia Sophia, Istanbul, Turkey. Photo by Dr. Leonard Schloff.

are defined by the architectural features, from the ground-level colonnade to a second-level gallery balustrade to the arches, pendentives, and half-domes, and finally to the crowning circular dome. The dome is literally the centerpiece of the building. Set off from the pendentives by the closely spaced windows of the drum, it seems to hover on a ring of light. As one walks through the nave, the lower level of piers, colonnaded aisles, exedra, and apse forms a complex puzzle of receding and advancing spaces that even architectural historians have called visually baffling.[34] This ground-level maze, however, resolves into more easily read spaces as the eye moves upward to the dome. Here, the eye finds peace.

And this was the point. The form of the basilica led the worshipper directly to the sanctuary and the altar where the miracle of the Eucharist occurred, reifying the sacramental relationship between humanity and God, but at the same time the form of the domed church led the eye of the worshipper upward, to the heavens—God's domain itself. Indeed, the domes in this and similar Byzantine churches, hovering almost magically on rings of light created by windows, earned the name *domes of heaven* and frequently contained an image of Jesus looking down upon and blessing the people.

In Hagia Sophia, the dome hovered on its ring of light as no previous dome had. It was covered with gold mosaic, which picked up the light and reflected it all around the room. The other half-domes and vaults were also covered with gold mosaics, and the poured concrete of the piers and walls was covered with marble veneer. The light from the dome gleamed and sparkled on the shiny surfaces, making the building seem alive with light. In his laudatory book on Justinian's architectural production, the historian Procopius reported that Hagia Sophia had a powerful effect on Christians, serving not only as an important landmark in the city but as a means through which one could know and understand God. He wrote, "And whenever one enters the church to pray, one understands immediately that it has been fashioned not by any human power or skill but by the influence of God. And so the mind is lifted up to God and exalted, feeling that He cannot be far away but must love to dwell in this place which He has chosen."[35]

Domed Byzantine churches, then, were informed by a different purpose from the earlier Roman basilicas. This was architecture less focused on awe of earthly power, though that theme was present, as on awe of the divine itself. This was architecture less focused on the altar and Eucharist as the means through which one could know God, instead fostering an individual, personal, and spiritual reckoning with an awesome divinity seemingly made manifest and glorious through light and space. This trope of the indwelling presence of God echoes the purpose of a temple, a building wherein divinity dwells. Housing the Lord was a new role for Christian churches, one that the early Christians and even Constantine had never imagined. But Christians quickly embraced it. Indeed, the *Narratio,* a collection of stories of the period, relates that upon completing the building, Justinian exclaimed, "Glory to God who has thought me worthy to finish this work. Solomon I have outdone you."[36] With Hagia Sophia, church became temple.

The representational art in Byzantine churches contributed to the emphasis on the divine realm, although it, too, was tempered with references to Christ's humanity. The figure of Christ and his revealed divinity were common, appearing in such forms as the Word (his divinity expressed in the form of scripture), as the Flesh (in the form of the Eucharistic elements), and as the Judge.[37] New images of the Virgin, whose own miraculous story lent witness to the divinity of Jesus himself, also appeared. Nevertheless, images of the life of Christ also remained, referencing the humanity of the figure.

As mentioned before, religious architecture functions as a ritual practice itself, focusing the attention on what is cosmically significant. In the domed church, the focus is above, on the transcendent God. Yet Hagia Sophia retained a foot in both the classical and Byzantine camps. With its square imposed on a rectangle and culminating apse, the plan itself echoed the rational lines of the Roman basilica and centrally planned buildings. Soon, however, that classical influence would wane, and experimentation would take religious architecture in increasingly complex directions.[38] The development of the triple apse by the eighth century, for instance, indicated new levels of spatial freedom and experimentation. Abandoning the synthronon and placing two side apses on either side of the original west end apse, builders incorporated the newly influential symbol of the Trinity into the physical plan of the church.[39] This elaboration of what is now known as the *chancel* underscored the power of the group allowed access to these apses, the clergy and in some cases orders of religious. But it also fragmented what had once been a unified space, compromising the riveted focus on either the altar or dome. This profusion of spaces would be used increasingly through the Byzantine period. Imposing geometrical form upon geometrical form (e.g., a square upon a rectangle, an octagon upon a square), covering individual bays with domes supported on pendentives, and adding niches and *sacristies* in the corners, builders created highly complex spaces, fragmented by forests of columns and piers. Still, the lighted domes and decorated half-domes aloft offered some relief for the confusion below, physically evoking the sacred message of Christ's saving grace and providing focus and visual respite.

Transformations in these spaces were accompanied by transformations in services. The addition of sacristies, or rooms in which sacred vessels are kept, on either side of the chancel created a new north-south flow of clerical activity that countered the east-west axis of earlier times. With the elements of the Eucharist and the service now stored in these sacristies, processionals, which had earlier brought the elements into the church, now simply relocated the elements within the building. New processional routes emerged, inscribing a north-south or even circular movement as clergy walked from the sacristy to the central area under the dome, where they could be viewed by the congregation, and into the sanctuary.[40] Although these shorter, more convoluted processionals lacked the unifying power of the main processional down the nave, they likely enhanced the exclusivity and importance of the restricted clerical areas of the church. They also provide an indication of how space and ceremony impinge upon one another.

Complexities of Power in Constantinian and Byzantine Churches

We can see many ways, then, in which power was articulated within these early Christian churches. They represented a new understanding of divine power, which focused on the transcendence of God and the heavenly location of salvation, even as they asserted the political power of the state, represented by the emperor. From Constantine on, emperors and other political leaders sympathetic to Christianity, by serving as patrons of Christianity, as semidivine figures (in some cases), as worshippers, and as judges and rulers, guided religious practice through imperial conduits for the benefit of both Christianity and the state. Through this association, the clergy also gained power. Performing their sacred tasks within imperial buildings, wearing the robes of magisterial figures, reproducing the ceremonies of imperial events, and earning state support for a new theological orthodoxy, the clergy significantly increased their status and influence. The buildings of Christianity, both the domed churches and the basilicas, reflected this enhancement of power by replicating the awesome spaces of imperial Rome and restricting their holiest areas to the clergy.

Yet this display of social power did not preclude the possibility of personal empowerment. In the Byzantine church, the devotion of worshippers came to rely increasingly upon the supernatural character of Christ. Although Gnostics had struggled mightily to emphasize Jesus's humanity, the concept of the holy Trinity, and with it the divinity of Christ, became orthodox. Yet the Gnostics succeeded in the extent to which the awe-inspiring churches encouraged personal encounters with a spiritual being. Though the church asserted that an individual's relationship with Christ came through the sacraments, lay worshippers' exclusion from the most important sacrament, the Eucharist, required their finding other means of connecting with Christ. This would come through spiritual means, including the development of relationships with intercessory saints and the experiencing of aesthetically powerful spaces devoted to sacred knowledge and performance, in the form of these new churches.[41]

In developing a spiritual connection to the divine, lay worshippers turned to hierophanies, instances of the divine breaking through to human perception. The Eucharist service, in which the real presence of Christ was achieved, created a hierophanic moment. Martyria, like the Anastasis, marked the locations of historical hierophanies—the death and resurrection of Christ. Churches devoted to saints (or to Jesus himself, as with Hagia Sophia) became a trope for the ongoing reality of such occurrences in daily life. Further, within the imperial churches described above, worshippers found an impressive space of great wealth and power in which they might intimately connect with the penetration of holiness into human life.

Their experiences in these churches differed enormously, however, from those of their forbearers within the house churches and domus ecclesiae of the apostles' time, ordinary domestic buildings in which the focus was on the teachings of Jesus, the agape meal, koinonia, and eventually the Eucharist. Thus, the imperial churches of the Roman and Byzantine periods eloquently demonstrate significant changes taking place in Christianity itself.

The Legacy of Byzantine Churches

Strong influences from the Byzantine era are visible still today in Orthodox churches. As Christianity developed, differences over certain theological issues between "eastern" and "western" perspectives arose as early as the fourth and fifth centuries. It was not until the ninth century, however, that the divisions between Christian leaders in Constantinople and Rome became acute. The schism came in 1054. Through the centuries since, the eastern perspective expanded both north (into Russia) and east from Greece and present-day Turkey. Called the Orthodox or Eastern Church, this wing of Christianity is composed of a number of independent churches—Greek Orthodox, Russian Orthodox, and several others—that are in communion with one another and acknowledge at least the honorary primacy of the Patriarch of Constantinople.

Orthodox churches have continued the architectural and spatial legacy of • early Byzantine churches such as Hagia Sophia to the present day. Among the central features of Orthodox worship is the belief in the corporate character of the human relationship with God, part of the legacy of the Byzantine world. Focus is less on the individual and more on the church as a community joined in worship. The Orthodox service is fully liturgical, and it is through liturgy that the worshipping community communicates with God. The church building is the site of this meeting—the place where heaven and earth come together. Indicating this meeting is the dome that commonly tops Orthodox sanctuaries. Ringed by windows and painted with an image of Christ in glory, the dome is understood as the locus of the divine within the meeting—the vault of heaven.

Beneath the dome is the sanctuary, enclosed from the view of the congregation by an *iconostasis* or screen. The iconostasis developed over the centuries from what was a low balustrade around the sanctuary in early Byzantine churches to a high screen by the fifteenth century. The iconostasis is covered with depictions of holy personages such as Mary and Joseph, the Evangelists, the Apostles, saints, and church patriarchs, all arranged in rows. The holy place it shields houses the altar and is accessible only to the initiated, that is, priests, religious, deacons and the like, who move between the sanctuary and the congregation through three doors: the north and south doors and the central or "royal" door. Movement in and out of the sanctuary and processions through the rest of the church are key components in linking the congregation with the Eucharist celebration. During the service, the priest, accompanied by attendants, carries the Gospel out of the sanctuary through the north door and processes throughout the church, reentering the sanctuary through the royal door. Later in the service, the same route is followed during the Great Entrance, in which the priest and celebrants process with the vessels of unconsecrated wine and bread.

Due in part to the importance of the congregation as the central component in the relationship with God, the power relationships in eastern churches are somewhat belied by the exclusivity of the sanctuary. That exclusivity acknowledges and conveys the significant power residing in the clergy. Yet a significant corporate social power also resides in the congregation that occupies the nave. During services, some worshippers engage in personal devotions, often the veneration of icons. Others, however, may walk about and converse with friends and family. Orthodox lay people generally take communion only a few times a year, a tradition that reflects the lesser importance attributed the idea of individual salvation. Simply being present in community within the church furthers the corporate relationship with the divine.[42]

Thus, in the understandings of the function of worship as a meeting with the divine, of the central role of the laity in this meeting, and in the spaces in which the meeting takes place, the legacy of the Byzantine period continues to this day in Orthodox churches. We turn now from the Eastern tradition to follow the Western, the development of the Roman church, which would later be termed the Roman Catholic. As we shall see, this branch of Christianity would also carry on some elements of the earlier periods, but at the same time it would develop a host of new ideas and practices.

4

From Abbey to Great Church, Fortress to Heavenly City

With the collapse of the Roman Empire, which had concentrated both political power and religious authority in the body of one man, came the fracturing of political and religious power. Struggles over power ensued among nation-states and against new invaders. Within often violent contexts, Christians sought new ways of conceptualizing religious meaning and defining power. In small, isolated communities scattered from the British Isles to North Africa, Christians turned inward to protect themselves from invading forces. Christian building from the fifth through the tenth centuries was done primarily by small insular communities of men and women who integrated residential space back into Christian architecture, all with an anxious eye toward security. During this period, the abbey or monastery, a religious building that would remain important through the twentieth century, emerged as a prominent Christian form. As the eleventh century dawned, however, and social stability grew more prominent, a gradual accumulation of wealth gave new impetus to church building, and the era of the magnificent cathedrals of Europe was launched. From the abbeys of the eighth and ninth centuries to the great churches of the eleventh, transformations in Christian architecture demonstrated profound changes in Christian views of God, humanity, and power.

These periods witnessed the increasing importance of a tension in Christian worship and architecture that continues to this day— the tension between a model of worship that is individualistic and privatized and one that is communal and social, between an internalized, introverted performance of faith on the part of the individual and an externalized, extroverted performance shared with other believers. Although most worship practices fell somewhere between these dichotomous poles, negotiation between them, as we will see, became increasingly evident as Christianity continued its spread through Europe.

Monasticism and the Abbey

Monasticism—that is, the intentional living apart from society, either individually or with a group, for religious reasons—long predates Christianity but has been a part of Christianity since the third century. Saint Anthony is generally credited with founding the first monastic community, and his legacy was carried on by his disciple, St. Pachomius, who is said to have founded the first Christian monastery, on the Nile River in Egypt. Western monasticism traces its roots to St. Benedict, who in the sixth century developed a set of rules for monastic life called the Benedictine Order, which emphasized poverty, chastity, and obedience. Benedict established several monasteries, including Montecassino, southeast of Rome. Built over a Roman fort and temple for Apollo, Montecassino obliterated the previous religious site and claimed the ground for Christianity. Monasticism, like previous church building programs, went hand in hand with spreading Christianity.

Given the insecurity of the period—the roving bands of invaders, poverty, famine, and hunger—it is not surprising that abbeys frequently resembled forts or redoubts. The Romanesque architectural style (termed *Norman* in England and *Lombard* in France), developed between 1000 and 1100, emphasized massive, protective walls with small, round-arched windows.[1] Called *Romanesque* by later historians who traced the use of round-arch technologies back to Roman techniques, these churches followed the basilica plan, with its long nave terminating in an apse that housed the sanctuary. Constructed with thick stone walls, resistant to marauding invaders, abbey basilicas contained few windows, and those were usually quite small, making the interiors dark and shadowy. Yet these buildings were not without technical expertise or ornament. In Romanesque naves, barrel vaulting often replaced the post-and-lintel ceilings of earlier days, and in a few cases a dome covered the sanctuary. Renewed interest in the visual depiction of biblical ideas and events brought new art to these churches, in the form of frescoes, paintings, and sculpture. A variety of exterior features also emerged, including the round towers with pointed caps that would eventually evolve into the church steeples of the

Gothic period. Features designed specifically for defensive purposes were not uncommon: crenellations on the top of towers and narrow lancet windows, both intended to provide protection for archers defending the buildings, augmented the fortress function. Whether or not monastics actually defended themselves against invaders is less important than the fact that many abbeys were sacked and their residents forced to flee for their lives.

The paradox of monasticism lies in its bringing community and the individual into not just creative tension, but into creative dependence upon one another within confined quarters. Abbeys were multiuse complexes that articulated the tension between communal and individual religious practice. Benedictine monks divided their time between "liturgical devotion, spiritual reading and meditation, and manual labor," according to historian F. H. Crossley.[2] Abbeys, therefore, included spaces for communal worship, individual meditation, administrative and agricultural work, food preparation, dining, and sleeping in a single cluster of buildings. A basilica generally formed the heart of the abbey, and served as a worship space for the community, which gathered there several times a day. The communal character of monastic worship was evident in the development of unison prayer and Gregorian chant during the period, performative worship practices in which the several individuals come together in a single unit in a shared activity.

The communal character of monasteries was also evidenced in the spaces reserved for work and in many of those devoted to everyday life. The dining hall or *refectory*, kitchen, guest rooms, and offices for the abbot brought residents together in shared activities, as did the spaces designed to accommodate the particular work of the abbey, be it agricultural (e.g., workrooms or storerooms) or artistic and intellectual (e.g., a *scriptorium* for the copying of texts). Privacy, however, was also an essential element of the contemplative life. Monks prayed for the redemption of a troubled world, beseeching God for mercy toward sin-laden humanity. Individual cells doubled as meditation spaces and sleeping quarters. Gardens, chapels, and other rooms also allowed for individual devotional practice, creating islands of personal space within what was essentially a communal institution.

In southern Europe, abbey buildings often included an atrium, which, following the Roman house model, was an open area surrounded by colonnaded arcades that became known as the *cloister*. In the cloister, the arcades provided sheltered passage between buildings, and the open space provided spaces for spiritual meditation and contemplation. As abbey building reached its peak in the eleventh century, the cloister took its place as a prominent religious space and was replicated throughout Europe in a variety of churches and, later, universities, medieval religious institutions patterned on the monastic model.

Within the abbeys, power was ordered hierarchically, with the abbot (i.e., the head of the abbey) holding great social and political power over the community and often over the region.[3] To be a member of a monastery meant one was under the direct rule of the abbot. Nevertheless, the goal of living in community with others and following the discipline of the order was, for monastics, to develop as close a relationship with God as this world offered. Personal power in the form of individual spiritual fulfillment, regardless of the abbots' control over one's material life, lay at the heart of the monastic life. Communal practice by no means hindered the personal experience of the divine; indeed, it made such fulfillment possible.

Surrounded by high walls and focused inward, abbeys such as Mont-Saint-Michel off the northern coast of Brittany, France, protected Christian communities, religious orders, and ideas during periods of civil disruption (fig. 4.1). Yet more often than not, they too succumbed to invaders. The Abbey of Montecassino, for instance, was destroyed in the sixth century by the Lombards, rebuilt in the eighth century, sacked again in the ninth, and rebuilt once more in the tenth. Though not sponsored by rulers, abbeys were religious buildings as fortresses. A few enjoyed the assistance of powerful figures—Charlemagne, for instance, granted Montecassino various privileges in the eighth century—but many existed throughout Europe as singularly stable institutions in landscapes all too often wracked with violence. Sacralized as places of spiritual work and contemplation, monasteries were also places of physical refuge—sanctuaries in both senses of the term, where safety and respite might be found.[4]

The isolation of monasteries also led to localized forms of Christian practice. In a period well before seminaries provided uniform training for priests, monastic and town congregations were frequently led by priests who were themselves poorly educated and might have only vaguely grasped notions of Christian theology. Not surprisingly, Christian beliefs and practices were often blended with religious practices previous observed in specific localities. Historian Gary Macy points out that as Christianity slowly filtered into northern Europe, many who came to listen to the priests made little distinction between their old Saxon gods and the new Christian god.[5] Thus, diversity, syncretism, and idiosyncrasy in religious thought and liturgical practice remained strong throughout the early medieval period. This would change, however, with the formation of cathedral schools or "universities" for the training of those who would be priests in the eleventh and twelfth centuries, as well as the later requirement for seminary training mandated in the sixteenth century by the Council of Trent.

It was in the abbeys of Europe in which Christianity survived during this period of social disorder. The abbeys conveyed an idea of Christian life as

FIGURE 4.1. Mont-Saint-Michel, Brittany, France. Photo by Barbara Carlier.

sanctuary, a respite from insecurity, poverty, and hunger. Devoting one's life to praying for the world emerged as not only a reasonable vocation but a necessary one, as necessary as copying sacred texts to preserve them and raising food to sustain one another. Yet neither the sanctuary of the contemplative life nor the abbey walls fully protected the religious (those choosing a monastic vocation); in truth, most monks suffered right along with the lay population.

During the eleventh century, political turmoil eased to the point at which communities could put their energies to activities other than defense and survival, and Christianity emerged into a new period of creativity and reform. Theological questions once again came under scrutiny. The nature and character of Jesus was debated. Efforts to develop a uniform education for priests increased, and important elements of religious thought and practice religion were standardized. Yet change came slowly. For instance, it took about a century for the sacraments to be standardized to the seven actions now recognized by the Catholic Church. The seven sacraments, introduced together only in the twelfth century by Peter the Lombard, were slowly codified as universities adopted Lombard's book as a major text. Other changes occurred as well. A new emphasis on liturgy had begun to grow as clergy struggled to communicate religious meanings to an illiterate public.[6] At the same time, the personages of Christianity, from Jesus to Mary to a host of other saints, were perceived in more human terms. Such developments, Macy has asserted, combined to make the early medieval period "one of the most creative and formative eras in the history of Christian theology."[7]

The Gothic Church

A new type of church building also appeared in this period, the medieval great churches (often inaccurately grouped together and referred to as cathedrals).[8] One of the most significant transformations that occurred between the early Christian basilica and these new great churches had to do with light. Whereas the high walls and sparse windows of the Romanesque and later Norman basilicas of earlier periods resulted in dark interiors, efforts in the eleventh century to bring light into the church transformed Christian architecture. New engineering techniques taking hold in the twelfth century allowed for larger and more numerous windows in buildings, flooding church naves with light and propelling the craft of glassmaking to unprecedented achievements. Because of the profoundly visual character of these new churches, their dramatic light and stained glass, the Gothic great churches and cathedrals to this day represent what many Christians view as a quintessential Christian architecture.

The architectural basis for the shift from the dark spaces of earlier Romanesque buildings to the light spaces of the Gothic was the replacement of the round arch with the pointed arch as the primary structural element. Prior to the Gothic period, two main supporting techniques had been used in building. The simplest had been used since time immemorial—the post-and-lintel structure, formed by two vertical members called *posts* connected with a horizontal *lintel* resting atop them. Roman builders had adopted this structure from the Greeks, but soon developed a sturdier structure, the round arch, formed by piling stones in two parallel columns and placing atop them a series of wedge-shaped stones, which then met in the center at a keystone that held the structure together. Round arches had defined spaces for doors and windows and barrel vaults had supported the roofs of classical buildings since the Roman period. Yet round arches could not span large areas. If the sides of the arch were too far apart, the whole construction would collapse. Consequently, round arch windows could not be made very large, significantly limiting the amount of light filtering into buildings. Similarly, although barrel vaults could cover narrow halls, they could not span large basilicas, which were generally roofed post-and-lintel fashion with timbers. It was these technologies—post and lintel and round arch—that dominated abbey building in the earlier period, resulting in the dark basilicas of the Romanesque period.

The pointed arch, originally developed by Arabic builders, proved more versatile. To create it, builders eliminated the keystone and lengthened the wedge pieces so that they met at a point. With the keystone gone and the wedge-shaped stones aligned to meet one another at the top, the two sides of the structure leaned directly upon one another in counter-tension, thus allowing the arch to carry more weight and masons to build higher, particularly if they braced the sides of the arch with buttresses. In this way, the pointed arch could be used to cover wide expanses. Similarly, the pointed arch and its three-dimensional counterpart, the ribbed vault, could carry more weight than the round arch and barrel vault, allowing for higher walls and greater window space.

The imaginative use of pointed arches in both structural and ornamental capacities characterized Gothic architecture and the great churches of the medieval period. Experimenting with the technology, builders used pointed arches to create decorative fan vaults to replace the barrel-vaulted or post-and-lintel ceilings of earlier times. They created large windows that defined the bays of the nave and filled them with tracery and stained glass. "Pointed" architecture moved well beyond the capabilities of the arch as builders emphasized the new vertical thrust of the new buildings in other ways. In the front of many churches, such as the cathedral at Chartres, pointed arch doors organized in banks of three to indicate the Trinity, were flanked by soaring towers topped with narrow steeples, and delicate finials echoed and enhanced the vertical character of the architectural style (fig. 4.2). In many churches a large round window, called a *rose window,* ornamented with delicate tracery forming compartments for stained glass, floated above the pointed entry, hovering like a great wheel above those who entered the church. On the tower and the sides of these buildings, segmented buttresses aided the interior walls in carrying the weight of the building down to the ground, and in many cases flying buttresses flung out their sturdy arms over side aisles to do the same. All of these structural elements offered opportunities for ornament—from crockets and finials to sculptures of gargoyles and saints.

In erecting the churches of the Gothic period, craftspeople and artisans of all types came together to create buildings whose visual and tactile effects were awe-inspiring to the local gentry and peasantry alike. Carpenters erected the frameworks for stone structures. Stonemasons cut and placed stone. Glassmakers created the astounding colors and images that lit the church. Tile makers and mosaic craftsmen laid floors. Textile workers wove tapestries. Stone sculptors and wood carvers created altars, screens, window tracery, biblical

FIGURE 4.2. Cathedral of Notre Dame, Chartres, France. Photo by the author.

figures, and gargoyles, and metalworkers forged everything from fittings and joiners to ornamental cups and plates for the Eucharist. Massive public projects, the great churches launched or contributed enormously to the much-needed distribution of economic resources as well as to the development of these crafts.

The results of all this work were buildings that stood as unprecedented statements of Christian devotion and faith. To enter a cathedral or great church was to be almost overpowered by its physical features: the height of the nave, the streaming light, the dappled colors, and the ornamentation. Mostly, however, the sheer verticality of the space, lifting the gaze from the floor to the columns to the windows to the vaulted ceiling, beckoned one to look up to know God's power.

The Heavenly City in Stone and Glass

Gothic churches came to be seen as symbolic analogs of the Heavenly City itself. By the twelfth century, monumental and awe-inspiring great churches were widely viewed as metonymies of heaven. Frequent references to Revelation 21 ("I saw the holy city, the new Jerusalem, coming down out of heaven from God, prepared as a bride adorned for her husband. . . . It has the glory of God and a radiance like a very rare jewel, like jasper, clear as crystal," Rev. 21:2, 11) in church dedications, as well as the writings of a number of medieval theologians, explicitly invoked correspondences between churches and the Celestial City—the heavenly Jerusalem.[9] As reproductions of heaven produced by human hands, these architectural representations were, naturally, flawed; nevertheless, Gothic churches were meant as powerful *evocateurs* of divine power and the holy life. Like the transformation of heaven into a churchly trope, divine power and existence were translated into human metaphors.

More than the towering columns and vaulted ceilings, more than the peek-a-boo aspects of the screens that shielded the sanctuary, more than the sculptural images, this transformation was achieved through the manipulation of light. The towering walls of the Gothic style, constructed precisely in order to maximize window area and increase the amount of light filtering into the building, suggested a grandeur that, in the minds of many believers, must have come close to replicating divine magnitude. The manipulation of the light that streamed through the vividly colored stained glass signified a human manipulation of divine power in order to make it manifest to inferior human senses. Bejeweled light itself signified divine expression, and bringing it into church became the sine qua non of Gothic builders.

To step into the twelfth-century Basilica of Saint-Denis, for instance, even on a cloudy day, is to enter a shower of light cascading from high above (fig. 4.3). The light draws the eye up the long nave to the chancel and soon the body follows, compelled to move down the column-lined nave to the sanctuary. Discussing the work of Abbot Suger, who designed Saint-Denis, historian George Duby explains that "Suger naturally placed the glowing center, the point where the approach of God became most dazzling, at the other end of the basilica, at the culmination of the liturgical procession turned toward the rising sun." This culmination was then surrounded, in Suger's words, by a "semicircular sequence of chapels, which caused the entire church to glow with marvelous uninterrupted light, shining through the most radiant of windows."[10]

FIGURE 4.3. Cathedral of St.-Denis, Paris. Photo by Mark Carlier.

The use of space and light in these churches constituted a new language of the divine—a new form of "godtalk." The buildings drew attention to the disparity between divine and human existence. In Christopher Wilson's terms, the "sharp contrast between the ideal quality of the house of God and the low, cramped, irregular and impermanent character of men's earthly dwellings" were powerful statements in that new language.[11] The soaring columns and intricately vaulted ceilings emphasized verticality and spaciousness, drawing the eye upward. The astounding spaces enclosed the faithful within a metaphorical heaven of awesome proportions infused by divine light. Simply by being inside such a church or cathedral, one might experience divine power.

Perhaps the quintessential statement of this human effort to approximate a divine city is the Church of Sainte-Chapelle in Paris. Designed and executed within a decade in the 1240s, Sainte-Chapelle was constructed as the chapel of the royal palace of King Louis IX of France and intended to house a number of holy relics that the king had collected, including Christ's crown of thorns. The chapel comprises two levels, the lower dark and close, but the upper a wonder in the human manipulation of glass and light (fig. 4.4). Here, the walls themselves seem to be mere tracery, supporting tall, gleaming windows filled with deeply colored glass that dominate the room, refracting sunlight into a spectrum of shimmering color. Even twenty-first-century visitors can believe that this remarkable nave is host to the presence of God, an expression of the City of Heaven.

FIGURE 4.4. Church of Sainte-Chapelle, Paris. Photo by the author.

The Plan and Furnishing of Medieval Great Churches

Yet even more important than the structural innovations of the Gothic churches to the exercise and expression of ecclesiastical or social power was the transformation of the interior plans. On one level, changes in plan related directly to the growing collection of symbols associated with Christianity. Enhancing the Christian significance of the basilica, builders added a transept bisecting the nave to create a cruciform footprint. Although transepted basilicas had been built during the earlier Constantinian period, their intentional replication of the Christian symbol cannot be assumed, in part because the symbol of the cross was not used widely by Christians during the period. Only in the early medieval period did the cross, conveying meanings of suffering, death, and resurrection, become a widely adopted symbolic element.[12] Within this context, the new cruciform plan carried great significance for worshippers entering the great church, a topic we will return to shortly.

For clergy, however, the most significant changes in church plans appeared in that area of the church where the Mass was celebrated—in the sanctuary. By the eleventh century, the synthronon, which in the early church had lined the eastern apse, had been eliminated, replaced by the high altar placed against a *reredos*. Carved of wood or stone, this complex backdrop generally covered the entire east wall of the sanctuary, and although its main function was to house the consecrated Host in a niche, most were encrusted with statuary—figural sculptures of the Holy Family, the Evangelists, Apostles, Prophets, and other important Christian personages. The sanctuary also accommodated the celebrant and various attendants, deacons, and other officials, housing chairs and benches for them, along with the *cathedra* or bishop's chair in those churches designated as *cathedrals*, or the home of a bishop. In large and monastic churches, a new space, called the *choir*, was developed. Composed of rows of narrow seats facing each other across the main aisle, choirs were inserted between the crossing and the eastern apse to accommodate the religious—monks or nuns who resided in the monastery. The length of choirs varied from relatively short spaces to a proportion of the size of the nave, and in some cases lengthened churches by close to half. Choir seats, called *misericords* because of their uncomfortable character, consisted of individual hinged ledges, frequently decorated with carved figures on the underside that were displayed when the seat was not in use. Thus the medieval church considerably lengthened the sanctuary to create a *chancel*, an area that included the choir and extended from the *crossing* (the point at which the transept crossed the nave) to the high altar located against the reredos at the back.

The chancel, reserved exclusively for clergy and religious, was clearly distinguished from the rest of the church (that is, the nave) in which lay Christians gathered. From the nave floor, several steps led up to the choir and more to the high altar. Marking the boundary between nave and chancel was an altar rail or, by the thirteenth century, a *rood beam* raised several feet above the nave and supporting a large *rood,* or cross.[13] In many instances, a full *rood screen,* a tall, elaborately carved multisegmented lattice barrier, divided the spaces. The rood screen dwarfed the cross, and was often an elaborately detailed piece of architectural furnishing, with doors allowing access to the chancel. Some screens featured a series of arcaded openings through which the chancel could be seen, whereas others offered only a few *squints* (sometimes called *elevation squints*) or small holes in the *dado,* or lower portion of the screen, that afforded only glimpses of the activity within. In some churches, heavy curtains performed the task of shielding the altar.[14]

In large churches, particularly those that housed relics, the chancel was ringed by an *ambulatory,* which carried foot traffic around the outside perimeter of the chancel. Off the ambulatory were chapels in small apses with half domes. These chapels, devoted to individual saints and containing altars and devotional figures, afforded worshippers a much more intimate connection with divinity than did the high altar of the chancel, which was distinctly off limits to the laity. The ambulatory allowed worshippers access to these areas without disturbing masses being celebrated in the main church.

The nave, too, was transformed. Although the arrangement of a center aisle with side aisles (either two or four) remained, the nave in the medieval church featured clerestory windows that allowed light into its upper reaches. As fan vaulting became increasingly decorative, this lighting technique created an awesome effect within the body of the church. In addition, the nave was increased in width, another benefit of pointed arch vaulting. Despite the fact that the rood separated worshippers from the sanctuary, other opportunities for devotional activity abounded. Small chapels might line the transepts and aisles. These spaces, like those around the ambulatory, encouraged private devotions and more intimate worship experiences than the High Mass could offer. The baptistery, generally a small chapel-like room at the west end of the church, also proffered a more intimate connection with the divine when in use.

The Medieval Chancel and Mass

The sanctuary, the holiest part of the church, took on an entirely new character in the medieval great churches. With the addition of the choir and the placement of the high altar at the back of the apse, the distance between lay worshippers in the nave and the site of the Mass suggested an analog to the distance between humanity and God. It also indicated a significant separation between laity and clergy.

Reasons for this marked separation are varied. It is likely that both utilitarian and ideological requirements were satisfied by separating the chancel from the nave. Some sources suggest that screens and curtains sheltered the priest and celebrants from the cold and drafts of winter, particularly during the many masses they performed when worshippers were not present. Although this may be true in some cases, these arrangements also created an architectural analog for the exclusivity of clerical power. The studied isolation of the high altar from the congregation suggested an ongoing veneration of the holiness of the altar and the rituals performed at it as well as a corresponding magnification of the mystical power of the clergy who performed those rituals. The sacredness of the space was not to be desecrated by even the gaze, much less the presence, of uninitiated lay people. Only those individuals fully initiated in spiritual matters were allowed to occupy the chancel, and even they had to engage in purifying rituals of prayer, confession, and vesting prior to entering.

This new spatial emphasis corresponded to a new theology of the Mass, which focused less on the shared community of the congregation than on the sacrifice of Christ, represented in the Eucharist and the miracle of transubstantiation. As historian Eamon Duffy writes, "The liturgy lay at the heart of medieval religion, and the Mass lay at the heart of the liturgy. In the Mass the redemption of the world, wrought on Good Friday once and for all, was renewed and made fruitful for all who believed. Christ himself, immolated on the altar of the cross, became present on the altar of the parish church, body, soul, and divinity, and his blood flowed once again, to nourish and renew the Church and world."[15] It was priestly intervention that brought about this miracle, and the power of the priest justified, indeed necessitated, his physical isolation from the ordinary congregation.

The medieval service began with the ritual vesting of the clergy, a practice continued since the days of the Roman empire and designed to distinguish the special power of the priest from the ordinary personal spiritual power of lay participants. Vestments constituted yet another demarcation between laity and clergy. Just as in Constantine's day, the elaborately clothed priest entered the church, accompanied by attendants. During services on Sundays and holidays, as the procession of clergy and assistants wound its way through the church, the priest might sprinkle the congregants with holy water. On other days, the procession might simply proceed from a side vestry to the chancel steps at the crossing and up to the high altar. There, the celebrant recited the *Confleteor*, or Confession. The Offertory proceeded, with congregants placing their gifts—perhaps a sheaf of wheat, some produce, or even a cow or goat—near the altar. Then the liturgy proceeded. During the main part of the Mass, called *the Canon*, the priest intoned in Latin a long prayer of consecration, upon completion of which the miracle of *transubstantiation* occurred, changing bread and wine to Christ's flesh and blood. Then, with a flourish, the priest held the consecrated Host high above his head and an attendant rang a bell, signaling the congregants to view the miraculous presence of the Lord.[16]

By the thirteenth century, this Elevation of the Host was the climax and, in the minds of many congregants, the singular purpose, of the service. Indeed, most congregants could not understand the Latin language used throughout the Mass and consequently occupied themselves by chatting and even carrying out business deals during most of the service. The devout, however, were encouraged to engage in private devotional exercises and contemplation of God during the Mass. In fact, theological arguments of the period suggested that reciting private devotions during services was as effective a means toward union with God as was partaking of the bread and wine during communion.[17]

As the bell rang and the Host was raised, congregants roused themselves from whatever they were doing, craned their necks for a glimpse of the Host, fell to their knees, and prayed. Rarely, however, did they partake in the communion by sharing in the bread and wine, for the Eucharist meal itself was considered an awesome and dangerous feast. To partake of it when one's soul was in an unworthy state could have dire consequences. Only on Easter were devotees invited to approach the altar for a piece of the bread—at which time worshippers would mob the chancel to share in the union with God. Wine, being too easily spilled in the chaos of distribution, was generally withheld from congregants.[18] During most masses, though, communal lay participation ended after the Elevation of the Host; the priest intoned the Lord's Prayer, received communion himself and shared it with the attendants, presented prayers of benediction, and dismissed the congregants. In the medieval service, congregants participated privately through adoration of the divine from afar, rarely through communion.[19]

Concealing and Revealing the Divine

Although the chancel arrangement, with its separation of clergy, monks, and laity, contributed greatly to clerical power, congregants were not without some access to divine presence. That access, however, was fragmented, concealed and revealed with a drama that rivaled the most theatrical of spectacles. Lay Christianity in the medieval church took a decided turn toward privatized experience.

Historian Eamon Duffy has argued that complex notions of seeing and not seeing, of concealing and presenting, hearing and not hearing, distance and proximity, lay at the heart of these services, and the architecture of the large cathedrals and great churches both enhanced and naturalized these strategies. Indeed, the redesigning of the chancel itself helped to both produce these revealings and concealings and make them seem entirely natural and necessary to the service. The relocation of the altar to the far end of the apse all but removed the proceedings of the Mass from the visual and aural range of congregants gathered in the nave. The position of the celebrant's body between the altar and the congregation, with his back to the nave, further ensured that the audience would see little of the critical act of consecration. The rood screen, of course, also obfuscated worshippers' view of the event and played an important role in fragmenting congregants' view of the altar and simultaneously revealing and concealing the mystery of the Mass and the Host.[20]

The crucial moment of the "concealment of things holy" occurred during the moment of transformation when the priest's prayers brought about the consecration of the Host. This was immediately followed by a partial visual revelation as the Host was elevated above the head of the priest.[21] Viewers caught glimpses of the consecrated Host through the crosshatches of the rood or, if they were kneeling, through the squints.[22] To view the Host was to be blessed, but, again, the concealment, exposure, and voyeurism involved enhanced the mystery of the consecration and underscored the powerful and "forbidden" nature of that blessing. The priest's actions, perceived by the laity as all too momentous to directly cast one's eyes upon, and the holiness of the Host were constructed as deep mysteries that underscored the awesome nature of divine power.[23]

Given the divine power that resided within the consecrated Host, great importance was placed on its treatment. Clergy and patrons addressed the question of what to do with consecrated bread and wine remaining from the Lord's Supper, which, miraculously transubstantiated into the body and blood of Christ, could hardly be tossed into the refuse bin or fed to the animals. Responses to this problem resulted in the outfitting of many medieval sanctuaries with a *piscina*, a vessel or basin that drained through the floor or a wall onto the bare earth and through which holy water and consecrated wine could thus be returned to the earth in a respectful manner. During the medieval period, remaining pieces of the consecrated Host were generally placed in a small box or *pyx* for later distribution or in a *ciborium*, a lidded cup on a pedestal. These receptacles were then placed in a niche in a wall, called a *columb* or *aumbry,* or in a cabinet in the reredos. In some cases, small caskets made of precious metals in the shape of a dove (*columb*) or tower (*turre*) were used to house the remaining Host. Columbs were generally suspended on chains from the altar canopy, whereas turres were housed in cabinets. By the late medieval period, *sacrament houses* appeared, small boxes in the shape of houses or churches, often with latticework walls or doors that allowed the Host to be seen once placed inside. During the Renaissance period a new receptacle, a large box or cabinet called a *tabernacle,* came into use. Tabernacles spacious enough to house a pyx or ciborium were often suspended above the altar. To alert people of the presence of the consecrated host within in the sanctuary, a lamp was sometimes kept lit when the Host was present, but this practice did not become widespread until a later period. All of these measures, however, were informal and varied from town to town.

Another receptacle for the Host was the *monstrance,* which was used in the medieval period not simply to house the consecrated Host between masses but to display it for public viewing, particularly during festivals. A monstrance, usually a silver or gilt box on a pedestal with crystal windows surrounding the Host, could be displayed in the sanctuary or carried through the streets as in the popular Corpus Christi celebration. Monstrances, sometimes called *ciborium* or *custodia,* also were used to display the relics of other holy figures.

The new significance ascribed the Host was seen not only in the new receptacles created to house it, but also in new architectural features, including cabinets and niches. Among these was the unique Easter Sepulchre. Parishes throughout Europe and Britain developed Easter Sepulchre rituals known as the *Depositio* and the *Elevatio*. On the morning of Good Friday, devotees carried the consecrated Host and a cross in procession through the church and symbolically buried them in a niche or freestanding cabinet called the Easter Sepulchre located near the high altar (*Depositio*). Candles were then burned in front of the symbolic sepulchre throughout the following two days. On Easter morning the Host was removed from the sepulchre (*Elevatio*). This reenactment of the death and resurrection linked the clergy ever closer to the risen Christ, but it also provided an opportunity for lay people to interact with the Host. Freestanding cabinets and niches inserted into stone walls were becoming common throughout Europe and Britain.[24]

These features of the great church enhanced clerical power by providing glimpses of priests' direct connection to the supernatural power of the Body of Christ while at the same time indicating the fearful nature and awesomeness of that connection. This contrasts sharply with the more straightforward display of secrecy that obtained in the Constantinian chancel described in the previous chapter. To see glimpses of a powerful event is much more impressive than to simply be assured that it is taking place outside of one's view. In both cases, priestly power resided in the ability to accomplish the mysterious transformation of ordinary bread and wine into divine substances. For laity, the ability to see but not fully understand this performance heightened its mystery and enhanced the importance of the priest's power.[25] It also underscored essential differences between the powerful priest, united with God, and the searching individual, yearning for union with the divine.

Yet this situation also brought a new type of individual power to bear. Straining to see the High Mass and the Elevation of the Host, whether through screen or squints, worshippers became active seekers of religious understanding during the Mass. The act of adoration constituted a new physical component of this search. This active search was not limited to the Mass, however, for it was articulated in the architectural and ornamental features of great churches—in the vaults of the nave, the shadows of the side aisles and the profusion of ornament. Architectural historians William Anderson and Clive Hicks hold that the interior space of the Gothic great church—with its complex patterns of aisles, transepts, ambulatories, and apses all defined by towering shafts splaying into webbed vaults—constituted a built equivalent of a forest. Unlike the easily understood spaces of the Byzantine church, which made the great power of the emperor and clergy transparent, the complex Gothic spaces required the faithful to peer into and search through them, replicating the need to search through the awe-inspiring mysteries of the medieval Eucharist service for an understanding of the divine.[26] Within the medieval space, the worshipper became an active, if sometimes frustrated, seeker. And the architecture itself helped to naturalize the alignment of the clergy with the object of the search: divine, supernatural power.[27]

The Power of Patronage

Regardless of the strengthening of clerical power achieved by the great churches, the social power of certain congregants was also strongly expressed in medieval churches. Indeed, if the early churches of Constantine were intended to cement the relationship between divinity and the empire, the churches of the medieval period, particularly of the Gothic period, were meant to clarify the nature of humanity through patronage aimed at obtaining divine mercy. The wave of great church construction from 1100 through 1400 in Europe and Britain was fueled by wealthy individuals, both lay Christians and clergy, and by local communities determined to demonstrate their devotion to God and Christianity. Indeed, without the amassing of great wealth by small groups that wielded enormous power over the poor and laboring classes, no cathedrals would have risen on the landscape. Yet patronage was understood as not just a means of expressing devotion or demonstrating power, but as a mode of penance. By endowing or contributing to a building that glorified God, individuals might atone for their sins while at the same time discharging their Christian obligations through munificence to the community.[28]

This is not to say that church building was devoid of political meaning. To the contrary, the expression of social power and the quest for personal spiritual solace intersected for the wealthy laity. The initial wave of church building, for instance, was initiated by monasteries intent upon consolidating regional power. Further, the creation of each church was driven by multiple motivations. Bishops, local nobles, religious orders, and even townspeople gave money, time, and materials to building projects, and all had their reasons for doing so. Henry III, for example, funded the construction of a Lady Chapel in Westminster Abbey (completed in 1245) not simply as "an act of piety, the consequence of a devotional habit," according to historian Paul Binsky, but also as "an acknowledgment of the political centralization of the kingdom."[29]

The interiors of medieval churches provided countless opportunities for claiming and displaying social power. Tombs, dedicated chapels, windows, murals, paintings, furnishings, service pieces, vestments—all were occasions for patronage beyond the construction of the building itself. In fact, such patronage often altered the design of buildings as patrons vied to present churches with altars and dedicated chapels. As the number of faithful and clergy rose, altars were installed in various locations throughout most churches. Some thirty-one chapels graced the cathedral in Barcelona, for instance.[30] Not only could a patron pay for the construction of the chapel and donate the altar itself, but each chapel could then be decorated as the patron wished with murals, paintings, mosaics, sconces, and the like. This profusion of altars affected even smaller churches, where altars might even be pushed up again the rood screen itself. Those who donated the altars often wielded great influence over the prayers and services said at them. The donation of an altar or a chapel granted significant power to wealthy laity, but at the same time mitigated the distancing effect of the placement of the high altar in the western apse by allowing congregants a much closer approach during masses performed at the side altars.[31]

Other architectural and decorative strategies also broadcast the rank of the wealthy in medieval churches. Although most worshippers stood or kneeled on the floor during masses, some families constructed high-sided box pews in the nave for their exclusive use. Patrons also paid for vestments, Eucharist plates and chalices, altar cloths and candles, stained glass, paintings, frescoes, and a host of other ornaments. Donations demonstrated piety and might help elevate one to God's good graces. They also demonstrated wealth and social position, and significant competition existed to outdo others' beneficence. In sum, the patronage system wove together complex meanings and the desire for personal spiritual power and social recognition.[32]

The most powerful symbol of this commingling of personal, social, and divine power was the entombment of members of important families within the church. In late medieval England, funerary chapels were often constructed within the aisles of the church, whereas in Europe it was more common for chapels to be built out from the side aisles.[33] Under what amounted to a new understanding of the dead body, the dead themselves were no longer deemed "holy," as were those laid in the martyria of the early Christian era, but now money and social power could increase the proximity or nearness of the dead to the sacred center and thus help to ensure and broadcast the individual's salvation. In the more elaborate examples, such as Westminster Abbey in London and Saint-Denis in Paris, kings and their families were interred under the chancel and transept floors or in large, elaborately carved sarcophagi placed in the aisles and side chapels. Saint-Denis, in particular, has been the favored burial place of French kings, and has reputedly held royal remains from Dagobert in the seventh century to Louis XVIII in the nineteenth. Such close connection with a church like Saint-Denis, in which coronations and other important state events were held, underscored and naturalized the divine right of kings to rule.

Regardless of political expedience, the desire of pious Christians of all types to locate one's eternal resting place within or at least near the sacred space of the church indicates that proximity also fostered personal power. Only the wealthy and powerful, however, would enjoy interment within the building; most lay people would have to be content with burial outside the church walls in the churchyard.

Humanism and the Divine Narrative

These material displays of social power occurred in a new intellectual context that tempered their impact. A new humanist philosophy gained increasing acceptance and significance through the medieval period, culminating in the twelfth century in a flowering of connections between the supernatural and the earthly, between divine and personal power. Through humanism, the laity gained unprecedented access to the divine.

An important element in this humanism was the re-visioning of Christian figures as more distinctively human and thus more accessible to human understanding and entreaty. Jesus, Mary, and the saints were increasingly understood through the events of their earthly lives, an approach that emphasized their humanity and made them seem more accessible to individuals. For instance, St. Bernard of Clairvaux (1090–1153) encouraged his followers to practice the devotion to the five wounds, a devotion focused on the physical human suffering endured by Jesus. Through empathy based on shared human experience, worshippers could understand Jesus' physical sacrifice and gain stronger, more personal understanding of his significance as the savior. By transforming empathy with human experience into a form of mystical connection with the divine, religious leaders like Bernard, according to historian Albert Storme, "appeal[ed] to feelings of the audience, by making them aware of the humanity of the Savior."[34] This representation of human experience made divine figures much more understandable and more accessible to the vast majority of Christians, who were illiterate.

The great churches participated deeply in the development of this new emphasis on the human aspects of divinity. The iconography of the Gothic churches specifically located humanity within the divine realm and invited individuals to participate in the Christian narrative. In fact, one of the most striking aspects of medieval great churches is how fully "peopled"—crowded with human images—they are. Almost any great church of the medieval period can serve as an example of the architectural emphasis on humanism. At Chartres Cathedral, for instance, each exterior façade of the building is replete with statuary. Above the central entry—the Royal Portal—the tympanum depicts Christ enthroned on Judgment Day (fig. 4.5). A common image of the promise of the Gospels, it shows Christ seated within a *mandorla,* an oblong shape indicating divine light, with a halo encircling his head. With his right hand he gives the blessing, and with his left holds the Bible. At his feet is the heavenly city. He is surrounded by the symbols of the four Evangelists and below him file the apostles.[35] Great arcs of other figures line the tympanum and doorjambs. Most striking, however, is the parade of saints, kings, queens, prophets, and other biblical figures that march across the world that centers on Christ. Covering the doorjambs and moldings, these human figures create a medieval crowd scene, welcoming worshippers into the building. The doors flanking the Royal Portal also contain a myriad of human figures. The central figure on the right is the Virgin and that on the left is Christ in Ascension. Surrounding these images is yet another host of human figures, including men and women bent over writing desks symbolizing the liberal arts and scholarship, great scholars like Pythagoras, and the labors of man corresponding to

FIGURE 4.5. Tympanum, Cathedral of Notre Dame, Chartres, France. Photo by author.

the signs of the zodiac. Elsewhere on the exterior appear images of working people, including the stone carvers who produced the sculptures.

This elaborate sculptural program was intended to instruct illiterate worshippers in the lessons of Christianity. Biblical personages peer down like silent teachers, catechizing those who enter. But these figures are not static; they spring out from their moldings to mimic human forms and to remind worshippers of the human condition that dwells at the heart of Christianity. It is human accomplishments that are heralded here, within the context of Christ's saving grace.

These increasingly lifelike sculptures, like a number of other features of medieval churches, performed a new building narrative, a story that stressed human agency by physically linking the human and divine worlds. This human narrative is also evident in stained glass and murals populated with human figures of all kinds performing biblical stories.[36] The images served as heuristics or teaching tools to bring the viewer and the Christian message into dialogue through the narrative structure of crucifixion, resurrection, and salvation, as well as numerous other biblical stories. The realism of stone, wood, and glass figures emphasizes the human character of the lesson, opening up a narrative space into which viewers can insert themselves either in sympathy with the human characters or as a figurative participant in the story.

The ambulatory at Chartres cathedral illustrates this narrative phenomenon. Along its inside wall, detailed sculptures positioned about five feet above the floor present major scenes in Jesus's life. From the manger in Bethlehem to scenes of Jesus's childhood, to his baptism, ministry, crucifixion on Calgary, entombment, and resurrection, the story is peopled with a variety of figures—Mary, Joseph, John the Baptist, the disciples, Mary Magdalene, and so forth—all playing their well-known roles. As an individual slowly walks around the ambulatory, the whole story is played out, with one's own motion signifying a personal role. As one walks and learns the story, one actually participates in the Christian narrative, envisioning oneself as yet another character in the drama.

These visual images constructed a new God-language, a new articulation of notions of divinity and supernatural power through iconography. As a representational or symbolic language drawing upon human form, it placed each individual worshipper in a unique relationship to the ideas it conveyed. Just as ferocious gargoyles lunged out from under eaves to frighten both saints and sinners, the narrative elements of the building similarly targeted worshippers and welcomed them in, encouraging believers to insert themselves as sympathizers or actors in the divine narrative.

Christian Pilgrimage: Individual and Communal

This combination of a metaphorical language locating the worshipper in "heaven" and the didactic iconographic programs telling the divine story as a human narrative requiring human actors produced buildings that physically placed the worshipper within the Christian narrative of crucifixion, resurrection, and salvation. Worshippers were assigned distinct roles to play within these extraordinary buildings. Not only were Christian narratives played out in the windows and on the walls of the great churches, but real Christian actor-worshippers or pilgrims were to play their parts, slowly moving through the landscape and through the church toward union with God within the heavenly spaces of the buildings. In this way, perhaps more than any other, the privatized, individual nature of medieval Christianity was embodied.

The performance of the faithful actually began outside the medieval church buildings, and the journey to the "heaven" they reproduced gained enormous significance through the medieval period, as pilgrimage to churches housing relics of saints became a quintessential expression of faith. Believers embraced pilgrimage in part because it mediated divine power and personal spirituality by physically situating pilgrims within the Christian narrative. Although devotions to saints dated back to the early Christian period, during the early medieval period the cult of saints grew to enormous proportions, providing a focus for individual worship, which connected worshippers to supernatural power without being so audacious as to approach God directly. Saints were believed to provide an intercessory between the individual and God, who was viewed as much too powerful to be approached directly. Praying to the Virgin Mary and a host of other saints constituted central devotional practices of the medieval period. The devout lit candles in front of images of the saints, carried talismans of the saints, and clothed statues of them in finery and carried them through the streets and fields in processions. Viewing and being near to a relic of a saint was deemed auspicious, providing healing, blessing, or other boons and demonstrating the depth and sincerity of the pilgrim's faith.

Pilgrims took to the road for a variety of reasons, some of them having more to do with commercial or social incentives than spiritual meaning, but religious sincerity fueled by desire for access to divine power commingled with such prosaic intentions on every level. For Christians of the fourth century, pilgrimage to Jerusalem allowed the devout to retrace the steps of Jesus and thus become actors in a symbolic reiteration of the Passion. At that time, this journey took place out-of-doors, along the newly established *Via Dolorosa* (path of suffering). Only devotions within the Church of the Agony and the Church of the Holy Sepulchre brought the new pilgrims indoors. Outdoor pilgrimage was also kept alive during the medieval period through the preservation and veneration of relics of the Passion and of the saints in individual churches, resulting in another type of devotional journey: pilgrimage to the cathedrals and churches that held relics of saints. Relics of St. Mary Magdalene and of St. James the Great in churches at Vézelay and Santiago de Compostela, respectively, drew thousands of pilgrims yearly, and whole towns sprang up along the routes to provide for their needs. The statue and tunic of the Virgin at Chartres Cathedral, the shrine of St. Thomas à Becket at Canterbury, and objects at numerous other sites produced towns that enjoyed the economic boon of pilgrims seeking spiritual power in their cathedrals.[37]

In these towns and along the roads leading to them, pilgrims socialized with one another, sharing their experiences and faith along with their meals and living arrangements while in transit. Chaucer's *Canterbury Tales*, written in the fourteenth century as a satire of the church, provides nonetheless an idea of the diversity and social character of medieval pilgrimages. To be on the road as a pilgrim, headed for sites such as Vézelay or Chartres, was to be a part of a communal worship practice, albeit carried on outdoors and over time and territory.

Once arrived at their destination, pilgrims found that the great churches that housed the relics they sought had been carefully planned to accommodate their numbers and devotional needs. The popularity of pilgrimage required certain architectural accommodations, the most prominent of which was the development of the ambulatory around the east end of the choir to effectively route the pilgrim traffic into the church to see the relic (typically housed near the high altar) and then out again without disrupting the purity or exclusiveness of the sanctuary. Screens separating the ambulatory from the chancel provided an effective barrier against lay encroachment while at the same time affording pilgrims a fragmented view of the divine objects that underscored their mystery and power. As noted, chapels devoted to saints also became sites for individual devotions and provided another means for the faithful to gain personal spiritual power though a close connection to divine power.

Journeys to distant towns, however, were not possible for most Christians. As a substitute, many great churches of the Gothic era offered local opportunities for worshippers to actively engage with Christian narratives. An early example of this appeared in the Church of San Clemente in Rome, rebuilt between 1120 and 1130. In this church, an intricate Tree of Life mosaic dominates the ceiling of the eastern apse and is reiterated on the floor of the nave, where a circular path of branches leads the worshipper from the west entrance to the full flowering of the tree in the apse above the altar (fig. 4.6). Proceeding up to nave from the narthex, the worshipper physically walks the metaphorical path of Christian life from west to east, figuratively "climbing" the Tree of Life to the altar.[38] Within this sacred site, worshippers' actions were integrated into the Christian story itself. This was not a wholly new concept given the use of cruciform churches since the fourth century, for in any cruciform church, a person moving from west to east literally ascends the crucifix to the altar. The Tree of Life at San Clemente required the same action but broadened the metaphorical context well beyond the Passion. Here the nave itself was transformed into a *via sacre*, or sacred way.

Many medieval buildings incorporated similarly unique means of physically locating worshippers within Christian narratives. The inscription over the entry portal of the twelfth-century Abbey Church of Saint-Denis quoted the parable of the Good Shepherd (John 10:9): "I am the door: by me if any man enter in, he shall be saved."[39] The worshipper, having passed through the door found him or herself in a monumental space whose verticality demanded the physical response of looking upward to gaze at the awesome height of the heavenly surrogate. As historian Richard Schneider has argued, once inside, the worshipper followed an inscriptural and iconographic program that led him or her through a spiritual pilgrimage to God.[40]

FIGURE 4.6. Apse, Church of San Clemente, Rome. Photo by Marilyn Chiat, Ph.D.

The construction of labyrinths in the floors in Chartres and Rheims cathedrals similarly accommodated individual spiritual journeys. By following the winding path to the center, to the heavenly city, the pilgrim learned the lesson of the circuitousness of one's journey to God. These indoor pilgrimages foreshadowed the formalization of the internal spiritual pilgrimage of the Stations of the Cross, the indoor version of the Via Dolorosa, which developed in the latter fifteenth and early sixteenth centuries.[41] Here again, the spaces of the church offered the faithful a means of inserting the physical self into the Christian narrative. Here again, movement of the body within and through space constituted an important form of worship.

Medieval Christian Architectural Diversity: Stave Churches

As new regions became Christianized during the medieval period and converts erected new churches, local building traditions and techniques predominated. Among the local techniques drawn into service for Christianity was construction in timber, a material used for generations, particularly in northern areas. One of the most distinctive phenomena in church building was the development of the stave church in twelfth-century Norway. Among the extant examples is the Borgund Stavkirke (fig. 4.7).

FIGURE 4.7. Borgund Stavkirke, Norway. Photo by Jole Shackelford, 2006.

Whereas the medieval great church built of stone rested upon the integrity of the side walls and their connecting vaults, the stave church was supported by an internal framework. A dozen or more *staves,* or tall vertical posts, were erected in a rectangle on a sill or foundation. Atop the posts, lintels were attached and roof trusses mounted. Then a belt or girdle of bracing, about a third of the way down from the top of the posts, was added, along with brackets between the posts, to strengthen the connections between the vertical posts, which carried the weight of the building. After the structure was in place, a shallow apse and side aisles were built around the center post framework and attached to it. The whole structure was then sheathed in boards and wooden shingles. The result could be as simple as a single nave building with a steeply pitched room to a building with several adjoining aisles, cupolas, and apses somewhat resembling an Asian pagoda.[42]

Unlike the stone churches of the same period, the interiors of the northern stave churches were very dark. Windows were few and generally small, due to harsh weather and lack of glass, allowing in relatively little light and echoing the darkness and awe of Romanesque churches. Nevertheless, the churches offered a variety of artisans unparalleled opportunities for ornamenting the buildings' interiors. Elaborate painting, usually in organic designs, covered the walls and ceilings, and a few carved figures appeared, although the general reliance upon organic ornamental patterns was an indication that the humanism beginning to influence Europe had not yet reached the northern areas and that the traditional nature-oriented religions of the region still held some sway. Other non-Christian elements were also seen in these medieval churches, including dragonhead finials at the ends of the ridgepoles on the roofs. Though leaf and vine ornament generally replaced the intertwining animal carving of the pre-Christian era, some animal carving is also found within stave churches. In this way, these buildings attest to the fluidity between Christian and earlier belief systems and the gradual character of the processes of change. By the seventeenth century, however, Christian figural images had become common, including elaborate altarpieces depicting the crucifixion or other scenes of Christ.

Given their small interiors in comparison to European great churches, stave churches did not separate the clergy and laity to the extent that larger buildings did. The sanctuary was quite small, often holding just an altar. Altar rails provided the major separation. The small size of the buildings, however, created an intimacy quite different from the European great churches, and likely emphasized the personal character of salvation more strongly.

In summary, then, medieval churches visually and spatially represented divine power for the benefit of worshippers through their monumental size, extraordinary manipulation of light, integration of human iconography, and awesome presentation. Although the Gothic churches, understood as portrayals of the Heavenly City, may not have been constructed by supernatural forces, they certainly were humankind's attempt to manifest and evoke an understanding of divine power through a new language of representation. Medieval churches afforded lay worshippers extraordinary personal access to spiritual power through their evoking of divine power and their physical placement of the individual into the Christian narrative.

If we compare these buildings to those of the earlier Constantinian period, we see significant change. In the fourth-century churches, the procession of lay Christians into the unoccupied church building and the following procession of the clergy had infused the space with religious meaning and power based on that gathered community, the sanctity of the space relying upon human presence. By the medieval period, this had changed. In medieval churches—replicas of the Celestial City and surrogate sites for salvation—the power of the space preceded human occupation. The towering spaces and radiant light indicated divine presence, whether or not it was witnessed by a human presence. Consequently, any worshipper who entered, with or without the presence of clergy, conceivably had some access to the divine power present there. Despite its underscoring of the social power of the clergy and wealthy patrons, the medieval church was perhaps most distinguished by this creative enhancement of the personal spiritual power of ordinary congregants. Only the martyria of the early Christians came close to such a physical association between divine and human power.

5

Transformations of the Renaissance and Reformation

In the Renaissance period, the medieval notion of the church as the City of Heaven yielded to new ideas about church architecture and space—ideas engendered by the very humanism the medieval church had introduced. The most radical reorganization of space occurred in the liturgical areas and the spatial relationships between the clergy and laity. Whereas through the fourteenth century, churches separated clergy and laity into two distinctive, self-contained areas—the chancel and the nave—by the end of the sixteenth century, as we will see, revolutionary new churches reorganized the sanctuary entirely, bringing together everyone in a single, unified space. The space reserved for the worshippers would also undergo radical transformation as new understandings of worship itself emerged during the Reformation.

These radical transformations were brought about by a number of factors, most importantly a growing intellectual and philosophical bent toward humanism. By the fifteenth century, the growth of commerce, urbanization, and transportation and new accomplishments in science, philosophy, and the arts nurtured a growing confidence in human ability and rationality. This new humanism catalyzed a critique of the Christian church that launched a period of astonishing innovation and creativity in church architecture and ultimately changed the face of Christianity and church architecture forever.

Thus the period under scrutiny in this chapter, from the fourteenth through the sixteenth centuries, demonstrates an important feature of religious architecture, which is that cultural and social change frequently play a greater role in spurring architectural change than do evolving liturgical requirements. By tracing the changes in church space that occurred between the fourteenth and sixteenth centuries, along with the architectural debates that accompanied them, we will see that the function to which a church was to be put was not necessarily the driving force behind its design. Rather, while liturgy changed slightly, experimentation flowered; traditional spaces were rearranged and used for new purposes. Although many people assume that the design of religious space is dependent primarily or even solely upon the liturgical function to which the space will be put, the architectural disputes that arose during this period were more frequently ideological and cultural than theological. Struggles over Christian spaces during the Renaissance period belie the modernist adage "form follows function," which is too often assumed to mean that function dictates form. In fact, liturgical functions can be accommodated in a number of ways, and the motivations behind the spatial changes in this period were often independent of functional necessities.

Humanism and the Power of the Patron

By the fourteenth century, the assertion of humanism had significantly expanded, spurred in part by a horrific event. The bubonic plague, carried by fleas that clung to rats stowed away on ships returning to southern Italy from China, hit Europe at mid-century. Called the Black Death, the plague swept north across the continent between 1347 and 1352, ultimately reaching as far north as Scotland. Some twenty-five million people—over a third of the European population—perished. With bodies being carted through the streets to mass graves and everyone fearful of being the next victim, the tragedy posed tremendous challenges for the Church. Why, people asked, was God punishing them so? Why did neither good deeds, nor sacraments, nor faith keep one from contracting the disease? Was the fate of humanity simply suffering and death? What could the church offer in the face of such turmoil?

Sadly, the Church had few answers, and rather than reach out to minister to the survivors, too often religious leaders distanced themselves both physically and spiritually from them. Death on such a massive scale required some religious response, however, some integration with the Christian view of divine power, resurrection, and eternal life. As a result, grassroots, laity-instigated change flourished, spreading innovative popular devotions throughout Europe.

Purgatory, saints, and the Mass took on heightened meaning as people turned to the church seeking salvation for their souls and for those of their loved ones. The theological concept of purgatory, an intermediary space between heaven and hell, had been integrated into the church at the end of the twelfth century but took on new importance as people faced the possibility that sudden death would take them before they had confessed and atoned for their sins. Migration of the soul to purgatory offered the possibility that the soul could be cleansed of the sins it had incurred on earth and enter heaven.[1] Saints, particularly the Virgin Mary, were understood to have the ability to intercede in this process, and thousands of believers prayed to them on behalf of loved ones who had already departed the earth and presumably were sojourning in this intermediary realm. Many people also embraced the belief that a special Mass, dedicated to the salvation of an individual, could intercede to save the soul and reduce its time in purgatory, and consequently the practice of saying masses for individuals expanded enormously. Although the Fourth Lateran Council (1215) had banned priests from charging fees for masses, wealthy individuals were willing to offer significant donations to ensure that masses would be said upon their death or for loved ones who had already died.[2]

Societies created by guilds and other lay organizations for the sponsoring of such masses proliferated. Called *chantries,* these lay organizations began to build spaces, also termed chantries, in which to hold special masses. A chantry might be created by partitioning off a transept or side aisle within an existing church or by erecting a small, freestanding building to house an altar and a few worshippers. Some chantries of the fourteenth and fifteenth centuries were quite elaborate. St. George's Chapel in Windsor Castle, for instance, was outfitted for private masses by Edward IV during a refurbishing of the building in 1475. His chantry was to contain effigies of himself, but the project was left unfinished, although the elaborate ironwork gate intended for the chantry entrance has survived. Just down the north aisle from Edward IV's chantry was that of William Lord Hastings, a close confidant of the king who was executed in 1483. This chapel exhibits the detailing of English pointed Gothic, including a fan-vaulted ceiling and a carved stonework entry gate with tracery windows. Both of these rooms were intended to house the remains of the individuals (though Edward's body was likely placed in a vault below the chantry) and to accommodate almsmen paid to pray for their souls after their deaths.[3]

The growth of chantry endowments and proliferation of other types of Christian spaces during the late medieval period was made possible by significant economic changes during the period that more widely distributed wealth among the Christian laity. A smaller population, increasing trade with Asia, the plundering of the western hemisphere, and growing literacy and education accelerated by the development of the printing press and movable type resulted in putting greater economic means in the hands of a larger percentage of the population. Not surprisingly, investment in one's eternal salvation was perceived as an attractive use for disposable wealth, and religious expenditures grew rapidly.[4]

This increased lay participation in the creation of Christian buildings contributed to new understandings of divine and social power. In particular, the period is marked by a shift in emphasis from the mysterious nature of the divine that had been associated with the medieval church to a new emphasis on the rationality of humanity. Spiritual knowledge was increasingly understood to be available not only to the clergy but to the educated laity as well. Clerical power was placed in a new position of vying, or at least having to negotiate, with that of informed, well-to-do laypeople and an expanding class of educated artisans and merchants.

Spatial Innovation in the Renaissance Church

The expansion of education, commercial success, and foreign trade that brought wealth to nations such as Italy and Spain helped to also expand the building trades. Architects, who were increasingly educated, embraced new technologies and aesthetic ideas. In fact, the period marked the beginning of architecture as a modern profession. Patrons, who were also better educated, came to claim a greater role in architectural decision making. Wealthy aristocrats wanted churches that would suit their needs as a growing "public" class rather than simply individuals or families. As such, they sought greater participation in worship. Not surprisingly, the new diversity of participants in the design process brought a concomitant growth in theoretical and methodological discussion and, of course, disagreement.

One important debate among church designers, builders, clergy, and patrons concerned the proper plan for a Christian church—should it be cruciform or centralized? The Gothic cathedrals and large churches of the previous centuries had mostly adopted the cruciform plan, although the rectangular "hall church" or oblong plan was common for smaller churches. As we have seen in the previous chapter, the cruciform plan articulated the Christ story in a very physical way, allowing the faithful to metaphorically ascend the cross as they physically approached the sanctuary located at the crossing. It also provided a distinct separation between the space assigned to the clergy and the space assigned to the laity, a separation that severely hindered lay participation in Christian rituals and worship. The use of medieval styles waned over the course of the fourteenth century, however, and by the 1430s Rome had regained its architectural, as well as doctrinal, influence in the Christian world. Italian artisans of all sorts, from architects to sculptors to writers, recast the architectural conversation by reviving the forms of classical Greece and Rome.

Architects did not fuel this classical revival entirely on their own. New interest in classical thought had flourished as early as the thirteenth century among the Scholastics, a group of philosophers associated with medieval universities in Paris, Oxford, and other locations, who attempted to reconcile their Christian theological understandings with ancient Greco-Roman philosophy. Although Scholasticism as a movement waned over the course of the fourteenth century, interest in the ancient world remained, and by the 1480s, classical inspiration was informing the arts in paintings such as Botticelli's *Birth of Venus* and *Primavera*, which were received by appreciative patrons. Classical images also migrated into churches. In the 1480s, for instance, Domenico Beccafumi's mosaic of Hermes Trismegistus graced the floor of the Cathedral of Siena. Hermes, the Greek version of the Egyptian god Thoth, god of wisdom, learning, and magic, was best known through the so-called Hermetic writings, thousand of volumes of sacred writing on philosophy and theology that many during the period felt revealed the "wisdom of God and the soul."[5] The installation of the Hermes figure in churches would soon be followed by any number of classically inspired human images, culminating in Michelangelo's work in the Sistine Chapel, executed from 1508 to 1541.

This classical revival, of course, also had a significant impact on architecture. By the late 1400s, architects in Italy, where the Gothic style had never been strongly embraced, looked to their Roman heritage as a means of developing new approaches to Christian spatial organization and architectural ornament. Among the most influential architects of this classical revival was Leonbattista Alberti, who served as the canon of the Metropolitan Church in Florence in the late 1470s and later became the abbot of San Sorvino in Pisa. Alberti brought to light the architectural writing of Vitruvius, a Roman architect who had worked around 46–30 B.C.E. Vitruvius's *Ten Books of Architecture*, which codified strategies for achieving the fundamental architectural elements of proportion, harmony, and simplicity, would spur a continent-wide revival of architectural classicism. Influenced by Vitruvius's delineation of architectural virtues, Italian architects of the Renaissance period, including Alberti, Palladio, and Michelangelo, launched a full-fledged classical revival in their efforts to emulate ancient Greco-Roman architecture.[6] Church leaders interested in reconciling Christianity and classical humanism helped to legitimize these efforts. For instance, Pope Pius II, who attained this office in

1458, was particularly interested in classical Roman culture and supported several projects.

The effect on religious architecture was significant. Classicism fueled a full-blown, if short-lived and fairly localized, rethinking of Christian architecture. Alberti himself reconceived of the church as temple, as the "Habitation of the Gods," in his words.[7] Because such habitation should be of perfect form, he argued, the plan of the church should be centralized, based on the "perfect" (symmetrical) forms of the circle, square, and other regular polygons, including the Greek cross with four equal arms. Similarly, Leonardo da Vinci favored centrally planned churches and developed a number of centralized plans for the "ideal church" as part of a series of architectural works depicting the "ideal city."

The radical character of the adoption of centralized plans for Christian worship is often overlooked. Earlier Christians had, of course, built centrally planned spaces, but as we have seen, these almost exclusively accommodated funerary or memorial practices. A centrally planned space focuses attention on one thing: whatever occupies the center. In a martyrium, this was the sarcophagus. Worship, however, requires multiple foci: the altar, the processional nave, the pulpit. Moreover, a centrally planned space allows all users, whether lay or ordained, to approach the center, which acts, in Mircea Eliade's language, as an axis mundi, a direct vertical and horizontal connection between the faithful and the divine. Christian worship, however, incorporated strong elements of hierarchy and privilege, distinctions between lay and ordained access to the divine, and these were not as readily designated spatially in the centralized plan as they were in the longitudinal plan. Not surprisingly, then, the use of centrally planned space for worship was for many church leaders unthinkable.

Nevertheless, interest in centrally planned churches caught on briefly, and between 1480 and 1510, several centrally planned churches were erected in central Italy, Tuscany, and Lombardy. Among these was Giuliano da Sangallo's Santa Maria delle Carceri in Prato (1485). Designed in the shape of a Greek cross, this church referenced the traditional use of the centralized form for funerary/memorial purposes but moved it in a new direction. The Carceri, as it was called, was built on or near the site of an image of the Virgin that many believed produced miracles.[8] Its relationship to this site was as a memorial. Nevertheless, the building also functioned as a parish church in which regular services were held. Thus the Carceri bridged the memorial and worship functions, incorporating both in a centralized space.

Yet centralized spaces were used in other ways as well. As classically inspired central plans gained popularity, builders did not simply copy buildings from earlier times but frequently modified the plans in new ways. For instance, Filippo Brunelleschi's Pazzi Chapel in the Church of San Croce in Florence, erected in 1429–1461, was intended as a chapter house or meeting space for the Santa Croce Franciscan abbey. The modest building featured an oblong plan that resulted from attaching barrel-vaulted bays to opposite sides of a central domed square. The chapel incorporated a blend of Greek and Roman vocabulary elements, including an exterior loggia supporting a frieze and a pedimented door sheltered by a barrel vault mounted on six columns. The interior ornament was understated, limited to pilasters, moldings lining the round arches, and round medallions housing images of saints.[9] In this room, the abbey community would gather for administrative meetings rather than worship.

Another example of experimentation with centralized plans was Donato Bramante's Il Tempietto of San Pietro in Rome (1502). This circular martyrium, whose location is said to mark the place where Saint Peter was martyred, consists of a central domed building ringed by a colonnaded porch of sixteen Doric columns supporting a ballustraded architrave. As architectural historians Trachtenberg and Hyman point out, the building was conceived of as a piece of sculpture, and it emits a "deep sense of Roman *gravitas*" [emphasis in original] in the "dense wall and deep niches of the interior and exterior of the cylinder," which are conceived "three-dimensionally, as sculpture in the round."[10] In this building, the interest in classical architectural theory complemented and merged with new understandings in the visual arts regarding optics, linear perspective, and proportion.

As we have seen previously, centrally planned spaces are readily understood by those who enter. Unlike the mysteries posed by the forest of columns within a Gothic church, centralized spaces create unobstructed sightlines and regular, symmetrical volumes. In the bright, uncluttered spaces of these Renaissance buildings, the mysterious character of the divine recedes. Human understanding and rationality are interposed. The central domes direct the gaze upward while at the same time bringing in light from above. These spaces suggest not mystery, but a human-based religious authority, powerful, even dramatic, yet understandable.

But the centralized spaces also hindered the traditional means through which clerical power had been demonstrated in the medieval church. For instance, the space limited the duration and impact of processions. Whereas the long naves of medieval churches and ancient basilicas had allowed for lengthy processions that underscored the power of the clergy, the new centralized spaces allowed for only short peregrinations, robbing clergy of an important means of demonstrating power and authority. The termination of processions was no longer in the distant chancel, as in the Gothic church;

instead, it was in a sanctuary located in one arm (the East) of the Greek cross building. Here, too, the plan obfuscated earlier strategies for indicating clerical authority. In these centrally planned buildings, the sanctuary was distinguished from the space of the laity by the use of elevation, as clergy ascended several steps from the main floor to the altar. This arrangement brought the laity closer to the altar, encouraging greater participation on their part and suggesting their growing influence. Given the growth of lay involvement in churches, this spatial arrangement both contributed to and expressed an embryonic egalitarian movement. The faithful were grouped together in the single space as a "public," a self-aware group, not isolated in their own privatized devotions, struggling with the mysteries of the church, but participating together in worship.

As intriguing as these centrally planned experiments were, the use of centralized space remained atypical during this period. Centrally planned worship space was a marginal alternative, used primarily for small parishes. Nevertheless, these early experiments laid the groundwork for more radical change to come.

The Council of Trent Transforms Catholic Architecture

During the late Renaissance, the Roman Catholic Church entered a period of internal reflection, reordering, and reform that was precipitated in part by challenges to church doctrine and polity that came to be known as the Protestant Reformation. The Council of Trent, a series of meetings of high-level church leaders that stretched from 1545 to 1564, attempted to respond to the dissatisfaction and criticism that had been launched at the church in the form of charges of corruption, liturgical heresy, and clerical disconnection from the faithful.

The Council brought about significant change, not in the doctrines or theology of the church but in its practices. Among the most far-reaching was the effort to standardize liturgies for all types of services and establish Rome as the sole arbiter of correct liturgical practice. As mentioned previously, liturgical variation within Christian churches was widespread, particularly because the church had few means of providing standardized education to priests or maintaining control over their work in the field. By the time of Trent, however, the printing press had been invented, allowing the participants of the Council to mandate the writing and publication of official liturgical forms and practices defined by the Council. In post-Trent Christendom, authorized versions of the Missal, the book of prayers and materials used by the priest during Mass, and the Pontifical, the book of bishops' services, carried the imprimatur of Rome, affording the pope and his top advisors authority and control over worship practice in ways not previously imagined.[11] Strictures for ordination were detailed, and mandates regarding clerical lifestyle, morality, and discipline were set into place. Local worship practices and celebrations that did not accord with church teaching were outlawed.[12]

Several specific liturgical pronouncements emerged from Trent. The taking of communion by the faithful only in the species (form) of bread was reaffirmed under the argument that Christ was fully present in either species and therefore the laity only need partake of one. In the view of historian Nathan D. Mitchell, this continued denial of the cup to faithful believers, a point of contention for over a century, signaled the church's determination to maintain its theological authority to "alter modes of sacramental celebration 'so long as their substance is preserved.'"[13] It was a show of power designed to demonstrate authority. Nevertheless, the Council left room for several innovations. For instance, the consecrated Host migrated out of the medieval boxes designed for its storage away from prying eyes and into a tabernacle or a transparent monstrance placed on the altar itself. The faithful could now view the Host at almost any time, taking in its miraculous character in a visual or "ocular communion."[14] In the view of liturgical historian James F. White, this innovation significantly transformed the role of the altar: previously a metonym for the sacrifice of Christ, it now became "a throne on which Christ could repose in the Host in the monstrance."[15]

Architectural innovations inspired by Trent were published in 1577 by the Archbishop of Milan, Carlo Borromeo. Perhaps most importantly, he recommended the removal of the rood and the use of a low communion rail in its place, a strategy that put the altar in full view of congregants. No longer were the mysteries of the Mass to be hidden from the gaze of the faithful. Now worshippers could see almost everything. The body of the priest, who faced the front of the church with his back toward those gathered, remained the single visual obstacle between the laity and the altar. In White's view, this new strategy transformed the Mass both theologically and architecturally from its earlier character of medieval mystery into an event similar to theater—a visual spectacle meant to be gazed upon, to be witnessed by the laity.[16] Watching became a new type of Christian participation.

Borromeo suggested other changes as well. For instance, given that the rood screen was where priests had previously listened to Confession, a new location for this sacrament was needed. He suggested the inclusion of "wooden furniture which serves to hear confessions in a convenient and proper way"— hence, the confessional.[17] He also urged the use of a partition in churches to separate men and women during services, believing that their intermingling hindered penance.[18]

Lastly, several other dictates of Trent had implications regarding lay participation. First, the Council recommended that priests intone the Canon of the Mass softly. Despite the fact that the view of the Host (the highpoint in the medieval service) and its consecration was made more available to the laity, the Mass itself remained distinctly exclusive, out of earshot. Thus the Council of Trent offered only an incrementally increased opportunity for lay participation in the Mass. Yet priests were encouraged to gloss portions of the Mass for lay congregants, an indication that the church hoped to use the liturgy itself as a teaching tool. Music, introduced by the choirs of religious orders in monasteries, was distinctly discouraged by Trent, placing another limitation on a part of the Mass most accessible and audible to the faithful. Preaching, on the other hand, was encouraged, even required at Sunday masses and solemn festivals. These somewhat contradictory adaptations show how the church was negotiating some new territory in the face of demands for greater lay participation brought to the fore by Protestant reformers of the period.

As White points out, these negotiations, like most of the Trent pronouncements, proved to be essentially conservative in nature. No radical change occurred in two important categories—clerical authority or doctrine. Gary Macy explains that the vast authority that the medieval church had located in the clergy remain unchecked by Trent; indeed, it was strengthened on the grounds that the clergy play a necessary, intermediary role between God and ordinary people. Ordination brought with it a special status that placed priests in "a whole new realm of existence above that of ordinary Christians."[19] As a result, while the new liturgies permitted lay spectatorship, the laity were no more integrally involved in the acts of worship than they had been in the Middle Ages. As Mitchell observes, Christians became more "intellectually 'engaged' and 'better prepared' for ritual," but no more engaged in the actual activities of services than previously.[20]

Revisiting the Centralized Plan

In the context of the Council of Trent, the church also began to rethink its earlier embrace of Greco-Roman classicism. Classical ideas about human virtues, many conservatives charged, were non-Christian (i.e., Roman or Greek) in origin and thus inappropriate models for Christianity. Striving to buttress its authority during a period in which many were calling for reform, the church looked to the spaces of the early Christians as a means of historicizing its legitimacy through association with those earlier practices.

Centralized spaces came in for particular attack. To the knowledge of church leaders, early Christians had used centralized space only for memorials or martyria, not for worship. The Roman groups that had used centralized spaces for worship in the ancient period were not Christian, but "pagan" in their view. Thus, although church leaders felt the use of centralized spaces for memorials was legitimate, they increasingly disapproved of their use for worship. Advocates of the cruciform plan argued that the adoption of what they viewed as pagan Roman temple architecture for Christian purposes was highly inappropriate. "The cruciform plan," wrote Charles Borromeo, "is preferable for such an edifice [a church], since it can be traced back almost to apostolic times." Regarding round or central plans, he continued, "the type of plan was used for pagan temples and is less customary among Christian people."[21]

Like many of the reforms of the Council of Trent, the move away from the classically inspired centralized spaces and back toward more traditional Christian spaces was not simply a return to a former strategy, but a new direction based on a rethinking of the past.[22] In the area of architecture, we see not a wholesale re-embracing of the cruciform plans of the medieval period, but a blending of the cruciform with the central plan, a strategy that attests to the essential conservativism of the church leaders of the period. Pragmatism entered into the picture as well, touted as a significant architectural criteria by designers unwilling to abandon the benefits of the latter in order to retain the traditions of the former.

An illuminating example of this blending of spatial strategies appears in what would become the most important church in the Christian world, St. Peter's Basilica in Rome. The site of St. Peter's has housed a major Christian building since the rule of Constantine, when a Christian basilica was erected there to memorialize it as the site of the martyrdom of Saint Peter, the apostle of Jesus who was instrumental in the institutionalizing of Christianity, served as the Bishop of Antioch, and later became the first Bishop of Rome. The centuries had not been kind to the massive basilica that Constantine's people had erected in 323–349; by 1500, it lay in ruins. In the early 1500s, Pope Julius II commissioned a new building, preferably, he specified, influenced by the classical revival and including a dome. Thus, the new St. Peter's was conceived as a classically inspired centralized building.

Donato Bramante's original plan for the building featured a Greek cross with a central dome (fig. 5.1). Structural problems, however, plagued the design, and it languished. Though not adopted for St. Peter's, the plan may have provided the inspiration for another building of the period, Santa Maria della

FIGURE 5.1. Bramante's plan for St. Peter's, Rome. Line drawing by Paul R. Kilde.

Consolazione, built in 1508 near Todi, Italy (fig. 5.2). This compact, centrally planned building, erected at a site believed to be sanctified by the mercy-giving presence of the Virgin Mary, featured a Greek cross plan similar to that proposed by Bramante for St. Peter's but is more accurately attributed to Cola da Caprarola. This building demonstrates the difficulties of the plan, however, with respect to the need for space for processionals and large groups of the faithful, neither of which were accommodated by it.

In 1546, thirty-two years after Bramante's death—a period marked by the unsuccessful efforts of a number of designers to develop a more structurally sound design—Michelangelo took over the project at the behest of Pope Paul III. He retained Bramante's basic Greek cross plan and dome, redesigning the latter feature to make it structurally sound and more fully integrated into the overall design. As architectural historian Vernon Hyde Minor has pointed out, Michelangelo's design made reference to the ancient Roman Pantheon (second century C.E.) by inscribing a circle within a square, "geometrical forms promoted by Vitruvius."[23] The resulting interior imagined with this new plan emphasized both the horizontal and vertical axes, dividing attention between the sanctuary and the dome, between earthly ecclesiastical authority and heavenly divine authority.

In the conservative post-Trent period, however, the Bramante/Michelangelo plan for St. Peter's was regarded by many in the church as dysfunc-

FIGURE 5.2. Church of Santa Maria della Consolazione, Todi, Italy. Photo by Marilyn Chiat, Ph.D.

tional, in part because it lacked the traditional auxiliary spaces of chapels, sacristy, narthex, and benediction loggia, but also because it was centralized. Muncante wrote in 1595 that "the new church of St. Peter's is really unsuited for the celebration of the Mass; it was not constructed according to ecclesiastical discipline; the church will therefore never become apt for celebrating any sort of holy functions decently and conveniently."[24] In 1606, at the behest of Pope Paul V, architect Carlo Maderno lengthened the nave to produce the

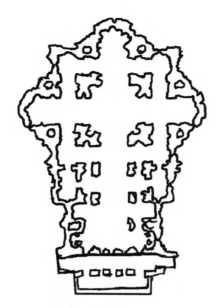

FIGURE 5.3. Maderno's plan for St. Peter's, Rome. Line drawing by
Paul R. Kilde.

cruciform plan that exists today (fig. 5.3).[25] Thus, in this single important
church we can trace the architectural discussion over the course of the sixteenth century, from the initial revival of interest in classically inspired centralized spaces, through the efforts to discredit them by connecting them with
pagan sources, and finally to their modification (by extending a portion of the
building to create a nave) and adoption. By the time Maderno created his
resolution for the plan of St. Peter's, a number of similar mergers of central and
cruciform plans in churches existed, including Alberti's St. Andrea Church in
Mantua, for instance, which featured a Latin cross plan with a particularly
strong central crossing.[26]

The New Spatial Setting of the Tridentine Mass

Yet more radical transformations of Christian space were already being imagined and constructed by the closing decades of the sixteenth century. As mentioned above, the Tridentine Mass, or that mandated by the Council of Trent,
required more preaching during Sunday services. A number of new orders of
religious embraced this directive, including the aptly termed Oratorians and
Theatines, the Capuchins, and the Jesuits, or Society of Jesus, a group estab-

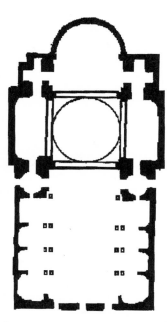

FIGURE 5.4. Plan of Il Gesú. Line drawing by Paul R. Kilde.

lished by Ignatius Loyola in 1540.[27] The Society of Jesus positioned itself on the front lines of Catholic reform, not as adversaries to the papal leadership but as defenders. With respect to the religious politics of the day, they blended Tridentine conservativism with both militancy and intellectual creativity.

The Jesuit's first church building, the radically new Church of Il Gesù in Rome (1568–1576), attested to all of these qualities. The plan was unlike any previous Christian church building traditions. Designed by Giacomo Barozzi da Vignola, this startlingly innovative church combined the simplicity of a hall church, a single rectangular space, with a gigantism that signaled enormous power and strength. The plan merged a central dome with a longitudinal nave (fig. 5.4). The nave, almost sixty feet wide and flanked by three shallow chapels on each side, was covered by a barrel vault, into which clerestory windows were cut, supported by external buttresses. A dome covered the crossing, and its massive supporting piers housed small chapels. The high altar, located in the apse, was bathed by the light streaming down from the dome. Somewhat similar to St. Peter's, though lacking transepts, the plan has been described by architectural historian Norberg-Schultz as a "centralized longitudinal plan."[28]

The walls, though highly ornamented with double pilasters supporting a large entablature, were painted white and the light streamed into the nave through the untinted glass in the clerestory windows (fig.5.5).[29] Stripped of the

confusing architectural and visual elements of earlier periods, Il Gesù redefined holy light and space in a way that eliminated the mysterious elements
of the Gothic period and emphasized the meeting of the individual rational
soul with God. Nevertheless, the interior of Il Gesù was intended to elicit an
emotional response from both laity and clergy in order to deepen Catholic

FIGURE 5.5. Andre Saachi and Jan Miel, *Urban VIII Visiting Il Gesú, Rome,* 1639–1641.
Oil on canvas. Courtesy Galleria Nazionale di Arte Antica, Roma, Palazzo Barberini.

spirituality and piety as encouraged by the Council of Trent and embraced by the new Jesuit order. In both St. Peter's and Il Gesù, the dome, casting light down onto the altar, played a vital role in organizing and defining the spaces of these churches by interrupting the horizontal axis with an abrupt vertical ascent. The eye moves down the nave to the altar and rises immediately to the light above. The mysteries of the shrouded sanctuary were abandoned for the direct experience of divine light. As Norberg-Schultz notes, the space of churches like St. Peter's and Il Gesù "gives a new active interpretation to the two traditional motifs: the path of redemption and the heavenly dome"[30]— the former inscribed in the nave and the latter opening up an inspiring vista.

Moreover, the single unified space of Il Gesù demolished the earlier strategy of providing two separate and specific spaces for clergy and laity. Gone was the medieval chancel with its long choir and rood. The altar was made visible, located in plain sight in the shallow apse and was easily reached by ascending a short flight of stairs. The consecrated Host itself was frequently visible in the monstrance placed on the altar. The space aided what James F. White calls the new theatrical character of the Mass, its emphasis on visual participation. This new setting suggested a new type of lay participation in holy ritual, although, as we have seen above, this participation was primarily as spectators. Yet another important type of participation was considered in the construction of Il Gesù,: responding to the mandates of the Council of Trent, it was intended to accommodate the new emphasis on preaching and was designed with the congregation's need to hear the sermon in mind. Here was an architectural revolution of stunning magnitude, for this new unification of space, paralleling the somewhat contemporaneous experiments of Protestants to create unified auditoria spaces, would result in a fully transformed Christian architecture in the next century.

This transformation encompassed not only space, but meanings associated with spaces as well. The intimations of heaven embedded in churches such as St. Peter's and Il Gesù were qualitatively different from those suggested by medieval churches. In this and other late Renaissance or, more technically, Baroque, churches, the spaces and the dome are filled with light streaming in through unfiltered glass. Here human capability, artistic virtuosity, and plenitude reign. The Jesuit motto inscribed in Il Gesù, "For the Greater Glory of God and the Church," implied the human element in the equation: this *we do* "for the greater glory," thereby signifying the social power of the church builders and patrons. As James McEvoy has argued, these churches brought together heaven and earth in a new unity: "The church is nothing other than the earthward projection of the divine life and the court of heaven; it is part of the spiritual world of angels and saints."[31] As the court of heaven, the church indicates the absolutism of God while at the same time articulating its own earthly and hierarchical power. Whereas the heavenly city of the Gothic cathedral might elicit fear and trembling on the part of an illiterate worshipper, the urban classical-inspired churches of Renaissance Italy were more likely to elicit awe and/or admiration for the power of the clergy and the lay patrons whose wealth made the buildings possible and provided the foundation of their service to God.

Thus, these buildings effectively articulated messages about clerical hierarchy even as they encouraged new forms of participation in services by the faithful. They welcomed the laity into spiritual life as spectators and listeners in ways that appealed to the intellect rather than inspired fear. The clerical hierarchy remained well defined within the spaces of the new buildings, which at the same time acknowledged lay worshippers' contributions. At St. Peter's, for example, the sheltering arms of Bernini's colonnade (1656–1667) that forms the elliptical piazza in front of the basilica reiterated the importance of the laity, circumscribing a space that invites the multitude to join and participate in worship.

Lastly, a rethinking of the past is evident in the exteriors of these churches as well, which took on new significance also traceable to classical ideas about proportion, harmony, and order. These buildings played a new role within the urban landscape. The renewed interest in temple architecture also extended to city planning, with church sites being selected for their ceremonial and monumental capacities. Noted designer and architect Andrea Palladio, for instance, argued that "if in the city there be hills, the highest part of them is to be chosen; but in case there be no elevated places, the floor of the temple is to be raised, as much as is convenient above the rest of the city."[32] While some Renaissance churches adopted such sites and emphasized their monumentality, the Baroque facades of many buildings, including Il Gesù, integrated the church into the streetscape, functioning much like gateways, opening the longitudinal axis of the interior onto the street, much as did early Roman basilicas.[33]

Humanism and the Baroque Aesthetic

The term *Baroque* is generally applied to art and architecture from the seventeenth century through the mid-eighteenth. The fundamental components of the Baroque are spaciousness (even gigantism), an emphasis on the visual, and visual and spatial complexity. By the latter part of the sixteenth century, these strategies grew exaggerated. The use of basic geometrical forms—circles, squares, oblongs—morphed into experiments with ellipses and elongated forms, which, when combined with new understandings of the optical trick of perspective, could be used to create spaces in which perspective seemed to bend. Rational spaces gave way to visual mazes. Multiple axes in Baroque buildings competed for the attention of the worshipper—longitudinal axes intersected with vertical ones, and apses softened the power of both. Further, the multiple axes and elliptical perspectives brought a feeling of movement to the buildings. Within these spaces, ornament proliferated. Baroque buildings featured an intentional integration of the arts. Spaces for frescoes and paintings were designed into the architectural features, and subjects became indicative of humanistic interests, with the depiction of psychological states—ecstasy, conversion, vision—of great interest to artisans and viewers alike.[34]

Baroque art's embrace of visual realism defined a new relationship between the faithful and the Christian narrative, reducing though not eliminating opportunities for worshippers to insert themselves into the narratives. The realistic depiction of biblical personages dressed in contemporary clothing, particularly clothing indicating wealth, popular among Baroque artists, for instance, reduced the narrative space available for ordinary people to identify with the stories depicted, while opening it for the wealthy. Artists of the period, for instance, often painted portraits of their patrons as characters in their religious works. Such use of the specific might encourage viewers to honor such patrons and follow their example, but it hardly invited viewers to insert themselves into the story. At the same time, however, the use of perspective techniques that led the eye deeply into pictures seemed to invite viewers into the work in a startlingly new way. Invitation and exclusivity created an interesting tension, emphasizing, as did the Mass, the role of the faithful as gazers upon the sacred narrative. As much as one may visually admire an image such as Leonardo da Vinci's *Last Supper* (1498), painted on the wall of the refectory in the Dominican Convent of Santa Maria delle Grazie in Milan, and imagine oneself at that table, the physical barrier that the table creates between the subjects and the viewer keeps the latter at arms' length, and the realism and concentrated activity of the people depicted allows little narrative space for another imagined participant. Similarly, the self-contained action of the work of Caravaggio during the Baroque period conveys important religious meanings but rarely encourages viewers to identify with the on-going action. Thus, while medieval art with its generalized depictions of religious figures had provided ample narrative ambiguity into which the faithful could imaginatively insert themselves, Baroque art set up a more complicated and frequently more distant relationship between the worshipper and religious narratives.

Baroque spaces also had a different kind of impact on the faithful than did medieval ones. The awe associated with entering a medieval analogue of a heavenly Jerusalem—a place infused with divine power—gave way to a different kind of awe, one inspired by equally breathtaking spaces and artworks that derived their power not from their link to the divine but from their human creators. A Sistine Chapel celebrates human achievement. Art patronage and art criticism in the sixteenth century evaluated this achievement and publicly proclaimed it to the world. Carrying on the didactic functions that medieval church art had so effectively advanced, Renaissance and Baroque artists took the didacticism to a new level by realistically depicting divine power within the human context of social and political power. While the bejeweled light and vaguely abstract quality of medieval art in medieval churches emphasized the metaphorical nature of human representation of the divine, complex Baroque spaces and images such as Michelangelo's rendering of God touching fingertips with Adam in the Sistine Chapel strove to depict actual power in realistic ways, and in the process necessarily emphasized human power. God is man in Renaissance art, a depiction that, unlike the tropic use of light as a metaphor for divinity, elevates human power by minimizing differences between it and divine power. God as Renaissance man is readily accessible to human understanding. Perhaps more importantly, the reverse—man as god— is also implied.

In the Italian church, the elevation of human power extended to the worship service, particularly through music, despite the Tridentine reproach of its use during services. Trumpet fanfares accompanied spectacular processions of the episcopacy, clergy, and ruling families. Elaborately choreographed musical performances, such as Giovanni Gabrielli's four-part antiphonal compositions, accompanied the Mass. Locating musicians in each of the four corners of a church to create what we would today recognize as a stereophonic effect, Gabrielli incorporated the acoustical properties of new buildings into their works and dazzled listeners with astonishing musical effects.

In these ways, then, Renaissance and Baroque churches and services directly celebrated human creativity and accomplishment on an unprecedented scale.[35] It did so at a time of particular turmoil within the church—a period in which the church itself was accused of corruption and being out of touch with the faithful. The churches of this period can be seen as part of the church's response to such charges. As historian James McEvoy has argued, the Catholic artists throughout Europe were encouraged to use the decisions of the Council of Trent as a guide to "replac[e] the pagan tendencies of the High Renaissance [neo-classicism] in art and sculpture by a new Christian synthesis of painting, the plastic arts, and architecture."[36] Just as the Council of Trent in the mid-sixteenth century instigated behavioral reforms among clergy, it also renewed attention on the setting of the service, at once humanizing it while at the same time articulating the church's social power through gigantism in space and the sumptuousness of ornament.

Yet this extravagance also laid the church open to continuing charges of corruption. Among the earliest critics had been Girolamo Savonarola, a Dominican who gained notoriety in Florence during the 1490s. Appalled at the resources and wealth being directed into the church and the moral corruption it implied, Savonarola preached apocalyptic sermons about the coming destruction of the church, which he saw as mired in greed, opulence, and immorality. He encouraged lay people to demonstrate their devotion to God by eschewing their luxuries and burning their lavish clothing, books, and jewelry in his famed "bonfires of the vanities." Although warned by the church to end his public criticism, Savonarola persisted. He was tried for religious error and sedition, and in May 1498, he was executed.

Others critics of the church would follow. As the construction of St. Peter's in Rome proceeded in the early 1500s under Julius II, corruption within the church seemed to many to grow deeper. Construction costs were offset through the selling of religious favors—papal indulgences or guarantees that an individual soul would be released from purgatory quickly upon its arrival after death. Among those outraged by the expansion of traffic in religious favors was a monk named Martin Luther, whose efforts to urge reform resulted in his excommunication and a firestorm of critique that washed across Europe: the Protestant Reformation.

The Protestant Reformation

Given the relationship between religious favors and architecture, the role and function of religious space lay close to the heart of the sixteenth-century Protestant reformation. Certainly, as the desire to display wealth through the construction and ornamentation of churches grew with the economic shifts of the late fifteenth and early sixteenth centuries, critics like Savonarola and Luther found receptive audiences. Sumptuous churches, paid for through the sale of indulgences and granting of special masses to big donors, would become symbols of the church's corruption and, soon, targets for iconoclasm, radical Protestant vandalism.

In fact, the act most frequently heralded as the catalyst to the Protestant movement involved a church building. When Johann Tetzel, a Dominican monk, began selling indulgences in Saxony as a means of raising funds for the reconstruction of St. Peter's, Martin Luther, an Augustinian monk who had previously expressed grave reservations about this practice, wrote up a list of concerns that he felt needed to be addressed by the church. To publicly post his now-famous ninety-five theses in October 1517, he supposedly nailed the text to the door of the Wittenberg Cathedral. This use of the church would become iconic. It was customary to post public announcements on the church door, but in this case the location underscored and magnified Luther's charges of clerical abuse of authority because the cathedral served both as a symbol of the institutional church and as a physical manifestation of its perceived corruption. Into this door, Luther hammered a single nail to attach the sheet of paper on which he had written the criticisms of current Christian practice, a transgressive act that has dominated the Christian cultural imagination about the period ever since. In the story, the nail, like those used to wound Christ, wounds the church door, a portal that should mark the entry into incorruptibility but, according to Luther's theses, is an entry into corruption. The wounded building becomes a physical metonym for the wounded body of the church. But the nail violates at the same time that it attempts to reform, to offer salvation, or at least a path out of corruption. This powerful image has resonated with generations of Protestants, for whom it unites a critique of the religious organization and its physical manifestation in the building.[37]

In the ensuing years, what began as an effort to reform the Christian church from the inside grew into a division between Protestants and Catholics that has defined Christianity ever since, one marked by frequently differing theologies, worldviews, worship practices, and aesthetics. It also ushered in radical architectural transformations in the spatial arrangements and clergy/laity relationships within churches and in the ornamentation of Christian churches. These architectural changes attested to Protestants' fundamental revisioning of Christianity's understanding of divine, social, and personal power.

The Protestant Reformation embraced and boosted the influence and power of the laity, which, as we have seen, had been growing within Christianity throughout the Renaissance period. Whereas in the papal system, lay influence came mostly in the form of fairly wealthy individuals' relationships with local priests, as Protestantism developed, a broader swath of lay people became actively involved in the religious life and leadership of communities, serving in such offices as elders and deacons and on consistory boards charged with maintaining church governance and monitoring the moral behavior of parishioners. In these ways, the laity (almost exclusively the male laity) gained social power by taking on duties previously reserved for clergy and patrons.

Understandings of clerical power also changed substantially. Priests' power derived in large measure from their knowledge of the mysteries of the

Mass and the transformation of the Eucharist, as well as from their function as mediators between the divine and the human. Protestants denied the mysteries of Eucharist transubstantiation, however, and thus eliminated this supernatural source of clerical power. By adopting a philosophy of what Luther called a "priesthood of all believers," Protestants repudiated another source of power, apostolic succession, or the belief in the succession of the priesthood from the original apostles. Luther encouraged direct, individual relationships with God, based on sound understanding of scripture. No special mediation was needed between individual faith and God's grace and salvation, and therefore, there was no need for clergy to claim lineage back to the apostles of Jesus's time. Consequently, this source of clerical power was also eliminated. This is not to say that Protestant clergy repudiated religious or social power, but simply that they developed new approaches for claiming authority and grounding their influence. The most critical source of Protestant clerical power was their relationship to scripture, the final authority for all things having to do with God.

For Protestants, divine power centered on the Word of God as delivered to human society in scripture. The Bible was seen as God's revelation, his primary effort to communicate with society—a conduit for divine power. One knew God through Jesus, and Jesus through scripture. The Word was thus understood by Protestant reformers as the primary concern of the church. Consequently, the focus of worship services shifted from the Eucharist transformation and sacrifice celebrated in the Mass to the sermon, a lengthy discourse on scriptural text preached by the minister. And thus preaching became the primary locus of power for Protestant ministers. Martin Luther reportedly believed that "When the preacher speaks, God speaks!"—an idea with far-reaching ramifications.[38] As historian Fred W. Meuser explains Luther's thinking, "If the pastor is not sure that God speaks through his mouth he should leave preaching alone for he surely denies and blasphemes God."[39] Clerical power, for Protestants, depended upon the individual preacher's ability to convincingly deliver God's message, to interpret scripture for congregations of believers gathered to hear the Word. Imagine the experience of late-sixteenth-century adult lay Christians, moving from growing up attending masses that provided only glimpses of God in the Host (and actual communion with the Host only once a year) to attending services in which God actually spoke through a preacher. In this situation, God was understood as drawing much closer to worshippers, answering questions, explaining things that once were mysteries. The minister, of course, played a critical role in this shift, but the individual was also empowered by this new situation, for he or she could also read the scripture, which was translated into the vernacular and made available through the development of the printing press, and evaluate the minister's interpretation of it. Here was a very new and very personal relationship with the divine.

This is not to suggest that the Eucharist was forgotten. Indeed, Luther embraced this sacrament, along with baptism, and encouraged weekly communion of the faithful in both species. As a result, the Communion service became a vital site of congregational participation in Lutheran worship and was retained by other Protestant groups as well.

Lutheran and Reformed Worship Space

These new understandings of divine, social, and personal empowerment, the reinterpretation of the Eucharist as one of congregational participation, and the new emphasis on preaching the Word of God inspired new approaches to religious architecture and space. The first space designed specifically for Protestant services is reputed to be the Schlosskapelle or castle chapel at Hartenfels Castle in Torgau, Germany (fig. 5.6). Designed by Nickel Gromann with input from Luther and noted artist Lucas Cranach, the chapel was dedicated on August 5, 1544, with Luther himself in attendance. The chapel consisted of a small rectangular hall with a narrow vaulted nave composed of four bays. A main gallery wrapped the entire room, providing seating for the congregation on three sides and for the choir on the east end above the altar. Above this main gallery a clerestory gallery flanked the nave on the north and south. An elaborately carved pulpit with a small sounding board hung halfway down the south wall of the nave, and at the east the altar table was topped with a carved altarpiece. Organ pipes hung on the east wall high above the altar and choir.

Torgau illustrates several fundamental elements that would become common in Protestant, and particularly Lutheran, churches of the sixteenth and seventeenth centuries. First is the emphasis placed upon the pulpit, in terms of both its location and its ornamentation. Here, the adage "form follows function" is appropriate. Although preaching had been an important feature of Christianity prior to the Reformation, the pulpit had barely been conceived of as a liturgical center until then. Tertiary to the altar and sanctuary, it previously had usually been located on a pier at the transept. This location, however, often rendered it impossible for many of the congregants to hear the priest's sermon or homily. Luther and his followers changed the location of the pulpit, moving it down the nave to a midway point as in Torgau. They also elevated it well above the heads of those on the main floor to make it readily visible from almost every point in the nave. To further attract worshippers' attention to the

FIGURE 5.6. Hartenfels Castle, Torgau, Germany. Courtesy Foto Marburg/
Art Resource, N.Y.

pulpit, Protestant designers, including those of Torgau, decorated their pulpits
with high-relief painted figures carved into the sides. Frequently, pulpit images offered distinctive lessons, following Luther's belief that although images
should not be worshipped, they can have a legitimate didactic or instructive
purpose by enhancing believers' understanding of Christianity and the life of
Christ. In Torgau, the pulpit figures depict Jesus during teaching moments
that overturn the usual course of events: as a boy in the Temple, with the
woman taken in adultery, and driving the moneychangers out of the temple.
The overall message was clear: the bold challenges to traditional Christian
thinking wrought by Protestant reformers took their model from Christ himself, who bravely challenged religious authorities in his own time.

The elevated pulpit, then, became a visual mnemonic for the new understandings of divine and social power. Like the earlier Elevation of the Host
during the Eucharist service, the elevation of the pulpit signaled its divine
association with the Word of God. More specifically, its elevation signaled the
importance and authority of its occupant, the minister who preached the Word
of God. Its ornamentation, designed to attract the attention of congregants,
further signaled the importance of the preacher. Pulpits would become larger
and even more ornate in the next two centuries, particularly as Calvinist or
Reformed congregations focused their services on sermons.

Yet in Torgau and later Lutheran churches, we see less of a single focus on
the pulpit than a dual focus on it and the altar. For although the sermon gained
in importance, the celebration of Communion, as mentioned above, also remained near the heart of Luther's efforts to reform the church. For Luther, a
strong advocate of the empowering of lay worshippers, the traditional with-
holding of the Eucharistic elements from the laity was anathema. The sharing
of the elements was an important sacrament, he felt, in which all Christians
should be allowed to partake frequently. The prominent presence of the altar at
the east end of the Torgau chapel, elaborated with the visually interesting choir
and organ pipes above, constituted a permanent visual reminder of Christ's
sacrifice, through which he atoned for the sins of humanity.

Thus the new Lutheran churches of the Reformation actually had two focal
points of relatively equal importance: the elevated pulpit halfway down the
nave and the altar at the end of the nave. Many authors have argued that in hall
churches like Torgau, the pulpit served as the focus of the room because of the
high ornamentation frequently given it.[40] Yet the architecture itself tends to
belie this claim. As pointed out previously, the spatial mass of the oblong hall
church, comprising a nave constructed with repetitive bays and lofty vaulting
and with the door located at the west end, naturally points the viewer in the
direction of the east end. That is, the whole architectural movement directs the
eye to the end of the room. At Torgau and many later churches, the Lutherans
abided by this movement and retained the altar table in its traditional location.
With their continued emphasis on the significance of the Eucharist service, the
spatial emphasis on the altar was appropriate and even necessary, even if it
created a rather awkward dual-focused room with the altar and the pulpit vying
for the attention of the worshipper. Indeed, one could argue that the spatial
tension created by early churches like Torgau in which the altar and the pulpit
are both distinctly elaborated parallels the ideological tension between the
primacy of the Eucharist and that of the Word, which lay at the theological
heart of the Reformation.

In ensuing centuries, designers of Protestant churches would struggle to overcome this fundamental problem—how to incorporate two liturgical centers, the pulpit and the altar (or table, as we shall see below) into a single room. Solutions to the problem generally hinged on the position of the altar and the meanings ascribed to the Communion ceremony. For Lutherans, who believed in the real presence of Christ in the Eucharist elements (though not precisely in the same way that in Catholic doctrine the *substance* of Christ was present), the altar, like the pulpit, was a central liturgical site. Thus they tended to treat them as relatively equal, elaborating their altars with distinctive altarpieces while ornamenting their pulpits as well. The development of the pulpit-altar or the *kunzelaltar* in the late seventeenth century was perhaps the most eloquent statement of the Lutheran view of the equal importance of Word and Communion, combining the two sites into a single piece of furniture in which the pulpit hovered directly above the altar.

Reformed Christians, like Catholics, solved the problem by reducing the importance of one liturgical center—the Catholics minimizing the importance of the pulpit, Reformed Christians the importance of the altar. This latter group was influenced by Ulrich Zwingli, who argued against Catholic and Lutheran understandings of the real presence of Christ in the Eucharist. Drawing a sharp distinction between things material and things spiritual, he argued that the Eucharist presence was wholly spiritual, and that sacramental communion through the Eucharist was a spiritual communion, not a ritual of sacrifice. John Calvin, who would become even more influential than Zwingli, argued something of a middle ground between the Catholic view of transubstantiation and Zwingli's idea of spiritual communion. Calvin felt that an exclusively spiritual communion neglected the human element of Christ. But in his view, the elements had no supernatural significance. The bread was bread, the wine was wine. The Lord's Supper was a means by which the community affirmed their belief and trust in Christ's promise of salvation.[41]

Because Calvinists understood the Eucharist as a communal sacrament of the Christian community, they reinterpreted the altar as not a place of sacrifice but a table for communion, a place for the Lord's Supper. Followers of Calvin participated in the Lord's Supper frequently; he recommended that they do so every time the community gathered. Thus the communion table was a fairly prominent feature in Calvinist churches, as least in the early years. Followers swayed more by Zwingli's views also used a modest table but tended to observe the Lord's Supper ritual less frequently; as a result, the table was not a prominent feature in their churches and may not even have been present most of the time, removed to another part of the building when not needed. When

Calvinist and other Reformed groups celebrated the Lord's Supper, they moved the table to the center aisle or another convenient location and placed chairs all around it for the participants. For such groups, the Lord's Supper was a meal among equals, although restrictions were placed on who could participate.

Another solution to the tension between the pulpit and table as competing liturgical centers was the elaboration of the pulpit in order to heighten its visual appeal. Reformed Christians, like Lutherans, favored large, elevated pulpits, and often placed large soundboards above them to help project sound out over the congregation. The high-relief carving and in some cases double speaking tiers (the top tier for the sermon and the lower for the Gospel reading) were not adopted by the more ascetic Reformed congregations but were common strategies among Lutherans and Anglicans (Church of England).

The third liturgical center, the baptismal font, raised fewer tensions and concerns than did altars and pulpits. Although Protestants viewed baptism as a sacrament, they rarely created a separate space for the ceremony in the church as did Catholics, who traditionally performed baptisms in a separate room or building. Protestants did, however, integrate baptism into the congregational ritual and thus moved the font into the church. Lutherans and Anglicans generally placed a permanent, freestanding font near the front of the church. Reformed congregations brought out a modest bowl filled with water and placed it on a table during baptisms. By the late sixteenth century, the Anabaptists, or rebaptizers, who insisted on adult rather than infant baptism, had moved the ritual outdoors, performing their ceremonies in rivers or other bodies of water, following the practice they found in the Bible.

One final key element that bears heavily on the spatial orientation of these new Protestant churches is that of congregational seating. Unfortunately, obtaining reliable information on this subject proves highly problematic, as seating is the least permanent component in spatial arrangements. Although in earlier Catholic churches, pews were available only for the wealthy, who generally provided them through their own efforts, in these early Protestant churches, benches accommodated worshippers who were expected to listen to sermons that could sometimes last more than two hours. In fact, the inclusion of benches, not only in Protestant but in Catholic churches during the period, transformed groups of worshippers into "congregations." Early sketches of the interiors of churches, such as one from the early seventeenth century titled *The True Image of an Apostolic Church,* depicting a presumably French Calvinist church, perhaps Charenton (which will be discussed below), shows what we in the twenty-first century would consider a rather casual gathering of people (fig. 5.7). Beneath the pulpit, located midway down the nave on the right, is a box pew for the consistory, or lay officials of the congregation. In front of this

Vera Imago veteris Ecclesiæ Apostolicæ.   Ware abcontrofeitung der alter Apostolischer Euangdischer Kirchen

FIGURE 5.7. *True Image of an Apostolic Church*. Courtesy Bibliothèque nationale de France.

are benches, occupied predominantly by women and, presumably, the aged. A single bench located further up the nave is occupied by a few men, and several men stand randomly between this bench and pulpit. Such seating does little to help define the spatial orientation of the room; indeed, it disrupts an orderly orientation by emphasizing the multipurpose character of the nave.

Whether this type of seating was common is impossible to say. And to make judgments on the basis of contemporary or even nineteenth-century seating arrangements is, of course, highly problematic. Various photographs of Torgau, for instance, depict two approaches to seating. In an early image, benches reach from side aisle to side aisle, a strategy that would become common during the eighteenth and nineteenth centuries. This arrangement creates a distinctive barrier between the worshipper entering the room and the altar and consequently tends to emphasize the pulpit, which is more visually accessible. A later image, however, illustrates how profoundly a single alteration to the seating can affect the orientation of the room. In it, pews are arranged with an aisle down the middle of the nave, a pattern that enhances the spatial emphasis on the altar. However the seating was arranged in the sixteenth century, we can be sure it did affect the visual emphasis within the room.

Although ground-floor seating likely varied widely from place to place, almost all Protestant churches shared one key feature: galleries. In fact, given the ubiquitousness of galleries in Protestant churches, we may well consider them to be on a par with elaborate pulpits as being among the most distinguishing architectural features of Protestant reform. The purpose of galleries grew directly out of the theological and liturgical transformations of reformation thought: they brought worshippers closer to the two liturgical centers, pulpit and table.

Nevertheless, just as in earlier Christian churches, galleries became enmeshed in systems of delineating social rank, with the different levels being reserved for different ranks, a practice that also grew common in the theaters of the period. The main floor of the castle church at Stettin, for instance, was occupied by servants and ordinary townsfolk, according to historian K. E. O. Fritsch. The first gallery level seated squires, nobles, magistrates, and other civic leaders; and the second or highest gallery housed royalty.[42] Here we see the architecture reinforcing understandings of social power, not the power of clergy but of congregants. Further, within such a hierarchical seating arrangement, the placement of the consistory below the pulpit on the main floor takes on greater meaning, as it suggests that church officials deemed the ordinary laypeople sitting on the first floor in greater need of monitoring than the occupants of the higher levels. In Protestant churches a new interest in surveillance arose, as congregation leaders watched worshippers and worshippers watched one another.

Calvinist architectural strategies brought further transformations to Christian architecture. Like the German Lutherans, the Calvinists in Geneva, France, the Netherlands, and later Britain converted many existing Catholic churches to suit their own worship practices. Just as with the Lutherans, this meant moving the pulpit down to a center point on the south wall of the nave. The Calvinists, however, made more significant changes to the chancel. Depending on how often the congregation celebrated the Lord's Supper, the tables were either placed to a side or removed from the room entirely when not needed. By the eighteenth century, a new location for the table, beneath the pulpit, became relatively common.

Among the earliest Calvinist or Reformed churches were those erected in France after the Edict of Nantes in 1598, which granted Protestants religious freedom to openly practice their faith. Several churches, or "temples" as they were more frequently called, were built between the passage of the edict and its revocation in 1685, when most of the Protestant temples were destroyed.[43] The most striking commonality among these French temples was the frequent use of centralized plans. Calvin's close friend and teacher, Martin Bucer, argued that the central plan linked Protestant worship to that of the Early Christians, whose temples, he claimed, were "usually round." Clergy in these ancient temples, according to Bucer, occupied the middle of the room, "and from that position divine service was so presented to the people that the things recited could be clearly heard and understood by all who were present"[44]—a description that suggests a relatively egalitarian relationship among worshippers.

The fact that French Protestants adopted the centralized plan just as Catholics were rejecting it with the Council of Trent invites speculation. Given the historical strength of the Roman church in France, it is likely that the debates among Italian architects over longitudinal and centralized space also influenced the French designers. Clearly, the architectural vocabulary of Italianate classicism was integrated into many French chateau and government buildings in the sixteenth century, and the adoption of centralized plans for churches likely had similar roots.[45] The architect most influential in the French adoption of centralized plans was Sebastiano Serlio, whose five-book treatise on architecture included, in the final book, twelve church designs featuring several plans, including circular, oval, and polygonal ones.[46] But Serlio and his predecessor, Philibert de l'Orme—whose chapel at the Château d'Anet echoed Bramante's Tempietto with its circular plan covered by a dome—built for Catholic patrons, not the new Protestant groups.[47] It is an open question whether Protestants adopted centralized plans when Catholics began to eschew them as a way of distinguishing themselves from Catholics or whether early Protestant adoption of the plan influenced those Catholics who came to disparage the plan as pagan. In any event, Calvinists erected several churches in France, although little is known about them, given their untimely destruction.

One invaluable piece of information about the early French Calvinist churches comes in the form of a painting by Jean Perrissin of the temple called Le Paradis in Lyon (fig. 5.8). Though Le Paradis may not have been built as a church, it was obtained by Calvinists in 1564 and refurbished for worship, only to be razed a mere four years later. Perrissin's painting provides valuable information about this early Calvinist church interior. The room is round, with a conical roof supported by a timber frame mounted on four posts. Leaded glass dormer windows pierce the roof, casting daylight into the space. A frame gallery supported by corbels encircles the room, and a few oval windows also pierce the walls on this level. The main floor is arranged with a large wineglass-shaped pulpit (a large bowl on a narrow pedestal) occupying one side. Above it

FIGURE 5.8. Temple Paradis, Lyon, France, 1566. Courtesy Fondation Pasteur Eugène Bersier and the Société de l'Histoire du Protestantisme Français.

a soundboard is mounted on the gallery. Beneath the pulpit two rows of pews on either side offer seating to children and a few men, perhaps consistory members, and a semicircle of crude benches placed around the rest of the room and horizontally to the pulpit in the center of the room provide seating for more men (around the ring) and women (in the center).

This seating arrangement evidences a significant transformation in church architecture. The people gathered in this space are organized by the seating into a *whole,* into a corporate entity—a congregation, an audience. Rather than benches sprinkled here and there for individual worshippers, the benches occupy the entire room and are carefully arranged to indicate that congregants are supposed to sit and listen attentively to the service. The seating arrangement suggests that a higher level of discipline was required of congregants in this church than in others we have examined in which areas devoid of seating allowed and perhaps even encouraged milling about and distractions. Another critical feature of the Temple Paradis example is that it allowed congregants positioned around the edges of the room to watch their counterparts throughout the room, a situation that discourages aberrant behavior while underscoring the fellowship of shared worship. This is not to say that the seating arrangement determined people's behavior; indeed, the casual character of the two men speaking to each other in the gallery on the right side of Perrissin's painting suggests that discipline was not fully achieved. Nevertheless, congregants, as an attentive and disciplined audience, played a crucial role in these new Protestant services, a role that was articulated in and fostered by this unique seating arrangement.[48]

Given the importance of the congregants to this new faith, it is not surprising that Perrissin carefully depicted the people gathered for worship. Children, women, and men occupy specific areas of the room. Some individuals wear brightly colored outfits, while others are garbed predominantly in black. Such details convey information about the social class and stature of these worshippers. A man and a woman sit in a framed space just below the pulpit, and the minister seems to be directing his remarks to them, an arrangement that adds a dramatic element to the painting and suggests that some sort of ceremony is taking place. Perhaps the couple is joining the church, or perhaps they are being married, an interpretation supported by the presence of the dog, a symbol of fidelity, to the left of the couple. In any event, it is likely that whatever ceremony has placed this couple in the fenced area under the close scrutiny of the minister has also occasioned the painting of the picture itself.

Lastly, it is important to note that the painting depicts a room that though not highly ornamented is certainly not devoid of decoration. The leaded dormer windows with their diagonal panes house colorful insignia in stained glass, as do the oriel windows on the gallery level. In fact, French churches typically sported municipal insignia and private coats of arms. The gallery is faced with hand-turned balusters and the corbels, carefully depicted, which add a decorative fringe to the edge of the gallery. The pulpit pedestal consists of several carefully curved legs, and the walls of the pulpit itself may depict scenes of some sort. Two tablets appear on either side of the medallion centered above the pulpit and are most likely inscribed with the Decalogue, or Ten Commandments. In some Calvinist churches the Laws of Love also appeared as inscriptions: "Love the Lord thy God with all thy Heart" and "Love thy neighbor as thyself." Italian classicism is seen in many churches of the period, not only in their plans but also in such architectural details as classical orders, dentils, and decoration. Such details belie the common generalization that Calvinists forbade ornamentation in their churches.[49]

A much different church, the Temple of Charenton in Paris, built in 1648, is perhaps the best-known early Reformation church. Unlike the Temple Paradis, Charenton flaunts its classicism. Featuring a rectangular plan with double galleries all around and a barreled ceiling supported by columns, the building, according to architectural historian Andrew Spicer, was modeled on "Vitruvius's description of his basilica at Fano."[50] Yet this is no Roman basilica. Resembling a lecture hall and somewhat reminiscent of Torgau, though much larger, the spatial arrangement of Charenton lacked, or more accurately, resisted, a longitudinal orientation (fig. 5.9). A towering, freestanding pulpit stood at one end, with a horseshoe or ring of pews at its feet. Beyond these, horizontal benches spread down the nave to the door and rows of raked benches occupied the aisles beneath the galleries. No aisle led from the door to the pulpit, and thus the seating disrupted the longitudinal axis. Only the

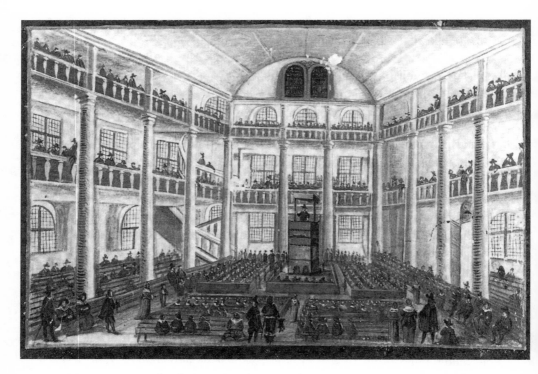

FIGURE 5.9. Temple of Charenton, Paris, 1648. Courtesy The Royal Library, Copenhagen.

moldings in the ceiling and the parallel columns suggested movement from one end of the space to the other.

In a room of this size, the designations of social power attached to the various seating areas were highly complex. Although specific information on who sat where is not available, we can make some observations about the relative spatial relationships among the various participants in the service. Here again, the minister is enshrined in a pulpit elevated several feet above the heads of the worshippers. In the illustration of Charenton, the pulpit and the preacher who occupies it appear to be gigantic, drawn disproportionately large in comparison to the rest of the room. This artistic strategy for depicting ministers addressing a crowd would become common in later years, for despite widespread knowledge of perspective, artists wishing to signify the great authority of preachers did so by making them appear larger than others in the scene. In this depiction, the room is relatively full but not packed with worshippers. The main floor pews nearest the pulpit are fully occupied, as are the galleries, an indication that these seats were considered most desirable. Indeed, individuals sitting on benches at the sides under the galleries very likely had difficulty hearing the minister, and the columns would have blocked their view. Those sitting on the straight benches at the rear of the nave may also have had difficulty hearing. Though we cannot be certain of the customs at Charenton, some Calvinist and Reformed congregations separated seating by sex and some had separate doors for men and women to enter. Some churches also contained special doors for the exclusive use of community leaders or the aristocracy.

In many churches, social status and position within the congregation became marked through individuals' efforts to claim a particular pew or bench. Some people furnished their particular seat with cushions, drapings, and even foot warmers, leaving the items in place between services as a means of reserving the spot. Some churches included cabinets or small booths attached to the exterior of the building with a window placed to allow the occupant to observe the service. Historian Raymond Mentzer, for instance, has found that by 1600, the temple at Nîmes housed some 242 private benches. These "luxury boxes" were generally built and furnished through the efforts of an individual or family. Not surprisingly, stories of acrimonious relations and even actual fights over benches are not uncommon.[51]

Iconoclasm

As innovative as the new Protestant architecture may have been, the Reformation period is better known for the destruction of religious buildings and artifacts than for their creation. Debate and, in many cases, violence sprang from differences of opinion on a range of aesthetic and theological questions. Should churches be ornamented? If so, how? Should the divinity or the life of Jesus be depicted visually? Should other Christian figures be depicted? Theological perspectives frequently informed the positions taken in such disputes. If the Word were all-encompassing and uniquely sufficient in depicting the divine, attempts to visually depict religious figures resulted inexorably in idolatry, some argued. An image of Jesus or of Mary or any other scriptural figure necessarily led to the worship of that image. Within the context of the sometimes overwhelming abundance of images and iconography in late medieval and early Renaissance Catholic churches of the period, this stark or ascetic view of visual art was all too frequently expressed in violent attacks on church ornament.

Among the first of hundreds of such incidents occurred in Wittenberg in 1522, when university students who were followers of Andreas Karlstadt, a reformer who had taken up the mission of establishing a new and fairly radical order within the Wittenberg church, destroyed several objects in the church when the council proved slow in carrying out its order to remove several altars and paintings from it.[52] Martin Luther, arriving in town shortly thereafter, took steps to quell the violence by preaching a series of sermons that refined the function of images within a word-centered theology. Luther took a moderate approach to figural images, condemning the belief in the intercessory abilities of saints and the veneration of their images, but allowing the use of figures for didactic or educational purposes. In fact, some years later, he suggested that a new altarpiece for the Wittenberg church depict the Lord's Supper, a suggestion that his close friend and artist Lucas Cranach the Elder and his son followed when they created the retable in 1539.[53] Luther took a moderate approach to figural images, condemning idolatry but allowing the use of figures as didactic tools. As a result, Lutheran churches tended to allow figural images. Altarpieces depicting scenes from the life of Christ or images of the evangelists were common in Germany, parts of Eastern Europe, and the Nordic regions. Reformed theologians, in contrast, tended to condemn visual depictions of religious figures and themes. An influential tract written by Martin Bucer in 1530 encouraged iconoclasm, the destruction or removal of religious images, which spread through the 1530s and 1540s.

In England, where church reform took a more complicated turn, the destruction of religious buildings and artifacts stemmed from a merging of religious convictions and political aspirations. Henry VIII, though more religiously conservative (i.e., Catholic) than his close advisors, agreed that the power of the church over the state was unconscionable and threatened his own authority to rule. Upon Pope Clement VII's denial of Henry's request for an annulment of his marriage to Catherine of Aragon, he claimed authority as the supreme head of the English church and officially broke with Rome. Henry's advisors, sympathetic to the slowly growing influence of Protestant reformers in the country, urged him to press for a number of church reforms. Henry issued the Bible in English and at least briefly urged it be read widely (though he later put restrictions on who could read it).

With respect to architecture and iconoclasm, Henry and his Protestant advisors, like the German reformers mentioned above, attempted to suppress the common practice of praying to saints for their intercessory power. In 1536, the Acts of Parliament issued under Henry prohibited devotional practices associated with saints (prayers, lighting candles, pilgrimage, etc.) and required that all statues of saints be literally defaced. Carried out under the administration of Thomas Cromwell, the Earl of Essex, the ensuing period of destruction was the first of what would become many episodes of iconoclasm in England. Church after church was visited by Cromwell's men, who destroyed the faces and hands of all statuary.

Also perceive as threatening Henry's authority as head of the church were the monastic societies, which, though relatively small in terms of population, had significant monetary resources—or at least Henry and his advisors believed this to be the case. Many monasteries collected donations from pilgrims who came to see the sacred relics of the saints placed on display there. The 1536 act also mandated the dissolution of the monasteries, which obviously had an enormous effect on religious buildings in England. Starting with the relatively small monasteries, those whose net worth was £200 or less, Cromwell's men visited hundreds of establishments and found them in violation of an array of requirements. Dissolution, or suppression, invariably followed. The residents were dispersed (in some cases pensioned off by the king) and the buildings seized. All valuable items, from liturgical silver to furniture to the church bells and lead roofs of the buildings themselves, were confiscated. The fate of the buildings varied. Some were sold to nearby landowners, others were saved as parish churches or cathedrals of the Church of England, some were dismantled, and others were simply left roofless to the elements. The ruins of many of the latter remain visible (and popular tourist sites); Tintern Abbey, immortalized in the poem by William Wordsworth, is perhaps the most well known. Whitby Abbey, dismantled in 1538, also remains as a ruin, its lead roof having been dismantled and then recycled as a new covering for the nearby St. Mary's Church, which had previously been thatched. Waltham Abbey, in 1540 the last monastery to be suppressed, was partially torn down, though its nave was left standing for a parish church.

Many abbey churches, however, were spared and converted for the new Church of England services. Several larger Benedictine cathedral priories—Ely, Durham, Winchester, Canterbury, and Bath, for instance—became Church of England cathedrals.[54] In these cases, few alterations were needed beyond minimizing the amount of statuary, usually by removing it. Stained glass, high in the Gothic walls, was generally spared, as it was deemed less likely to be used idolatrously due to its distance from worshippers. The traditional spaces of the churches, their naves and chancels, proved quite workable for services that retained the flavor of the earlier Mass while simplifying it and making it more accessible to lay participation and understanding.[55]

Thus it is in the Renaissance and Reformation periods that we begin to see clearly the many ways in which Christian architecture was made to serve theological, political, social, and cultural ends all at once. Catholics experimented briefly with centrally planned buildings as part of an aesthetic or cultural trend, but after the Council of Trent they quickly retreated in favor of more traditional plans. Lutheran and Reformed religious leaders urged a rethinking of church space that would serve the requirements of their new Word-centered services while also allowing a sacramental element. Their buildings reflected these new worship requirements and social arrangements.

Protestantism in the seventeenth century, then, reconceptualized religious space and architecture just as it revolutionized Christian creed, code, and cultus. New relationships among worshippers and between worshippers and clergy required new spaces, which in turn helped to naturalize those relationships. The new spaces also articulated new ideological perspectives. The Protestant creed assigned greater power and responsibility to each individual, which was articulated in congregations' closer proximity to clergy. This was especially true during Communion services, which were celebrated at tables around which all communicants gathered. Nevertheless, during sermons, ministers hovered above their flock, a position that signaled the importance and power of their words as, if not the precise language of God, certainly as close as the human voice could speak.

This period also opens a window onto the vulnerable character of church buildings. Successive waves of destruction, from Karlstadt's attacks on images in Catholic churches to the Catholic attacks on Calvinist churches in France after the repeal of the Edict of Nantes to Cromwell's iconoclasm in monasteries, point up the contested character of religious space. In each case, the destruction of certain Christian spaces and material objects constituted an expression of faith, the action resulting from differing theological understandings of true or "proper" worship space and practice. As we have seen throughout this book, of course, Christian worship space has been constantly changing since the first century, making the idea of a "true" Christian architecture historically untenable.

6

Formalism and Non- or Antiformalism in Worship and Architecture

The separation of Protestant worship from Catholic worship led to new and differing emphases in worship practice or cultus. To understand this expansion of Christian cultus, historians and theologians have conceived of the breadth of worship practices since the Reformation as a continuum of organizational and aesthetic characteristics. *Liturgical* services, for instance, are those that proceed according to a set order of service and include standardized materials—prayers, invocations, and the like—that are repeated service after service. The content of liturgical services is generally overseen by a member of the episcopate, who wields a high degree of interpretive authority over the ritual. The quintessential liturgical service is the Catholic Mass, which proceeds in the familiar manner guided by the presiding priest or bishop. The antithesis of the liturgical service is a service that is wholly spontaneous, proceeding idiosyncratically to include prayers, exhortation, sermon, testimony, scripture reading, hymns, and the like and lacking an individual presider. Quaker services, for instance, proceed through the actions of the gathered congregation and conform to no specific pattern or series of actions, and are thus *nonliturgical*. Most Christian services fall somewhere between these two poles, incorporating some liturgical elements but retaining some amount of freedom for the presiding clergy or even the congregation to add elements as desired.

The terms *High Church* and *Low Church* are also often used to correspond loosely with the terms *liturgical* and *nonliturgical*. *High* and *low* in this context originally described distinct positions or parties within the Church of England during the late seventeenth century, referring to those who accorded a *high* degree of authority to the priesthood and episcopate, the sacraments, and the liturgies of the *Book of Common Prayer* and to those who accorded a *low* degree of importance to these elements. A strong aesthetic element figured into the High Church/Low Church debates, with High Churchmen favoring the incorporation of vestments, crosses and/or crucifixes, stained glass, paintings, and sculpture into worship services and churches and Low Churchmen favoring the minimizing of such elements. Among the Low Churchmen of the seventeenth century were the Puritans, a group who remained within the Church of England despite the affinity between their views and those of dissenters, separatists, and other Protestant nonconformists. As the Puritans evolved into the Congregational Church in North America, the terms High and Low Church occasionally took on a more generalized application to Protestant services.

Although useful in their own right, all of these terms prove somewhat misleading with respect to the study of religious space and architecture, particularly as we move into the eighteenth century and the modern period. With the disestablishment of religion in the United States (a process that was not completed until the 1830s) and the resulting voluntary character of religious participation, congregations found themselves functioning in a new and untested context of a religious "marketplace" in which religious groups competed for members. In this new setting, the worship experience offered inside the walls of churches, indeed the churches themselves, became commodities to be promoted, or at least placed on display for interested "buyers," or potential members.

In this context, the antinomies suggested by the High Church/Low Church, liturgical/nonliturgical categories blurred. Orders of service, particularly among the burgeoning evangelical groups, included both liturgical elements such as recitations and nonliturgical ones such as exhortations. Experimentation with material elements—from vestments to communion paraphernalia to stained glass—grew steadily throughout the nineteenth century even among Calvinist-based denominations that had eschewed such display in previous generations. Oppositional terms like High Church/Low Church and liturgical/nonliturgical direct our attention away from what was really a range of practices, a continuum consisting of highly structured services on one end and unstructured or loosely organized ones on the other.

If these terms are less than effective in describing religious services, material culture, and architecture over the last three centuries, then what terms should we use to describe these distinctive and changing elements? Theologians and historians, critical of the oppositions implied by that language, have employed the terms *formalist* and *anti-* or *nonformalist* to indicate the continuum of positions and preferences adopted by congregations. *Formalism* suggests an affinity for formal aesthetic elements as well as formal liturgies. Formalistic worship relies heavily upon clerical authorities, frequently signaled by architectural and sartorial elements, as well as standardized liturgies. Combining the meanings associated with both the High Church end of the first scale and the liturgical end of the other, *formalism* is readily applied to non-Anglican services as well as to services whose liturgical elements may be idiosyncratic. Thus, a Quaker service that follows a regular pattern of activities— even a pattern as nonliturgical as an opening prayer, messages from the congregation, meditation and experiencing the inner light, and closing—can be regarded as somewhat formalistic. Non- or antiformalism, at the opposite end of the continuum, is characterized by an eschewing of clerical authority and liturgical patterns in favor of spontaneous outpourings of worship and emotion. Again, however, these terms indicate a continuum, and most Protestant and, in the late twentieth century, even many Catholic congregations, fall somewhere between the two poles, incorporating both formalist and nonformalist elements within their services. Since the mid-eighteenth century, Christian worship within many denominations can be characterized by their negotiations regarding the level of formalism in their services. Those levels of formalism obviously have a strong bearing on the experience of power and influence on the part of both clergy and congregants.

Formalism in Anglican Worship and Architecture

In the seventeenth century, debates over formalism in worship blended with political struggle, particularly in England, where the monarchy's religious affiliation fueled sectarian antagonism beginning with Henry VIII's declaring himself the head of the Church of England upon its separation from Rome in 1534. Over the course of the next century, the Church of England developed into a distinctive sect with its seminal *Book of Common Prayer* (1549, 1552), which attempted to carve out a middle ground between Roman Catholic and Reformed worship practices by retaining some of the features of the Catholic Mass but eliminating Latin, the cult of saints, and certain liturgical elements. This effort launched a turbulent controversy over formalism in worship, which focused on such aspects as the understanding of the Eucharist service as a "sacrifice" requiring an altar or a "communion" taking place at a table, the wearing of vestments, and the liturgical elements of various services. By the early seventeenth century, efforts to retain or reinstate several formalist elements of the Catholic Mass, including using certain vestments and restoring the altar, were advanced by William Laud, who became Archbishop of Canterbury in 1633, and his followers. Their efforts toward formalism fueled an opposition movement bent on "purifying" the Church of England of the vestiges of Catholic ritual in such High Church elements. As religious and political tensions grew throughout the country, these reformers, called Puritans, aligned politically against the monarchy, which was associated with the High Church position of the Church of England and suspected of having Roman Catholic sympathies. They joined with others, the Parliamentarians, seeking the elimination of royal privilege. In 1642, civil war broke out between the monarchists and the Parliamentarians, and the king, Charles I, an Anglican sympathetic to the High Church aesthetics of Laud, was captured and imprisoned in the Tower of London along with the archbishop. Laud was executed in 1645. Four years later, the Parliamentarians beheaded the king and took control of the government, establishing the Commonwealth under the leadership of Oliver Cromwell, the Lord Protectorate, and banning the *Book of Common Prayer*. The Commonwealth was short-lived, however. Within three years, Charles II returned from exile in France and in 1660 ascended to the throne, reestablishing not only the monarchy but also the Church of England with the High Church liturgies of the *Book of Common Prayer*. By the late seventeenth century, then, religion and politics, monarchy and parliamentarian government, and High Church and puritan worship had been under dispute— and often violent dispute—for several generations.

Then, in the early hours of September 2, 1666, a fire broke out in the City of London. Carried along by strong winds, the conflagration swept westward through the city for five days. The half-timbered houses, businesses, and churches of the medieval city, with their thatched roofs and lathe-and-plaster walls, succumbed quickly. Additional buildings were pulled down by firefighters to create firebreaks. By the time the fire was extinguished, the central city lay in ruins. The Great Fire had claimed an untold number of lives, some 13,200 houses, and most of the buildings in the central core, including 93 churches and chapels. Rebuilding began almost immediately, and high on the list of priorities was the restoration of the city's churches, including the Church of England's Cathedral of St. Paul.

Under the leadership of Christopher Wren, a mathematician and astronomer turned architect, the construction and restoration of some fifty London churches would transform Protestant architecture in England and eventually provide the prototype for church construction in Protestant North America. Wren, a member of the Church of England, put an indelible stamp upon

Christian architecture for generations to come as he adopted neoclassical architectural vocabularies that, although popular for domestic and civic buildings in Britain since the mid-sixteenth century, had not been used for Anglican churches, which had generally retained medieval Gothic forms. At the same time, he altered the footprint and interior space of churches in a way that carved a compromise between the differing views of formalism within worship held by Catholics, Anglicans, and Puritans within the context of political struggle. The Great Fire of London and the subsequent rebuilding of the Christian landscape of the city occurred twenty years after the end of the English Civil War and six years after the restoration of Charles II to the throne. Laudism once again held sway within the church, and Puritans once again feared that "popery" threatened, given that Charles's Roman Catholic brother, James, was in line for the throne. But the Puritans and Parliamentarians were far from vanquished and would rise with new force in 1688, bringing William and Mary to the throne and shifting power from the royal court to the Parliament. Rebuilding the churches of the established Church of England in this complex context of religious and political loyalties took on great public significance.

The city's flagship church, St. Paul's Cathedral, was naturally considered of particular importance. Pronounced structurally unsound even before the fire, the medieval cathedral was all but destroyed in the conflagration. A new building was needed. But on what design? Should the old medieval footprint, with its cruciform nave, transepts, and deep choir, simply be rebuilt? Should something new be erected? Most of the city leaders agreed that the rebuilding offered an opportunity to create something new, but just how new or unprecedented the building should be was a point of contention. The formalism of Anglican services would provide the background against which decisions regarding the plan of the new cathedral went forward.

Wren's initial plans for the cathedral were striking in their innovation within the British context. The first plan, which has not survived, featured two distinct parts, an *auditory* consisting of a rectangular room lacking aisles, and a centralized, circular space or vestibule at the west end, designed for gatherings. Although little is known about this plan, it nonetheless was a startling departure from medieval English forms. Wren, who had recently designed the Sheldonian Theater at Oxford, envisioned the main part of the new cathedral as an auditory—a spatial type that would come to be known as a *preaching hall*— which would help worshippers see and, more importantly, hear the service. Clearly, the experience of working on the theater, a space in which audiences must be able to see and hear the performances, contributed to Wren's conviction that church buildings should also assist those gathered in them in experiencing the activities taking place.[1] Although earlier experiments among Lutherans and Calvinists on the continent had made some effort in this direction, in England, Wren's interest in preaching halls was unusual, given the formalistic leanings and prominence of Laudian ideas within the Church of England. It points up, however, the importance he and his supporters invested in the preaching component of services, as well as the need for congregants to hear, understand, and contribute to the liturgical components of the service.

In addition, Wren's startling new plan featured a massive dome, a classical feature that would have immediately drawn comparison to St. Peter's in Rome and suggested a sympathy with Catholic liturgical formalism. In fact, this similarity was made even more pronounced in Wren's second design for St. Paul's, developed after the initial plan was rejected on the grounds that it did not provide sufficient space for large gatherings. The second plan, which was realized not in the final building but in an elaborate model that survives to this day, borrowed almost directly from Bramante's original plan for St. Peter's, with its Greek cross plan topped by a central dome. This plan, like the original *Book of Common Prayer,* can be seen as an attempt to find a middle ground between the formalism of the medieval Catholic services and spaces and the reduction of liturgy in Calvinist services, for although the Greek cross space could be organized in a highly formal manner, separating sanctuary from worshippers and emphasizing the altar as in St. Peter's, it could also be organized so as to unite the oral and liturgical elements of the Anglican service. In Wren's plan, the elimination of the deep chancel of the medieval church acknowledged the Anglican shift away from the idea of the Mass as a sacrifice and brought the clergy close to the congregation. The altar, located on the east wall, could easily be surrounded by a railing by Laudian sympathizers, but the congregation still was allowed much nearer to it than in earlier churches. Most importantly, the domed crossing could function as an auditory, with a pulpit located at one of the massive piers. Such a plan offered a new opportunity to advance the personal power of worshippers by increasing their perception of and participation in the service, that is, by helping them to see and hear every part of the service.

Yet although this proposal was described by later historians as Wren's favorite, it, too, was rejected, this time on the grounds that the proposed building was not sufficiently cathedral-like. In all likelihood, the model was too much of a departure from the medieval Gothic form of the previous cathedral, with its Latin cross plan and deep chancel. It was not sufficiently formalist. A cathedral almost by definition was High Church, with its distinct separation of clergy and laity and lengthy processional space that characterized medieval churches. Because the second plan united clergy and laity in a single space, and thus

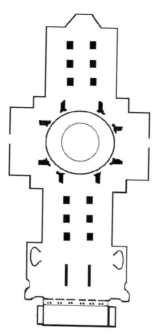

FIGURE 6.1. Christopher Wren's plan for St. Paul's. Drawing by Paul R. Kilde.

compromised the formalist of the space, it too was rejected. In the end, Wren developed an innovative—one might even say postmodern—compromise, erecting his St. Peter's-inspired neoclassical domed cathedral on the medieval Latin cross footprint and situating the dome at the crossing (fig. 6.1). For Wren, the success of the classically inspired building resulted not from the building's replication of the divine beauty of heaven, the view taken by the medieval builders of the Gothic cathedral, but from its spatial rationality, derived entirely from human knowledge and ability. This was a building determined, in the words of historian Lydia Soo, "by society and man," not by God.[2]

The new St. Paul's, harking back to Rome but at the same time offering innovative new spaces, satisfied the High Church sympathies of both the government and the clergy, including the dean of the cathedral, William Sancroft, known for his Laudian views (fig. 6.2). The building would become a symbol of Anglican formalism for generations to come. It would also function as a symbol of the nation itself. The first service held in the not-yet-completed building (held in the choir) occurred on December 2, 1697, when Bishop Henry Compton officiated at a thanksgiving service commemorating the end of the war between England and France.[3]

FIGURE 6.2. Cathedral of St. Paul, London, 1697. Photo by Marilyn Chiat, Ph.D.

In the debate over the plan for St. Paul's, then, as with that over the plan for St. Peter's in Rome, we can see the strong influence of a political context, in this case that of a continuing dispute and struggle for position among Laudian, Puritan, and Catholic perspectives. Here we can see that political realities do influence architecture and worship, and thereby religious systems, discourse, communities, and institutions themselves. Although we tend to be quite aware of instances in which religion influences the political, it is helpful to be reminded once again that the political realm also influences the religious.

The popular realm also has influence on religious spaces. Almost immediately, Londoners and visitors from throughout England flocked to see the new building, making St. Paul's into a pilgrimage site. But this pilgrimage destination was of a significantly different type than earlier Christian ones, for the Anglicans had long since eliminated the cult of saints, the collection of relics, and the practice of pilgrimage from its catalogue of approved worship practices. Saint Paul's was destined to become a new type of religious site—a tourist attraction, a remarkable building that many visited not out of religious motivation but out of a desire to see and experience the architecture. As early as 1709, for an entry fee of two pence, one could gain access to the nearly completed building between services. Visitors to this day wander up the nave to be astounded by the massive dome hovering above the cavernous crossing, climb the steps to the "whispering chamber" between the walls of the double dome to experience how this astonishing feature carries one's voice around the dome to the opposite side, and step out onto the cupola to view all of London at their feet. Although by the mid-nineteenth century many religious sites would similarly become tourists sites valued more for their architecture than for any spiritual meanings associated with them, St. Paul's was the first such building in Great Britain. In this example, we can see how a populace can claim influence over a religious building in ways completely unanticipated—and frequently unstoppable—by religious leaders.

Despite the fact that St. Paul's would achieve worldwide renown, Wren's rethinking of Anglican worship space can be seen even more clearly in the many London parish churches he designed in the wake of the Great Fire. Again working with the footprints of the medieval churches that had been destroyed, Wren developed new spaces that supported the High Church services by maintaining clerical authority while bringing the pulpit and communion table into a kind of balance. Most importantly, however, congregants' need to hear the services was acknowledged and accommodated by the rectangular preaching hall plan that Wren favored. To aid worshippers, Wren employed his understanding of acoustics, which included, according to Soo, the view that the "main space be approximately 60 feet wide and 90 feet long" and that it "should not be so crowded with pews that the poor could not see and hear from the aisles."[4] As we can see, the "science of sound" was still in its infancy. Projecting one's voice ninety feet is an uncommon skill, fifty feet being more realistic. Wren also believed that "one use of Pillars in great

Churches was to facilitate hearing, by breaking the sound and so preventing Echoes."[5] Pillars, of course, also create obstacles that block sound while at the same time visually impeding the reception of the proceedings. Nevertheless, the preaching halls Wren designed were more conducive to worshippers' seeing and hearing services than were the earlier medieval buildings. To provide additional seating and unobstructed sightlines, he placed raked galleries above the aisles. The dome-covered centralized spaces in such buildings as St. Mary Abchurch and St. Swithin's and the oval spaces in St. Benet Fink and St. Antholin reduced acoustically "dead" areas and provided a scale suitable to the human voice. Thus, although these spaces remained acoustically rudimentary in comparison to later buildings, they were miles ahead of the medieval buildings they replaced.

With Wren, Christian architecture achieved a variety and spatial freedom never before seen.[6] The lots in place for the London churches were often irregular, a situation that seems to have freed Wren to experiment widely.[7] His interiors featured large windows with clear or nearly clear glass that allowed in as much light as possible in an increasingly overgrown city in which neighboring buildings loomed, shutting out the sun and darkening the streets (fig. 6.3). The interiors also had a more domestic feeling than medieval buildings, projecting an intimacy through the richly hued wood of the pews, wainscot, and gallery fronts and the ornamented ceilings with their plaster moldings of intertwining vines and flowers. Whereas the earlier Gothic spaces were designed to elicit awe of the power and mystery of God, the London churches, like those of the Italian Renaissance, exuded confidence in the accomplishments of humanity and rationality. Wren did borrow one tactic from Gothic builders, marking his London churches with a tall steeple. Each of the churches sported a multistaged steeple that distinctively announced its presence in the building-congested urban landscape, and with dozens of new steeples rising above the city, panoramic views of the London skyline soon became iconic of the city itself. Here was a city marked by Christian spaces.

Many architects would follow Wren's lead in these areas, most notably Nicholas Hawksmoor and James Gibbs. The latter's St. Martin-in-the-Field on Trafalgar Square in London would serve as the prototype for church builders operating in the new republic across the Atlantic, the United States (fig 6.4). With its pedimented porch supported by six Corinthian columns in the front and pilasters defining the side and rear façades, St. Martin's is a Christian version of the Parthenon. The multistage steeple rising just behind the porch served as the key external marker of the Christian purpose of the building. Inside, the building echoed the preaching halls of Wren, though Gibbs's strategy of

FIGURE 6.3. Saint James, Piccadilly, London. 1684. Christopher Wren, architect. Frederick Nash, watercolor, 1806. Courtesy Guildhall Library City of London.

hanging the gallery fronts on the columns created a more unified space. Like Wren's churches, however, the space was readily used for either High or Low Church services, depending upon the arrangement of the furnishing.

Formalism in architecture and liturgy was also being modified as Christianity swept into the western hemisphere. Since the sixteenth century, Franciscans, Dominicans, and Jesuits had been spreading Christianity throughout Central and South America, and by the eighteenth century, the use of Christian buildings as a colonizing strategy had been perfected by the Spanish, who established a series of mission churches that ran from central Mexico to the present-day San Francisco. These missions served as a means of linking the

FIGURE 6.4. Church of St. Martin-in-the-Field, London, 1726. Photo by
Marilyn Chiat, Ph.D.

far-flung territories of New Spain with the administrative center of the vice-
royalty, located in Mexico City. These walled colonial outposts, enclosing residences, workshops for ironwork and other crafts, grazing animals, gardens,
and churches, brought Christianity as well as European governance and

FIGURE 6.5.   Mission Nuestra Señora de la Concepción, San Antonio, Tex.,
1755. Photo by author.

authority to the indigenous peoples of the region and supported Spanish and
Mexican settlers.

Mission churches, such as Mission Nuestra Señora de la Concepción, in
San Antonio, were generally modest buildings constructed of local materials
including timber and adobe. They simplified and even abstracted the Baroque
architectural vocabularies popular in Europe at the time, blending the native
architectural vernacular with the European (fig 6.5). The iconography within
these modest churches and settlements also evidenced a similar blending or
syncretism, as symbols and images from indigenous religious systems appear
within several of these buildings. A starburst sun, for instance, appears on

FIGURE 6.6. Sunburst in Nuestra Señora de la Concepción, San Antonio, Tex., 1755. Photo by author.

the ceiling of a room within the convento of the Mission Concepción (fig. 6.6). Images of corn, a staple food of the region that was infused with spiritual meaning for the Native peoples, appear in several missions. Such syncretic blending suggests that Spanish control over these buildings was not all-powerful, that mission priests were willing to make room within their churches for at least some of the traditional beliefs of those they colonized. Although we must not romanticize this willingness to stretch Christianity a bit, for the colonizing process wiped out far more of the traditional belief systems and practices than it incorporated, such activity can help us to understand the ways in which formalism in Catholic worship was challenged and modified. Syncretism allowed for the retaining of some measure of personal power among those being colonized, some preservation of the familiar by a religious and administrative system that was, in almost every other way, highly dictatorial and totalizing.

The Growth of Antiformalism in Evangelical Worship

At the same time that Wren and his confederates were designing preaching halls, separatists and Puritans and their descendents were holding their services in meeting houses, simple buildings designed for both civic and religious assemblies and community gatherings. These antiformalist buildings, such as the still extant Old Ship Meeting House in Hingham, Massachusetts, built in 1681, featured a simple two-story rectangular meeting room, with a pulpit centered on the long wall opposite the door and simple benches or box pews arranged to face it. In these rooms, as in the earlier French Protestant churches, the minister hovered above the gathered congregation, with a view of all that occurred within the pews (fig 6.7). In the Puritan meetinghouses, however, inattention to the sermon was not tolerated, and officers of the town stood at watch, ready to reprimand anyone who might disrupt the service.

A further challenge to formalism developed in the mid-eighteenth century, when a new conception of religious authority produced a significant shift in worship practice and architecture. This was a period in which interest in philosophical humanism grew rapidly. Theologians and philosophers were interested in the efficacy of human action, knowledge became a tool for change and betterment, and the perceived relationship between the divine and human society was transformed. Although the Calvinism of previous generations posited that the individual's fate rested solely in the hands of God, a more theologically liberal position (that is, one that assigned greater responsibility for salvation to the individual) gained influence among Protestants. Adherents to this view argued that human responsibility for the state of one's own soul played a significant role in salvation, and that to seek conversion, to acknowledge one's own unworthiness and sin and accept God's power over the fate of

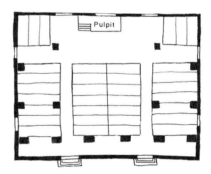

FIGURE 6.7. Typical meetinghouse plan. Drawing by Mark Carlier.

one's soul, was possible—indeed, necessary—for salvation. Although early Calvinists felt that conversion would happen only through God's agency, in this new evangelical view, God had in fact already offered humanity salvation through the death and resurrection of Jesus Christ, but only those who accepted his offer and embraced Christ would receive this boon. The acknowledgment and acceptance of God's offer of salvation as the responsibility of the individual created a new understanding of the relationship between God and the individual. It was up to each person to seek out and accept God's love and salvation through his or her confession of sin and subsequent conversion.

In order to spread this message, preachers developed new strategies for warning their listeners of the consequences of ignoring God's invitation. These strategies not only targeted the emotions (called *affects*) of the individual—fear, desire, comfort, love—but also restructured and legitimized new, more emotional forms of piety. Evangelicalism developed as an affective religion, or one centered on the affections, the emotions. To know God or Christ within one's own heart became the central desire of believers, and certain emotions and emotional responses became signs of the authentic experience of the divine. Clearly, evangelicalism allotted individuals a vast amount of personal empowerment. Not only was the individual responsible for instigating the conversion experience, but the authenticity of the experience could be judged solely by the individual, though often in consultation with a clergy member. Over the course of the eighteenth and nineteenth centuries, affective religion spawned any number of individual-based practices and experiences that signified an empowering personal connection with the divine.

The fundamental shift in religious creed brought about by evangelicalism significantly altered religious practice, or cultus, and, in turn, religious architecture. Perhaps the most distinctive and far-reaching new practice involved the gathering of large groups of people for the purpose of hearing a specific individual expound on the need for conversion and the consequences of ignoring God's invitation—that is, to experience evangelical preaching. In England, George Whitefield and John Wesley preached to gatherings of hundreds, even thousands, of people eager to hear the Word. Such massive gatherings, however, posed spatial problems. Few buildings of the mid-eighteenth century were designed to accommodate such crowds. In many areas, particularly rural ones, these renowned preachers delivered their sermons outdoors, as no suitable building was to be had. Outdoor sermons constituted a fundamental shift in Christian worship practice, which had for centuries eschewed outdoor observance, associating it with non-Christian ("pagan") religious practices.[8] Wesley, in particular, was initially repulsed by the idea of preaching outdoors but was convinced to do so by Whitefield.

Among the many outdoor locations used by these mid-eighteenth-century evangelists was a large depression in the earth near Gwennap, Cornwall, created by the deposits of mining operations there. Called Gwennap Pit, this natural amphitheater of about a hundred feet in diameter offered evangelists and their congregants a number of advantages—advantages well known to the ancient Greek performers who used similar amphitheaters in which to perform plays. First, amphitheaters efficiently accommodate a large number of individuals. Second, the steeply sloped sides create unobstructed sightlines for audience members looking across or down the slope. Third, assuming the performance takes place at the base of the amphitheater, a location which places the performers lower than the audience, the sound of the human voice is carried naturally up the slopes of the earthen formation and dispersed to even the farthest members of the audience.

Christian services, however, had never been held in amphitheaters, and although Whitefield's and Wesley's sermons in Gwennap Pit had the potential to transform Christian worship space in ways never conceived by earlier generations, it appears that neither evangelist took full advantage of the amphitheater formation. Wesley, for instance, delivered his sermon not from the base of the amphitheater but from about three-quarters of the way up one side, from which position he shouted across the pit to audience members.[9] This physical position was paramount. Like the elevated pulpits in churches, this location placed him above most of his audience, and spatial elevation had signaled the power and authority of Christian clergy for centuries. To stand beneath a congregation at the bottom of the pit was simply unthinkable at the time, no matter how expedient doing so may have been. Despite the frequency with which sermons were delivered outdoors, centuries of practice locating the minister well above the audience mitigated against even these highly innovative evangelists using the natural landscape to full advantage.

Yet revivalists' success depended in part upon their ability to make their voices heard at a great distance. The scientifically minded Benjamin Franklin assessed, with some awe, the power of Anglican revivalist George Whitefield's voice during revivals in Philadelphia in 1739:

> He had a loud and clear Voice, and articulated his Words and Sentences so perfectly that he might be heard and understood at a great Distance, especially as his Auditories, however numerous, observ'd the most exact Silence. He preach'd one Evening from the Top of the Court House Steps, which are in the Middle of Market Street, and on the West Side of Second Street, which crosses it at right angles. Both Streets were fill'd with his Hearers to a considerable Distance.

Being among the hindmost in Market Street, I had the Curiosity to learn how far he could be heard, by retiring backwards down the Street towards the River, and I found his Voice distinct till I came near Front-Street, when some Noise in that Street obscur'd it. Imagining then a Semi-Circle, of which my Distance should be the Radius, and that it were fill'd with Auditors, to each of whom I allow'd two square feet, I computed that he might well be heard by more than Thirty Thousand. This reconcil'd me to the Newspaper Accounts of his having preach'd to 25000 People in the Fields, and to the antient Histories of Generals haranguing whole Armies, of which I had sometimes doubted.[10]

The human voice has limits, however, and generally does not carry well in the open air. Though a handful of individuals like Wesley and Whitefield had enormous vocal projection, ministers of more moderate abilities sometimes struggled to make themselves heard even within church walls.

Evangelical preaching thus gave rise to even greater interest in the construction of spaces and buildings that helped congregants to see and hear the preacher. Whereas the rectangular preaching halls popularized by Wren and Gibbs remained most prominent, patrons of Wesley and Whitefield experimented with round and square centralized spaces. The Wesley Chapel in London, for instance, erected in 1777, featured a nearly square room with galleries on three sides. Similarly, Whitefield's Tabernacle in Tottenham Road near London, erected by evangelical benefactress Selina Hastings, Countess of Huntingdon, featured a round room with the pulpit elevated on one side. In spaces such as these, which accommodated several hundred people, fiery evangelists delivered sermons designed to convince each person present of the danger of damnation that threatened their mortal soul and of the need for immediate conversion.

A striking paradox lay at the heart of this new evangelizing in which a profoundly personal message was delivered and received in the presence of hundreds, during large gatherings or *revivals*. Revivalism transformed Christian experience; personal access to the divine was no longer a private affair but a highly public event in which participants freely watched as individuals around them wrestled with their consciences. Buildings like the Tabernacle and the Chapel, though designed mainly to accommodate large numbers and to facilitate hearing the preacher, fostered this public and communal character of evangelical revivalism. Worshippers were increasingly united physically and visually in the evangelical experience of conversion. In the next century, this communal character of evangelicalism would increasingly influence the shape of Protestant churches.

The Versatility of Centralized Space

The evangelical chapels mentioned above, square and round in shape, are, of course, examples of centrally planned space. We have seen the recurrent use of centralized plans for Christian purposes since its use for martyria and baptisteries in the ancient period. In the sixteenth century, Italian Catholics in the midst of a renewed interest in classical architecture adopted it for highly formalist services, and Protestant reformers employed it for Calvinist preaching services in Lyon's Temple Paradis. Wren employed it for Anglican services in several of the London churches. Accommodating practices from across the spectrum of formalism to nonformalism, from Catholic to evangelical worship, centrally planned spaces can be arranged in ways that foster clerical power and liturgical formalism, on the one hand, and congregational spontaneity and participation, on the other.

German Lutherans, for instance, negotiated formalism during the eighteenth century within centralized churches. During this period, church leaders enforced a high level of liturgical orthodoxy. Liturgical portions of Lutheran services could last over an hour and included not only traditional prayers and recitations but also hymns and other music. The musical compositions of Johann Sebastian Bach, for instance, not only significantly transformed but also significantly lengthened services. The sermon following the initial liturgical component of the service could continue for an hour or more, and was then followed by the Communion service.

These highly formalist services took place in new buildings such as the innovative Frauenkirche in Dresden, a centrally planned church covered by a huge, bell-shaped dome, designed by Georg Bähr and completed in 1743. Like Wren's London churches, this Baroque church united its congregants in a uniform space beneath the dome. Differentiation between the space for the congregation and that for the clergy was created through the use of steps that elevated the sanctuary above the communal seating area. The stunning chancel consisted of two parts (fig 6.8). The first, marked by a balustrade that incorporated the pulpit, raised a relatively modest three or four feet above the congregation floor, was closest to the congregation. Three steps on either side led up to a second level, on which the baptismal font was located immediately behind the pulpit. Another set of three steps led to the top level, dominated by

FIGURE 6.8. Die Frauenkirche, Dresden, Germany, 1726. Reconstructed plan. Drawing by Mark Carlier.

the stunning altarpiece, which was surmounted by the organ pipes. The setting placed the three main liturgical sites (pulpit, font, and altar) on a single axis with the organ, indicating its centrality to the service as well. Moreover, the gradual rise of the Die Frauenkirche chancel, as in theater stages of the eighteenth century, allowed the viewer to look deeply into the space to witness the ceremonies.

A kinship with the architecture of theaters is also evident in Die Frauenkirche, particularly in the congregational seating. Here, perhaps for the first time, pews were designed to follow the curve of the circular room, enhancing the line of vision to the chancel. The seating also emphasized the public experience of worship, allowing clear sightlines across the seats to other congregants as well. In this church, Bähr carved out a Lutheran middle ground between formalism and nonformalism. Whereas the chancel arrangement and ornament strongly suggest highly formalist services born out by the formal liturgies, the seating arrangement hinted of the kind of communal experience more typical of revivals. The evangelical nature of Lutheranism, though defined differently from that of other Reformed groups, shared an affinity for communal experience.

The seating in Die Frauenkirche was a first architectural step in creating a new understanding of the role of lay Christians. Just as the sixteenth century fostered the creation of "congregations" by lessening the physical distance between clergy and laity and providing seating for the latter, the centralized plans and evangelizing of the eighteenth century were reconstructing worshippers as a "public," a corporate group with shared interests and, to borrow a political term, rights. Being able to watch one another during worship created the feeling of what Rudolph Arnheim calls a "corporate body," a group that held an awareness of itself as a group with shared interests and experiences.[11] Here was an unprecedented religious situation, in which the design of Christian space fostered congregants' sense of themselves as worshippers and of their centrality as a group to worship itself. Yet the curved seating of Die Frauenkirche proved to be more idiosyncratic than trendsetting, and the use of curved seating within centrally planned spaces remained unusual. The consolidation of this new religious public would not be celebrated and fostered architecturally for another century.

Affective Antiformalism and the Revolution in Christian Space

Revivalists Whitefield and Wesley saw themselves as reforming the Church of England from within, though they would eventually preside over the establishment of what would become a new Protestant denomination, the Methodists. Theologically, however, they disagreed with each other on a number of matters, most particularly on the relative roles of God and humankind in the salvation process. Whitefield embraced a more conservative, God-centered, Calvinist position that assigned the greater share of power to the divine. If a person was sufficiently penitent for his or her sins and sincerely sought conversion, Whitefield preached, God *may* grant it. Wesley, in contrast, embraced a more Arminian position that allotted greater power to humanity. If an individual were sufficiently penitent for his or her sins and sincerely sought conversion, he believed, God *would* grant it.

During the eighteenth century, Arminianism, which replaced the Calvinist belief in absolute predestination with belief in the possibility of salvation for all who sincerely sought God, opened the door to a host of new worship practices that sprang up outside of traditional ecclesiastical structures. Nonconformist groups flourished in England at mid-century. Quakers, a dissenting group that had emerged in the seventeenth century, embraced the view that all humanity had been saved by Jesus's atonement. For them, salvation raised individuals to a new level of direct communion with the divine, a communion that not only provided the foundation of Quaker worship practices, but also was deemed to place individuals outside civil law, a position

FIGURE 6.9. Arch Street Friends (Quaker) Meeting House, Philadelphia, Penn., 1803–1805. Courtesy Library of Congress, Prints and Photographs Division, Detroit Publishing Company Collection [LC-D4-70253].

known as *antinomianism*, that, not surprisingly, resulted in a tense relationship between members of the sect and civil officials. Quaker worship took place in meetinghouses somewhat similar to earlier Puritan meetinghouses, but in the seventeenth and eighteenth centuries, the rooms were arranged not with a pulpit on the long wall but a low *bema* or raised area. The Arch Street Friends Meeting House in Philadelphia, for instance, featured a rectangular room oriented on the long wall that housed a bema on which the elders were seated (fig. 6.9). Congregants sat on benches placed in rows facing the bema, with men on one side and women on the other. Services proceeded without a stated order as spontaneous testimonials were offered, most often though not exclusively by the elders, along with some hymn singing and bible reading begun spontaneously by individuals. In the nineteenth and twentieth centuries, Quaker congregations eliminated the bema, placing congregants in a square facing one another and in some cases designating an administrative leader or "friend" by a specific seat on the center pew. Except for this designation, which does not indicate authority over the format of the service, the arrangement was uniquely egalitarian.

FIGURE 6.10. Shaker Meeting House, Pleasant Hill, Ky., 1821. Courtesy Library of Congress, Prints and Photographs Division [HABS KY, 84–SHAKT, 4–11].

An offshoot of the Quakers, the Shaking Quakers, or the Shakers, as they became known in the United States, similarly viewed worship as an opportunity for immediate connection with the divine, but they invited that communion through highly formalistic dance and body movements. Shaker meetinghouses, like Quaker ones, were simply frame buildings, but inside the Shakers cleared the floor to provide a large space for their ritual dances and placed the benches around the walls (fig 6.10). The Shaker meetinghouse at Pleasant Hill, Kentucky, for instance, featured a rectangular room in which the floor was cleared of furnishings. Designed for *a cappella* musical performance, the room has extraordinary acoustical properties, projecting the human singing voice throughout the room despite its fairly low ceiling. With the Shakers, too, we find formalism and nonformalism in a unique balance, for although the dances were highly ritualized (i.e. formalist), repeating the same motions in each performance, the lack of clergy, vestments, and ornament indicated their antiformalist leanings.

Such groups had little need for ornament in their worship spaces. Because they believed that people learned about God from the Bible, the preacher, and the testimonials of others (whether inspired directly by the Holy Spirit or not), didactic elements such as pictures were of little importance. Similarly, they had little need for a trained clergy, for a mediating knowledge of theology was not required. Reading the Bible brought all the knowledge of God that one needed, and by the late eighteenth century, scores of preachers, both educated and not, roamed the new United States, England, and Europe gathering listeners wherever they could. For these groups, direct access to the divine brought not only personal spiritual empowerment, but salvation itself.[12]

Antiformalism was most profoundly illustrated in the practices and spaces of camp meetings held in the new United States in the late eighteenth and early nineteenth centuries. Cane Ridge, Kentucky, was the site of what was likely the first of hundreds of such meetings held during the next several decades. During several days in August 1801, hundreds of people traveled to the isolated site to share in the preaching, extorting, prayer meetings, Bible reading, singing, prayer, communal meals, and worship. The spontaneous character of the extemporaneous preaching, heart-wrenching testimonials and stories of conversion, and emotional fervor—expressed in such physical behaviors as jerking, barking, and fainting—articulated the personal spiritual empowerment experienced by believers at these meetings as they were filled with the Holy Spirit. Although the spontaneity of camp meeting was strongly antiformalist, these meetings did exhibit some underlying formalist elements, not the least of which were patterns in the timing of activities (however spontaneous) and, by the 1820s, standardized patterns in the organization of meeting grounds.[13]

Revivals and camp meetings made visible the centrality of the social or communal component of evangelical worship. As much as the evangelical experience was about the salvation of the individual, evangelical worship was about sharing that experience with others and watching how others experienced the divine. Evangelical worship, in effect, required social interaction and fellowship. It was, and remains, a social phenomenon. For evangelicals, worship was not only about the self, it was about everyone around the self as well. As a result, revival preachers often found themselves stymied by traditional Christian spaces. The traditional longitudinally oriented rectangular worship rooms of many churches hindered the ability of congregants to participate in the communal nature of evangelical worship. Congregants could not see one another. Further, the long rooms swallowed up the sound of voices—not only the voice of the preacher, who, ensconced in the pulpit, had at least the benefit of elevation, but also those of individuals in congregation who rose to give testimony and exhort those gathered to repent and convert. Similarly, the long rooms with their straight box pews limited congregants' ability to see the proceedings, for in such rooms many could not see over the heads of those seated in front of them. The centralized plan churches worked somewhat better with respect to acoustics, as the distances within the rooms were shorter, but the problem of obstructed sightlines remained, as congregants had to crane their necks to see around those closer to the front.

It would not be long before those who designed religious buildings would begin to take these problems into account. Whereas the spaces designed for evangelical worship in the mid-eighteenth century simply fostered large gatherings in which preachers could be heard more readily by as many individuals as possible, by the early nineteenth century church designers began to recognize the social, communal character of evangelical worship and started to design spaces that would foster this characteristic. The result was the development of a wholly new type of Christian worship space.

Among the leaders in this development was renowned revival preacher Charles Grandison Finney, who had swept through upstate New York in the 1820s stirring such evangelistic fervor that the area became known as the Burned-Over District. Then, upon launching revivals in New York City, Finney turned his hand to designing a church. The resulting Broadway Tabernacle, more akin to a theater than a church, embraced the lessons of the amphitheater with an unprecedented confidence and enthusiasm (fig. 6.11). In the circular room, a hundred feet in diameter, the floor sloped down to an elevated stage or pulpit platform located on one side, the pews curved around the platform following the curve of the wall, and a gallery with raked (sloped) seating swept around two-thirds of the room like arms embracing the circular space. From the platform, the preacher's voice carried easily up the ranks of seats and into the galleries. The platform also accommodated the choir and, following the example of churches like Die Frauenkirche, a massive organ case, ensuring that congregants would have much to keep them visually absorbed during lengthy services.

In such a space, not only could congregants see and hear the proceedings on the pulpit platform, but they could also see one another—they could hear those who rose to testify and they could watch those who descended to the "anxious bench" during what we would now call the altar call. On this bench, placed in the front of the room just below the platform, those in the throes of conversion wrestled mightily for their souls' salvation as onlookers prayed them through the process. In such a space, congregations gained a power unprecedented in the history of Christian architecture, for the space was designed precisely to accommodate their needs, both to see and hear the proceedings and to work together in the salvation of souls. Satisfying audience requirements—not liturgical or theological requirements—was the goal of the Broadway Tabernacle.[14]

LITH. OF T. PALMER & CO. 95 NASSAU STREET, N.Y.

THE BROADWAY TABERNACLE.

FIGURE 6.11. Broadway Tabernacle, New York City, 1836. Chromolithograph, 1845. Courtesy Eno Collection, Miriam and Ira D. Wallach Division of Art, Prints, and Photographs, The New York Public Library, Astor, Lenox and Tilden Foundation.

It would take another half-century before this spatial arrangement would be perfected and widely embraced, however, and then it would not be revivalists who ultimately made the auditorium space popular. Several experiments and prototypes emerged in the mid-nineteenth century, but not until the 1870s and 1880s did building technologies and the science of acoustics reach sufficient sophistication to bring the power of the preacher and of the audience into balance in a single room in the innovative auditorium church.

The auditorium church was designed around the congregation space rather than the liturgical space—that is, the features of the seating area were of a higher priority to church designers than those of the worship and preaching centers. As in Westminster Presbyterian Church in Minneapolis, the congregational space in auditorium churches consisted of a ramped floor that sloped gently from the back of the room to the front, filled with arcs of pews that curved in a semicircle (fig. 6.12). In the majority of auditorium churches, a gallery with raked seating also curved around the room. The focus of the room, located either in a corner or on one wall, was a pulpit platform raised some three or four feet above the main floor, which housed the central pulpit and, behind it, raked seating for the choir. Rising behind this pulpit stage was an impressive display of organ pipes and case. The communion table and font were generally placed on the main floor below the pulpit stage and often removed when not in use.

Auditorium churches, widely adopted by Methodist, Congregationalist, Baptist, and Presbyterian congregations in the late nineteenth century, were statements of the cohesion of a new social class as much as they were articulations of evangelical worship. The new middle-class laity, confident of their economic security and quite capable of leading their own religious organizations, wielded significant influence. Their new church auditoriums catered to their physical needs, thanks to new technologies. New roof truss systems eliminated the need for the columns that obstructed sightlines. Advances in acoustical science took advantage of the fact that sound rises and perfected the use of shallow domes and curved wall surfaces to help project even soft voices

FIGURE 6.12. Westminster Presbyterian Church, Minneapolis, Minn., 1898. Charles S. Sedgwick, architect. Photo 1905. Courtesy The Westminster Presbyterian Church Archive.

throughout the rooms. Central heating in the winter and dry-ice cooling in the summer kept congregants comfortable, as did cushioned pews with hat and umbrella racks and deep carpeting on the floors.[15]

The auditorium arrangement offered a more egalitarian spatial formation than had any previous church design. Educated, middle-class congregants in these new churches sat comfortably with a clear view of the proceedings. They found themselves members of a corporate body, able to watch one another across the curved seating. In curiosity and Christian fellowship, they viewed their coreligionists and merged into a single wave of humanity, which at least metaphorically threatened to overwhelm any authority in the pulpit. These congregations embraced the newly wrought social power reflected in this new church design to influence worship and religious practice that had previously been available only to clergy. They used their authority to demand expert musical performances, shorten the length of sermons, and influence the selection of liturgical components and orders of service. They also expanded church activities beyond the realm of worship into that of the educational and the social. For one thing, they demanded that these new churches include commodious accommodation for Sunday schools and recreation for members' children, resulting in the construction of gymnasiums, game rooms, and even bowling alleys and swimming pools in institutional buildings connected to the church. Even more common was the demand that the new churches include kitchen facilities and a dining hall to accommodate dinners and celebrations. All of these features, almost unprecedented in the history of Christian architecture, were born out of the needs and desires of these growing middle-class congregations.

Despite this newly found congregant power, clergy did not necessarily surrender their authority; power within church space is not a zero-sum game. Preachers were accommodated by new and sometimes elaborate pulpits that stood atop the platform like the prows of large ships. The placement of the organ case and choir behind the preacher also helped to ensure that congregations would focus on the activity in the front of the room. Influential preachers and ministers pronouncing the gospel from these imposing pulpits located at the center of the auditorium stages continued to captivate congregations just as their predecessors had.

This negotiation of social power among congregations and clergy went hand in hand with a negotiation of formalism within services. As evangelicals moved into the economic middle classes and their worship took on a corporate character, they moved back toward formalism in worship, viewing the spontaneous and affective aspects of the revivals and the camp meetings as ill mannered. Evangelical congregants and clergy—including Congregationalists, Presbyterians, Methodists, and Baptists—lobbied for services with regular orders, regular congregational participation in recitations and hymns, professional performance of some musical numbers, and in some cases, even robed choirs. Ministers embraced these formalist elements as a means of fostering congregational engagement and participation in services, and they adopted orders of services that included such formalist elements such as organ voluntaries, recitations of the doxology and invocation by the minister, recitation of the Lord's Prayer and the Gloria Patri, responsive readings of Psalms, anthems, hymns, and benedictions—all elements that their Calvinist and Reformed forbears had expunged from services long ago.

The new religious formalism that emerged with the auditorium church underscores the complex character of the relationship between formalism and power. Whereas antiformalist Quakers and evangelical revivalists in the eighteenth century had claimed personal power through individual experience of the divine, in the late nineteenth century middle-class evangelicals now combined an interest in formalism in worship with their claims to social power even as clerical power remained strong. With respect to formalist and nonformalist worship, then, Christian congregations have moved back and forth across the continuum, and that movement has reflected transformations in personal, social, and clerical power. Yet, as we have seen, the relationships between these matters are complex. Personal power can correlate with both formalist and anti- or nonformalist practices, for instance. Moreover, negotiations along the continuum do not occur in a religious vacuum but have frequently been influenced by social and political concerns, such as the need to rebuild London, the rise of industrialization, and the expansion of the middle class. The response of Christians, especially Protestants, to these transformations has been articulated in coterminous transformations in worship practice and in the very buildings that accommodated those practices. In the next century, Catholics would be similarly challenged by sociocultural developments.

7

Historicism, Modernism, and Space

Since the beginning of the modern period, dated here to the late eighteenth century, perhaps the central issue shaping Christian architecture has been its relationship to the past. The struggle of Christians to define authentic belief and practice in the face of increasing voluntarism, secularism, industrialization, and material abundance has brought little agreement. Creativity and diversity in worship practices has burgeoned. The result has been a clash between traditionalists and innovators that has spanned more than a century. Should Christian architecture echo ancient or traditional forms, be they classical or medieval, or should it draw upon the modern design movements of the day? What constitutes authentic Christian architecture and space?

The clash of opinions on this matter has most recently been articulated in debates about Catholic architecture in the United States. Those in the traditionalist camp, such as architectural writers Michael Rose and Steven J. Schloeder, argue that architectural modernism, relying upon a spare aesthetic and stark spaces that lack the previous richness of material culture expression—statuary, stained glass, and so forth—diminishes the individual worship experience by not sufficiently encouraging an encounter with the transcendent, with divine power.[1] In their view, modernist churches are instead mired in the everyday, in the ordinary rather than the extraordinary. Proponents of modernism, on the other hand, argue that Christianity's universal message can and should be articulated in contemporary architectural language and spaces—that Christianity's relevance in the modern period should be reflected in its dialogue with contemporary forms of architectural and artistic expression. Trappist monk and Catholic theologian Thomas Merton, for instance, argued in favor of the modernist position in the mid-twentieth century:

> One of the big problems for an architect in our time is that for a hundred and fifty years men have been building churches as if a church could not belong to our time. A church has to look as if it were left over from some other age. I think that such an assumption is based on an implicit confession of atheism—as if God did not belong to all ages and as if religion were really only a pleasant, necessary social formality, preserved from past times in order to give our society an air of respectability.[2]

For Merton, a contemporary faith required a contemporary architecture. He favored modernist buildings that connected Catholic faith to the contemporary experiences of believers.

Although this difference of opinion stems in part from aesthetic disagreements about the nature of the human experience of the transcendent, it also results from differing views of the history of Christianity and the function of church buildings. As we have seen throughout this book, church buildings function within both religious and social contexts. In the nineteenth and twentieth centuries, transformations in both areas have contributed to significant transformations in Catholic and Protestant architecture as well. As we have seen, aesthetic questions and judgments are shaped by matters of both belief and power, particularly social power, and, as we shall see in this chapter, the process of church creation in the twentieth century has continued to privilege social concerns over religious ones.

The Historicist Foundation of Church Architecture in the Modern Era

Coming to terms with the history of Christianity poses particular challenges during the nineteenth and twentieth centuries, eras in which an unprecedented diversity of religious practices and beliefs, including but not limited to the evangelical practices discussed in the previous chapter, grew and flourished. This expansion of Christian practices and denominations was prompted in part by a growing population with the economic and political wherewithal to wield significant influence in religious matters. In the mid-eighteenth century, the Catholic trustee movement in North America, for instance, attempted to shift religious authority away from parish priests and dioceses and into the hands of laymen. Though relatively short-lived, the movement did presage intermittent efforts toward increased lay participation in Catholic decision making through the nineteenth and twentieth centuries. Although in the nineteenth century the largely immigrant Catholic population in the United States was for the most part content to leave religious matters to the clergy, in the twentieth century the movement of more Catholics into the middle class resulted in a corresponding movement toward greater participation in services and church building decisions, much as it had among Protestants in the nineteenth century.

By the middle of the nineteenth century, U.S. Christians, increasingly affluent, influential, and concerned about perceptions of Christianity through-out society, particularly among nonbelievers, wrestled with the age-old question of what type of architecture was most suited to Christian worship. Many worried that the growth of denominationalism implied that there were many Chris-tianities (or at least Protestantisms), not just one, resulting in a diversity that threatened to undermine the legitimacy of the faith. Surely, many believed, Christianity should be *one* thing. At the same time, the practice of architectural design was becoming increasingly professionalized, with the development of pattern books that broadly disseminated the work of individual designers, trade journals that brought builders information on new and old buildings from all parts of the United States and Europe, and training programs for architects at schools such as the Massachusetts Institute of Technology. The intersection of these religious and professional concerns resulted in one of the most influen-tial church architecture phenomena to date—the Gothic Revival.

Starting in England and spreading rapidly to the United States and glob-ally, this architectural revival touted the medieval Gothic style as the sine qua non of Christian architecture. Historians, writers, architects and others of the period romanticized the Middle Ages as a period unmarred by the self-interest, materialism, and abject poverty brought by industrialization. It was seen as a time of virtue, chivalry, and Christian piety. Medieval craftsmen and artisans were nostalgically viewed as taking great care in their work, and, in the case of church building, dedicating their labors to God as acts of piety. Gothic church architecture, with its awe-inspiring height, vaulting, stained glass, and orna-ment, and understood as expressions of their builders' faith, satisfied the de-sire of nineteenth-century architects and congregations to locate Christianity in a purer realm than that of contemporary life, with its innumerable problems.

The Gothic Revival, advanced initially and most enthusiastically by An-glicans, spurred the restoration of medieval buildings throughout England and the construction of faux-medieval buildings in both England and the United States. The Gothic Revival was anticipated in the United States as early as 1816, when architect Ithiel Town enclosed a preaching-hall-type church, Trinity (Episcopal) Church on the New Haven Green, in a Gothic envelope (fig. 7.1). Soon, other denominations started to adopt Gothic architectural vocabularies

FIGURE 7.1. Trinity Episcopal Church on the Green, New Haven, Conn., 1816. Photo by author.

as well. Richard Upjohn's simple "Carpenter Gothic" building, First Parish Congregational Church in Brunswick, Maine, with its pointed arch windows and vertical board and batten siding, was an extraordinary architectural statement for a denomination descended from the antiformalist Puritans.

Just as the Romantic Movement in literature and aesthetics turned to an imagined preindustrial, pristine beauty and innocence to critique the growing inequities and privations of the industrial revolution, the Gothic Revival in church architecture was similarly a response more to social concerns than theological or creedal ones. Prominent among these social concerns was the desire to project a single, unified image of Christianity in a context of increasing secularization and denominational fragmentation. Many Christian church builders believed that the revival of earlier approaches to church building, and specifically the re-creation of the Gothic parish church building, would help stabilize and promote the church itself. According to architectural historian Phoebe B. Stanton, "To those who wished to restore the Church in England as an institution and to withdraw it from corrupting secular attachments, the return to this traditional English building type and to the ceremonial connected with it seemed not only reasonable but necessary, suggestive of a splendid moment in the national past."[3] By widely adopting medieval vocabularies for their churches, Anglicans in Britain and various Protestant congregations in America, including the Episcopalians, Congregationalists, Methodists, and Presbyterians, laid claim to an ancient faith as a means of bolstering their current situation.

Using historical architectural forms to allude to and claim kinship with an ancient or more authentic Christianity is a form of *historicization,* a process through which people claim connection to ideas, objects, or practices of the past in order to lend legitimacy to their own activities. Church architecture has a long history of doing this.[4] As we have seen, interest in classicism flourished in Michelangelo's time, and the work of Christopher Wren and other architects of the Baroque period drew upon classical vocabularies not native to their immediate culture and thereby associated Christianity with a new perception of the Greco-Roman or classical roots of Western society. Yet these sixteenth-, seventeenth-, and eighteenth-century architects were employing classical vocabularies not in an attempt to claim connection to a purer historical form of Christianity, as were their nineteenth-century counterparts, but to infuse their vision of Christianity with a set of non-Christian (i.e., Greek and Roman) values (i.e., rationality, republicanism). With the Gothic Revival (and the Romanesque Revival that followed it in the late nineteenth century), the borrowing of earlier architectural vocabularies was meant to convey specific ideas about the nature of Christianity itself, and particularly about Christian piety and the relationship between God and humanity. Towers, lancet and rose windows, pointed arches, stained glass, minarets, Romanesque arches lined by polychromatic voussoirs, and rough-hewn stone all signified the ancient character of Christianity. Tall Gothic spires signaled the Christian presence in increasingly crowded urban and residential landscapes. The rapid multiplying of these buildings throughout America gave the impression of a unified Christian faith, even though the congregations that constructed them could be Methodist, Congregational, Presbyterian, Episcopalian, Lutheran, or Catholic.[5]

One other crucial social concern that informed the Protestants' movement toward Gothic architecture at mid-century was their desire to attract more people to the church. As we saw in the previous chapter, Protestant revivalists in the first half of the nineteenth century had embraced affective religion and nonformalist worship that had given rise to experimentation with worship spaces and contributed to the development of auditorium worship rooms in evangelical churches. This spontaneous, emotional, affective religion, however, also prompted a backlash, particularly among congregations whose members were gaining greater economic resources and community standing. These middle-class congregations, seeking a more decorous, calmer, and rational approach to worship, gravitated toward more formalistic practices. Presbyterian and Congregationalist ministers, however, initially despaired that their congregants were being attracted to the formality of the Anglican (Episcopalian) and Catholic liturgies and the art and ornamentation of their Gothic churches; nevertheless, they soon began to also adopt medieval building vocabularies and they gradually incorporated greater formalism into their services, in effect acknowledging the growing power of their congregants. Gothic Revival buildings such as the Broadway Tabernacle Church in New York City, built in 1859, with its vaulted nave and stained glass windows, were intended to attract congregants by appealing to these new aesthetic and formalistic interests of this growing middle class (fig. 7.2). Worshippers flocked to these new churches, which would have shocked earlier generations of evangelicals and their Puritan forbearers. In this way, aesthetic and social motivations intertwined as churches competed for congregants in the religious marketplace.[6]

For Protestants, then, historicism provided a means of addressing concerns about Christian unity and the desire to attract and retain members. For Catholics, however, adoption of historicized architectural vocabularies worked a little differently. In the United States, where the flow of Catholic immigrants increased steadily through the nineteenth century, Catholics historicized their churches in two ways. Although they, like the Protestants, adopted architectural styles that harkened back to an illustrious Christian past, many Catholic congregations adopted styles that signaled various nationalist identities. For

FIGURE 7.2. Broadway Tabernacle Church, New York City, 1859. Leopold Eidlitz, architect. *Congregational Quarterly* 22 (Jan. 1860), 65. Courtesy Special Collections and Rare Books, University of Minnesota Libraries, Twin Cities.

instance, although Irish immigrant communities generally erected Gothic churches, they frequently included traditional symbols such as shamrocks in them to tie the buildings to their homeland. Italian immigrants also used architecture to make nationalistic statements, erecting not Gothic but neo-classical churches that alluded to their Roman heritage. For instance, churches like Our Lady of Mount Carmel in Worcester, Massachusetts, built just after

FIGURE 7.3. Church of the Assumption, St. Paul, Minn., 1874. Photo by author.

the turn of the twentieth century, and Our Lady of Mount Carmel in Altoona, Pennsylvania, erected from 1912 to 1923, are similar Italian Renaissance style basilicas.

German immigrants in the Midwestern United States also erected chur-ches inspired by medieval forms as a means of maintaining continuity with their national heritage. The Church of the Assumption in St. Paul, Minnesota, erected in 1874 by a German congregation, was intended to articulate to the urban community both the presence and the influence of the German church in the city. To design their church, the congregation turned to an architect of the ruling Wittelsbach family in Bavaria, Joseph Reidl, who patterned the building, with its twin 200-foot square towers, after the noted Ludwigskirche in Munich (fig. 7.3). Assumption's basilica form, small windows, and dark interior hinted at the medieval experience of worship space, but also encouraged the individual pietistic worship of the nineteenth century. To this day, the church greets the visitor with the odor of burning candles and the shadowy, hushed interior of earlier days. In such cases, the effort to connect new buildings with older forms and traditions and thus infuse them with a stronger legitimacy is clear. Although a variety of meanings were communicated through the selection of architectural style, the motivating impetus for those selections was predominantly social in character, rather than a matter of theology or worship practice, creed or cultus.

Modernist Tensions within Historicized Exteriors

Even as many Christian churches in the United States adopted these historicized architectural vocabularies, however, a tension began to grow between the earlier architectural models and the design of the new churches' interior spaces. During this same period, as we have seen, many evangelical Protestants had completely redesigned their interior spaces, and in church after church, the increasingly popular auditorium interiors had little to do with the eclectic medieval architectural vocabularies of their exteriors. In the Broadway Tabernacle Church described above, for instance, the cruciform nave was filled with pews that curved toward the pulpit platform that occupied the front of the worship room—hardly a medieval practice. By the closing decades of the nineteenth century, many architects abandoned the effort to replicate medieval interior spaces entirely, adopting square or round auditorium spaces but enclosing them in eclectic façades composed of a variety of Gothic and Romanesque features.

In contrast, Catholics during the same period retained the longitudinal plan that resembled the medieval church spaces precisely because their services had not altered significantly since the Council of Trent. The need to mark the separation between clergy and laity remained in these churches, resulting in the retention of the distinct chancel or sanctuary. Nevertheless, a disjuncture between the medieval and the more modern is evident here, too. For although the exteriors of Catholic churches sported Gothic and Romanesque

FIGURE 7.4. St. Patrick's Cathedral, New York City, 1870. Stereograph by Underwood and Underwood, Publishers, c. 1902. Courtesy Library of Congress, Prints and Photographs Division [LC-USZ62-112334].

vocabularies, the medieval chancel, with its long choir and isolated high altar, was not replicated, but replaced with the more unified space of the Baroque church that featured a visible pulpit and the smooth merging of the sanctuary into the nave.

Saint Patrick's Cathedral in New York City, perhaps the quintessential nineteenth-century Gothic Revival church in the United States, provides an illuminating example. Erected between 1858 and 1870 and designed by noted architect James Renwick, St. Patrick's, with its twin towers, huge rose window of stained glass, and vaulted nave seemed like a medieval European great church transplanted to Fifth Avenue (fig. 7.4). Yet the interior was a hybrid of medieval and Baroque references. The vaulted nave flowed into the readily visible sanctuary, which was approached by steps. As in Die Frauenkirche, the altar was located several feet further back and raised several feet above the main floor. As in St. Peter's in Rome, the altar was sheltered by a huge baldacchino, in this case of shiny brass. This arrangement, based on Baroque rather than medieval practices, was readily incorporated into the cruciform plan of the church. The result, though historically inaccurate, suited the services of the archdiocese, which in the twentieth century would alter the space even more.

Reacting against Historicism

By the early twentieth century, architectural change was occurring at an increasingly rapid rate. Changes that would have taken previous generations decades if not centuries to effect occurred within the span of a few years. Leading these changes were the professionalization of the building and design fields, as well as the development of new building technologies. At the same time, both Protestants and Catholics were transforming their worship practices in ways that profoundly affected church architecture. Most importantly, a new modernist aesthetic developed that consciously rejected historicism and tradition. Although historicization would never completely disappear from the practice of church building and would make a significant though short-lived comeback in the second decade of the twentieth century in the form of the Late Gothic Revival and a Colonial Revival, the modernist aesthetic would predominate in the twentieth century.

As an architectural movement, modernism attempted to free aesthetics from the grip of history, that is, from traditional ideas and practices, a goal that appealed to many Christian congregations eager, after a century of embracing historical architectural vocabularies signaling the ancient character of Christianity, to establish the ongoing relevance of Christianity. Embracing creativity and expressiveness while at the same time focusing on function, modernism spawned a host of architectural movements, from art nouveau and expressionism in the late nineteenth century, through art deco, prairie school, Bauhaus, internationalism, futurism, and postmodern in the twentieth, just to name a few. What these styles shared was a release from the past, an emphasis on the integrity of materials, a strong concern for function, and, by the mid-twentieth century, a disinclination toward ornament. These concerns, many theorists of architecture believed, signaled a decidedly "modern" view of the world, progressive, unhindered by the past, forward looking, and ultimately liberating for humanity.[7]

Congregations embraced modernism at precisely the same time that they were rethinking the role of Christianity in a now industrialized and urban world, increasingly influenced by science. Evangelical Protestant denominations, previously unified to some extent around shared beliefs in the inerrancy of biblical text, the importance of conversion, and the need for personal witness, split as some people embraced the new scientific developments and worked to reconcile them with an idea of an omniscient god, while others embraced more conservative and even fundamentalist views of the role of God and Christianity in the world and worked to retain their traditional beliefs. For each of these groups, "modernism" or efforts to be "modern" meant very different things.

Although the conservatives remained generally comfortable with the practices and churches of the previous generation, liberals and many middle-of-the-road Protestants (often called "mainline" Protestants) embraced a new liturgical movement, designed to increase the formalism of worship. The architectural result was the adoption of a new interior arrangement called the *split chancel* by Congregationalists, Presbyterians, Baptists, and Methodists, in particular. Based on the more formalist spatial arrangements of Episcopalian, Lutheran, and Anglican churches, split-chancel churches featured a longitudinally oriented rectangular worship room with a center aisle and (sometimes) side aisles. The front of the church eliminated the pulpit platform that had dominated evangelical Protestant churches for nearly a century, replacing it with a slightly elevated platform approached by a central set of steps on the main axis. This chancel area housed an altar table against the front wall at the termination of the axis. Above the table, most congregations positioned an altarpiece such as a portrait of Jesus or a large cross. At the entry to the chancel, a pulpit was located on the right and a smaller lectern for the reading of the Epistle on the left.[8] In the spilt-chancel arrangement, the table is given pride of place at the terminus of the axis, yet the large pulpit remains accessible and highly visible. The unique feature in the arrangement was the lectern, which had not been a worship center in the past, at least not among Presbyterians, Congregationalists, and Baptists, but was now elevated to a parallel position with the pulpit, signaling the importance of the scriptural reading, a clearly formalist component of the service. During a period in which liberal Protestants were increasingly adopting a historical-cultural understanding of scripture and moving away from the idea of biblical inerrancy, this new arrangement helped to legitimate their claim that they were not abandoning scripture but in fact increasing its importance within their faith and worship.[9]

Catholics also underwent a liturgical transformation in the early twentieth century, precipitated by a movement to encourage greater laity involvement in services. The first indications of the movement was an effort in the 1890s to incorporate more music into the Mass, supported by Pope Pius X, who upon taking office in 1903 mandated "the use of the Gregorian chant by the people, so that the faithful may again take a more active part in the ecclesiastical offices, as they were wont to do in ancient times."[10] By 1905, Pius X expanded his effort to encourage the participation of the faithful by decreeing that weekly, even daily, communion be made available to all those "in a state of grace, and who approach the holy table with a right and devout intention . . . free from mortal sin."[11]

The generations-old practice of observing private devotions during the Mass became increasingly untenable if the gathered congregation were to come forward to share in the Eucharistic meal, making it necessary to find new ways to engage the attention and participation of worshippers in the liturgy of the Mass itself. Although the Mass would remain spoken in Latin for several more decades, a new liturgical movement aimed at lay participation flowered within the Catholic church in the second and third decades of the twentieth century, under the influence of Lambert Beauduin, a monk of Mont César, Louvain. Beauduin argued that the liturgy was the defining act, "the prime and indispensable source," of Christian experience and spirit, and thus the "democratization" or participation of the faithful in the liturgy was vital.[12] In Europe, this movement centered on religious orders and clergy, and encouraged a shift away from individual devotional practices toward a stronger interest in communal liturgical activities. Although welcomed by many in the church, Beauduin's initial forays in this direction were not universally hailed, particularly among those religious and lay faithful who were dedicated to traditional saint devotions. In the ensuing decades, however, Beauduin's position urging "liturgical piety" even among the laity would become predominant, even commonplace by the late twentieth century.[13]

In the United States, this interest in liturgical participation would take a distinctively democratic turn, involving greater lay participation. Beauduin's ideas of liturgical reform were brought to the United States by one of his students, Dom Virgil Michel, a Benedictine of St. John's Abbey in Collegeville, Minnesota, who in 1926, founded the influential journal *Orate Fratres*, the central organ of the Catholic liturgical movement in the United States. *Orate Fratres* refers to an exhortation spoken during the Mass just before the secret act of consecration when the celebrant turns to the faithful and says, "Pray brethren that my sacrifice and yours be acceptable to God the Father almighty," to which the people answer, "May the Lord receive the sacrifice from thy hands to the praise and glory of his name, and for our benefit also and for that of all his holy Church." This key liturgical exchange, in which the celebrant acts on the behalf of the people and the holy Church itself, underscores the centrality and role of the gathered faithful. The name of his journal thus signaled Dom Michel's priorities: advancing the renewal of corporate worship and the corporate nature of the church and reengaging the liturgy as a vehicle through which to encourage laity participation and ultimately develop active parishes engaged in service to God. Michel and his coreligionists were also interested in fostering church interest in the daily lives and experiences of the faithful and serving the poor.[14] The American liturgical movement thus emphasized and focused on the role of the laity, providing a route through which influence and power began to shift away from the clergy and toward the people.[15]

Two other changes in Catholic thought during the first half of the twentieth century also prepared the ground for a greater participation of the faithful and the development of a modernist movement in Catholic church architecture. The first was the reinterpretation of the meaning of the Eucharist that focused on time and history rather than substance. For theologians like Odo Casel, a monk from the Maria Laach Abbey, an institution instrumental in the German liturgical movement, the mystery of the transformation of bread and wine into the body of Christ was more about *time*—the connections between Christ and the contemporary period—than about *space*—how Christ was present in the Eucharist. As historian James White explains, Casel was concerned with how "the events of salvation history become our contemporaries."[16] The historical bent of this new inquiry contributed to a second significant shift, a new willingness on the part of the church to apply historical analysis to Christianity. When historical criticism of biblical texts had emerged in German universities in the early nineteenth century, the Catholic church had opposed the practice of inquiring into the production of scripture. In 1943, however, Pius XII proclaimed that biblical scholarship would be allowed.[17] Together, these changes in Catholic thought and dogma demonstrated a new willingness to think of the church as undergoing change over time rather than being timeless in every way.

In the context of these efforts to engage the faithful in the liturgy, reinterpret the Eucharist, and explore the history of Christianity, the role of the priest—and thus power relations between the clergy and the laity—also began to transform. Although priests remained more fully initiated in the mysteries of the Mass and the liturgy than their parishioners, they were also adopting new roles and responsibilities and working with lay people on addressing various types of individual and community needs. Many priests took up social agendas aimed at bettering living conditions, labor conditions, education, and the like in their parishes. Pastoral counseling beyond the confessional also grew important in the twentieth century. The priesthood was "humanized" in new ways. U.S. popular culture began depicting priests as beloved figures, such as Bing Crosby's portrayal of Father Chuck O'Malley in *Going My Way* (1944) and *The Bells of St. Mary's* (1945), which depicted priests not as distant, all-knowing, authority figures but as "just people" with personal problems and joys like everyone else.

Thus, at the same time that the liturgical movement among liberal Protestants moved their services toward greater formalism, Catholics retained their original formalism in services but added a new layer of congregational participation. A generation later, some Catholics would move toward non-formalist practices and spaces.

Catholic Modernism

The willingness of Christian churches to modernize their worship services was paralleled by a willingness to modernize their church architecture, and new Christian churches of the twentieth century shed the historicizing aspects of their earlier counterparts. Architects and congregations adopted European aesthetic trends that grew out of the social, political, and cultural contexts of the late nineteenth and early twentieth century, including art nouveau, expressionism, and modernism. Art nouveau, for instance, embraced organic, "biomorphic," forms as a counterresponse to industrialization, launching a revolution in the decorative arts and architecture in the 1880s and 1890s. In the case of church architecture, Antoni Gaudí's Temple of the Sagrada Familia in Barcelona, begun in 1884 but still unfinished, referenced the Gothic in an expressionistic way as he encrusted the building's pointed features with a distinctively organic sculptural veneer that to this day is astonishing in its uniqueness. Called everything from brilliant to bizarre, the exterior of the church is overlaid with sculptural detail that suggests that the building itself is somehow organic, bending this way and that and sprouting features from unexpected sources.[18]

Despite this unprecedented character of the Sagrada Familia's envelope, its interior remains distinctly traditional, suggesting again the way in which church spaces become naturalized (i.e., considered natural or even inevitable) over many generations. The original cruciform plan included a central nave of some thirty meters wide and eighty meters long. Double aisles flank the nave, and the crossing is covered by a dome. The chancel is raised some two meters above the main floor, with the altar placed close to the center of the chancel and surrounded by a semicircle of seating (reminiscent of the synthronon in Roman basilicas) intended for the choir. Beyond this, a semicircle of seven chapels referencing the seven sorrows and joys of Joseph outline the outer wall of the chancel apse.[19] Combining classical Roman forms with the Baroque arrangement, this interior space, like its earlier Gothic Revival counterparts in the nineteenth century, abandoned the medieval chancel arrangement in favor of the more open view of the altar. Thus this art nouveau church replicated the authority relationships and formalism embedded in earlier churches.

Yet the organicism of the façade and ornament pointed to new understandings of the divine that were becoming popular during the late nineteenth century, in particular the notion that divine power was best understood through the natural world. Art nouveau postulated an organicism connected to a spirituality of creation. In the United States, this organicism was warmly embraced by artisans active in the arts and crafts movement, leading to an infusion of organic-based ornament in many Protestant and Catholic churches in the closing decades of the century. In Europe, Gaudí, a devout Catholic, believed that God's creation was continued through the works of humankind, stating, "those who look for the laws of Nature as a support for their new works collaborate with the creator."[20] The layers of organic detail, the pinnacles topped with piles of berry-like balls of green, yellow, orange, and red, or with sculptures of trees hiding birds and animals all suggest God's creation. Similarly, the tapered shape of the four main towers and their vertical rows of rectangular windows further suggest forms from nature—perhaps an ancient calcified stalagmite in an underground cavern—rather than the products of an increasingly industrial and mechanistic age.

Buildings such as this, which were closely identified with the artistic vision of a particular designer working in the new modernist idioms, would provide the Catholic church with claim to a forward-looking modernism, a demonstration that the church continued to be relevant in the lives of modern people even as their lives changed with the new demands of urban life, commercialization, and technology. Another notable example is architect August Perret's Notre-Dame du Raincy (1922) on the outskirts of Paris. Notre-Dame du Raincy was conceived as a distinctively modern building, evident most clearly in its use of materials and ornament. Following the modernist idiom of "truthfulness" to the building materials, the ferroconcrete (concrete reinforced with iron or steel) of the building's construction remains bare, from its walls and interior columns and vaults to the latticework of the glass sheet walls. Outside, the rough concrete and spare geometry of the front façade and central tower is relieved only by latticework strips on short pavilions on either side of the central door and tower and by a similar lattice of windows running from the door to the clock above it. At this point, the tower is broken into segments, a belfry and a cap consisting of a cluster of rectangular lattice steps leading up to a simple cross. Inside, as well, the building materials are allowed to convey their own meanings, a task the glass and latticework does to extraordinary effect.

Like most other modernist churches, the interior of Notre-Dame du Raincy remains strictly traditional, replicating the basilica space with a long barrel-vaulted nave, two side aisles (with traverse barrel vaults), and an apse. This arrangement still provides for a distinct separation between the clergy and laity while accommodating the new interest in fostering congregational focus on the liturgy during worship. The sanctuary platform consists of two levels, the lower housing a central pulpit and the upper, several meters above it, housing the altar. The latter, raised high above the main floor and backlit by the blue glass of the front wall, stands like a dramatic promontory. During the Mass, the celebrant is readily visible, if not particularly accessible. Each of his movements can be witnessed, and, if one sits relatively closely, each word heard. Through the simple device of elevation, clerical authority is maintained while the faithful are allowed far greater visual access to the performance of the liturgy.

Following centuries of efforts to bring light into church buildings, the nave of Notre-Dame du Raincy is enclosed on the north, south, and east with latticework walls of colored glass. The hue of the glass deepens from very light in the back to darker near the front of the church, flooding the apse with deep royal blue light, interrupted only by the red outline of a cross inscribed in the blue glass. The result is an interior awash in light with a dramatic, eye-catching apse. Just as Sainte Chapelle created walls of light using cut stone and medieval technology, Notre-Dame du Raincy used concrete and early-twentieth-century technology to do the same. As in Sainte Chapelle, light itself, shimmering through a thousand windows, offers the faithful a visually and spiritually inspiring experience.

The Modernist Ideals of Space, Material, and Light

The notion of architectural *space*, the analytical concept that informs this book, was introduced by the modernists in the context of church architecture. Though it appeared early in the nineteenth century, particularly in Hegel's *Philosophy of Art*, in which he describes the Gothic as "the concentration of essential soul-life which thus encloses itself in spatial relations,"[21] most architects of the time were not particularly interested in the idea, focusing their attention, as had their forbearers for millennia, on *structure*, not space. The lack of an analytical concept of space had consequences such as those we have seen in the instance of the revivalists at Gwennap Pit, who could not conceive of locating themselves at the base of the amphitheater but instead preached from its upper reaches. Escaping the received understanding of elevation and authority was simply not possible without some critical approach to the function of space. One early outcome of church architects' interest in the concept of space was the development of the auditorium space, although many of its conceptual properties, such as the organization of individuals and groups within it, remained largely unexplored.

Among those who did take notice of the possibilities of this new church space was a Unitarian minister, Jenkin Lloyd Jones, who claimed that the auditorium plan was particularly appropriate for liberal Protestant worship because the arrangement promoted an egalitarianism among the assembled congregation that echoed Unitarianism's understanding of universal atonement, or the idea that Christ's death on the cross redeemed all of humankind.[22] Architect Frank Lloyd Wright, Jones's nephew, would pioneer the idea of looking at enclosed space as a fundamental component of design and began to explore the design ramifications of the idea that spaces themselves play a role in the activities that are performed within them—that spaces make possible some activities and hinder others.[23] He put these ideas to work in a church of his design, Unity Temple, a Unitarian Universalist church in Oak Park, Illinois.

Although Wright rejected using the curved seating of the auditorium church in Unity Temple, his design nevertheless adapted elements of the auditorium, placing a by-then-common pulpit platform at the front of the nearly square room and focusing straight pews in a meetinghouse-type arrangement around it. Yet the auditorium was startlingly creative and modern in its use of the space (figs. 7.5 and 7.6). Double galleries enclosed the remaining three sides of the room, but the unique lower galleries were elevated only four feet above the main floor. These "alcoves" accommodated just over fifty people each. The very exceptionality of this seating, designed to create direct sightlines from the aisle and back of the room to the pulpit platform without the aid of a sloped floor, made those individuals seated in the alcoves uniquely aware of their position within the room and of the space of the room in general. In addition, entry into the room was through doors on either side of the pulpit platform on the front wall, rather than through the rear of the room. Thus, people entering and leaving the space in effect "trespassed" on the chancel, an area that had for centuries in the history of Christian building

FIGURE 7.5. Unity Temple, Oak Park, Ill., 1907. Frank Lloyd Wright, architect. Courtesy Library of Congress, Prints and Photographs Division [HABS ILL, 16-OAKPA, 3–4].

been reserved for clergy. For the strongly egalitarian Unitarian Universalists, such spatial distinctions of authority were anathema, and by routing all traffic around the platform, Unity Temple took a major step in countering long-held Christian practice.

As the century wore on, thinking in terms of space gained currency in architectural design, and by mid-century, awareness of space had been elevated to one of three fundamental aspects of modern church design, along with the use of truthful and unadorned materials and the evocative use of light. Furthermore, the latter two concerns were frequently employed in ways that prompted a heightened awareness of the space itself.

Not disguising structural materials or masking their function by covering them became a hallmark of modern architecture, and some architects made a further virtue of this by using the materials to emphasize space. Architects' initial experiments in this regard frequently employed poured concrete or ferroconcrete. Frank Lloyd Wright demonstrated the possibilities of concrete in Unity Temple, a building that offered something of a middle ground between

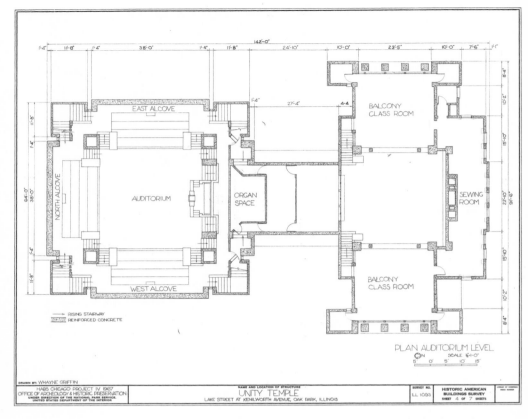

FIGURE 7.6. Building survey, Unity Temple, Oak Park, Ill., 1907. Frank Lloyd Wright, architect. Courtesy Library of Congress, Prints and Photographs Division [HABS ILL, 16-OAKPA, 3].

the nineteenth century interest in ornamentation and the twentieth century interest in minimalism. Unity Temple, with its geometric exterior massing and subtle external ornament, suggested a modernist aesthetic, but its interior was highly ornamented with geometric moldings. The unrelenting rhythms of the interior moldings drew attention to the space itself, creating a visual and physical sense of movement within the static space.

Five years later, Bernard Maybeck's design for his First Church of Christ, Scientist, in Berkeley, California, emphasized the spaces of the building by drawing attention to its materials and structure. Constructed of ferroconcrete and wood, the low-profile building with its large overhanging eaves looks more like a residence than a public church from the outside. Inside, the square worship room is dominated by a single vault composed of two intersecting concrete trusses supporting the roof. This huge X of concrete beams criss-crosses the room at right angles, directing attention to the space itself by drawing the eye first up to the crossing and then down in each of the four directions to the corners of the room. Like that of a Gothic cathedral, the vaulting in this church stirs a physical response to the space and emphasizes the dimensions of the space itself. The concrete of the vault, like that of the poured walls, is exposed, although Maybeck, like Wright, chose to provide some ornamentation, painting organic designs on the concrete itself, and thus accomplished a similar marriage between nineteenth-century ornamentation and the spare constructivist aesthetic that would later come to dominate modern architecture.

Light also became a critical factor in modern design, and it, too, was put to use to emphasize the spatial qualities of churches. In Unity Temple, Wright, again adapting auditorium church practices that were by then two decades old, covered the worship room with a ceiling made of colored glass, flooding the room with light from above during the day. By mid-century, architects were developing even more sophisticated means of using light to draw attention to space. Father and son Finnish architects Eliel and Eero Saarinen, for instance, designed two churches that featured a similar dramatic use of natural light in the sanctuary. In First Christian (Disciples of Christ) Church in Columbus, Indiana, completed in 1942, light enters the rectangular worship room from both the back and the front. In the back a glass-fronted façade pours light into oblong worship room. In the front of the church, in contrast, exterior light is carefully funneled by a narrow, recessed, floor-to-ceiling window positioned on the wall adjacent to the apse. This window allows a thin vertical wash of light to sweep the front wall of the church behind the altar. The wall itself, which is curved at the north corner, is almost bare, ornamented only with a single cross. As the sun moves across the sky, illuminating the wall through the narrow window, the cross casts a dramatic shadow that moves against the curved wall.

The Saarinens used a similar strategy in Christ Church Lutheran in Minneapolis, Minnesota, completed in 1949 (fig. 7.7). Here, rectangular windows placed low in the side walls of the nave allow some ambient light to enter the room. In the front (west end) of the worship room, the narrow, floor-to-ceiling window echoes that of the Columbus church, but here the brick sanctuary wall provides a more textured surface for the light and the simple cross is suspended a few inches from the wall, creating even more dramatic shadows as the sun, beaming in through the long, narrow window on the south wall, moves across the building. During the course of a sunny Sunday morning service, worshippers find their eyes drawn to the cross and the changing effects of the light as it passes across the sanctuary wall. In Christ

FIGURE 7.7. Christ Church Lutheran, Minneapolis, Minn., 1949. Eliel and Eero Saarinen, architects. Courtesy Christ Church Lutheran.

Church, the light brick of the walls provides a texture and warmth that softens the otherwise unadorned vertical walls and ceiling.

These buildings' use of materials, seemingly simple oblong design, and manipulation of light result in restful spaces intended to foster contemplation and prayer. Offering few cues to the Christian narrative, these modernist spaces rely heavily on the service itself to convey the required religious messages. But they also rely upon the inclinations of the individual to mentally fill in the meanings of the space, thereby fostering the empowerment of lay people, who bear significant responsibility for their experience within these buildings.

Perhaps the most renowned church to use these three modern design principles to extraordinary effect is noted architect Le Corbusier's chapel of Notre Dame du Haut in Ronchamp, France, often called, simply, Ronchamp. Although designed by the acknowledged master of austere modern architecture meant to erase cultural references from buildings in order to convey meaning through structure and materials alone, the completed building pushed beyond this paradigm by accomplishing the latter while embracing the former. That is, it emphasizes structure and materials while at the same time suggesting a multitude of cultural meanings.[24] Located at the top of a hill in

FIGURE 7.8. Exterior, Notre Dame du Haut, Ronchamp, France, 1954. Le Corbusier, architect. Photo by Jeffery Howe.

eastern France that reputedly was the site of a series of miracles effected by the Virgin Mary, the chapel occupies a location that has been the destination of pilgrims since the medieval period. The destruction of the previous chapel in World War II necessitated the erection of a new building, and a Dominican priest, Father Marie-Alain Couturier, commissioned his friend Le Corbusier to design it. Le Corbusier, who had been raised in a Protestant family but had abandoned religion by adulthood, focused his attention on the needs of pilgrims and an aesthetic derived from nature. The resulting chapel, a concrete building with a distinctive triangular roof that sweeps up to a peak, has been likened to mountain peaks, a ship, a nun's cowl, human figures, and a variety of other visual referents (fig. 7.8).

The design of the space, both inside and outside the building, was remarkable, though not as unprecedented as some have argued. The interior of the building consists of an oblong worship room with an altar at the far end (fig. 7.9). But Le Corbusier problematized the axial character of the room by placing pews only on one side, leaving the other open for gathered pilgrims to stand, kneel, or sit as they choose. An altar rail, which can also be used as a bench, cuts sharply across the space horizontally, separating the altar from worshippers. This untraditional arrangement disrupts the visitors' usual experience of church space, sending out mixed signals regarding where one should position oneself in the space. The space is further problematized by the boundary enclosures of the room—the walls and ceiling themselves. Above,

FIGURE 7.9. Interior, Notre Dame du Haut, Ronchamp, France, 1954. Le Corbusier, architect. Photo by Jeffery Howe.

the ceiling curves down into the space along the longitudinal axis, reversing the usual convex character of nave vaults, and slopes gently from the high wall on the right to the lower on the left. The thick concrete walls are *battered* (that is, larger at the bottom and smaller at the top), also resulting in a kind of trespass on the interior space. Encountering a ceiling and walls that thus seem to close in, to fold in on the room, visitors become acutely aware of the space itself.

The use of light within the building also contributes to a viewer's awareness of the space itself. The thick walls of the south wall are pierced with rectangular light wedges or *embrasures* of varying size, positioned randomly. Like spotlights, these embrasures funnel shafts of light into the room, creating an eerie effect of bright light contrasted by dark shadows. High on the front wall, however, a single rectangular window containing the image of the Virgin allows light to stream in.

The use of light and space as referents to the mystery of God, as we have seen, were particularly important during the medieval period, and this history of their use provides a clue to the religious meanings that have been associated with these modernist buildings. For Le Corbusier, the chapel signaled *l'espace indicible,* often translated as "ineffable space."[25] That sense of the ineffable, of something indescribable, unspeakable, irreducible, is readily formulated in spiritual terms—a sense of divine power that presses in on the individual while at the same time appearing mysterious and unknowable. In this sense, Ronchamp,the Saarinen churches, and many other modernist buildings that emphasize the influence of the effects of light and space on a sense of the spiritual, have much in common with the medieval Gothic.

Both the modern and the medieval church builders attempted to convey a sense of the power of the divine and of the fundamental difference and unknowableness of God, which they accomplished in two ways. First they created worship rooms that make the individual profoundly conscious of his or her position within the room and relationship to the space itself. In the medieval cathedral, itself a heavenly city, the forest of columns suggested the search for God, the soaring nave his power and distance. In these modern churches, a sense of power is accomplished not through grandeur, but through the subtle use of space that evokes a sense of personal positionality, both physically in the space and in relation to God and the infinite. Second, both the medieval and the modern churches use light to signal the divine. Carefully controlled light, filtered through colored glass or directed through precise embrasures, focuses attention on a narrow portion of the natural world, the light that floods our Earth, thereby suggesting that God is better seen or contemplated through an intensified, focused natural experience than through everyday experience of the natural world.

This mystical use of space and light and the spare aesthetic of plain walls and simple furnishings well suited the growing emphasis on the power of the liturgy and on lay participation. Distracting images, Stations of the Cross, and chancel furnishings were eliminated, leaving only the faithful, the celebrants, and the ceremony. These rooms were intended to help focus the attention of the faithful on the spiritual event taking place. As Jonathan Z. Smith reminds us, ritual practice and spaces focus the mind on the truly important, that which is spiritual or divine; they encourage us to pay attention.[26] Modernist buildings, by paring down the setting to space, light, and material, intended to accomplish exactly this.

Modernism and the Liturgical Movement Unite

Other changes began to occur in modernist buildings as well, the most important being attempts to diminish the distance between the altar and the

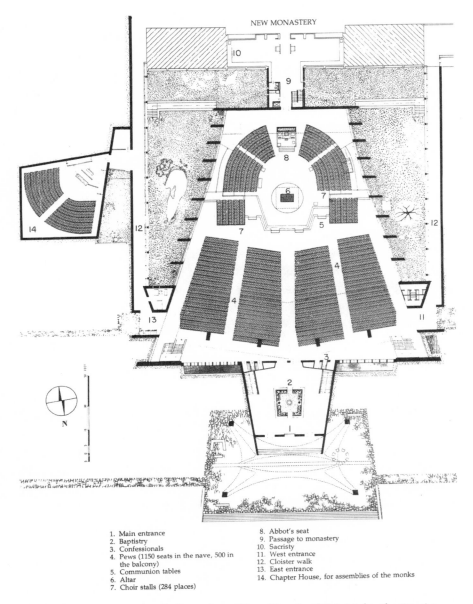

NEW MONASTERY

1. Main entrance
2. Baptistry
3. Confessionals
4. Pews (1150 seats in the nave, 500 in the balcony)
5. Communion tables
6. Altar
7. Choir stalls (284 places)
8. Abbot's seat
9. Passage to monastery
10. Sacristy
11. West entrance
12. Cloister walk
13. East entrance
14. Chapter House, for assemblies of the monks

FIGURE 7.10. Upper church floor plan, Abbey Church of Saint John the Baptist, Collegeville, Minn., 1961. Courtesy St. John's Abbey Archives.

faithful. As early as the second and third decades of the twentieth century, builders had begun to move altars away from the front wall and closer to the people. By the 1950s, the Baroque arrangement was being modified by a number of church designers, including Rudolf Schwarz, a German architect who experimented widely with many types of church plans and spaces, including centralized and elliptical plans, in which the altar was positioned at a focal point rather than against the front wall.[27]

In the United States, Marcel Breuer's Abbey Church of St. John the Baptist, commissioned by the Benedictines at St. John's University in central Minnesota and completed between 1958 and 1961, features a nearly square plan with the altar positioned in the center (fig. 7.10). A fan of pews for congregants faces the altar, and a semicircle of pews for the Benedictine religious is located opposite the congregational seating behind the altar. During the Mass, the celebrant originally faced the members of the order, but the seating arrangement did provide many of the congregants a view of the altar from the sides.

Spare in ornament, this church also uses space and light to convey the spiritual message of the building. Congregants enter the church into a low-ceilinged narthex, which serves as a baptistery (fig. 7.11). Rough-hewn concrete

FIGURE 7.11. Baptistry, with view of upper church, Abbey Church of Saint John the Baptist, Collegeville, Minn., 1961. Courtesy St. John's Abbey Archives.

walls seem to press in on the space, and the stone font surrounded by a rail contributes to the cave-like atmosphere of the space. The feeling of physical oppression continues as one leaves the baptistery and enters the main worship room, where a massive cantilevered concrete gallery hovers a few feet above one's head. As one clears the gallery, however, another world suddenly opens. The high ceiling and open space of the room immediately direct the gaze upward. A skylight located directly above the altar catches the eye, casting a ray of light onto the liturgical center. From the dark baptistery to the light-filled altar of the sacrifice and resurrection, the path one follows through the abbey church replicates the path of a Christian life, from baptism, marked by an awareness of sin, to the flowering of Christian life, forgiven of sin, filled with light, and focused on the Eucharist.

This physical strategy well suited the needs of the institution's leaders, who had since its founding been deeply involved in the liturgical movement. The arrangement offered an important model for recasting the hierarchical Baroque space that had dominated Catholic building for centuries and bringing the assembled faithful more fully into the Eucharist ceremony.

The Second Vatican Council

Despite the fact that changes in the placement of the altar and the embrace of a minimalist modernist aesthetic had begun in Catholic architecture well before the Second Vatican Council (1961–1963), they are frequently traced to the decisions regarding liturgy made during the Council. It is true that the Council mandated moving the altar away from the front wall of the church in order to allow the celebrant to position himself behind it and face the congregation. But as we have seen, this spatial transformation and the ensuing embrace of modern architectural vocabularies in Catholic churches had their actual roots in shifts in the social power of the laity and cultural and aesthetic architectural trends of the early twentieth century.[28] By officially sanctioning these changes, however, the Second Vatican Council legitimized them and accelerated their momentum. The result was the rapid transformation of large numbers of churches in the next decade and the construction of new churches with distinctively new interior arrangements and decor.

This sanctioning of the new architecture was also a by-product or corollary of a profound shift in the theology of the church articulated by the Council, which embraced the corporate ideal of the church of the faithful and lay-oriented practices championed by the liturgical movement. In this formulation, the church was reimagined as an institution of the people, not simply a community of clergy and religious, and therefore the liturgy was reimagined as an observance of the people, for the people. As stated in the Council's *Constitution on Sacred Liturgy*, "the Church reveals herself most clearly when a full complement of God's holy people, united in prayer and in common liturgical service (especially the Eucharist), exercise a thorough and active participation at the very altar where the bishop presides. . . ."[29] The responsibility for encouraging the participation of the faithful was taken seriously by the Council, which advised, "the rite of the Mass is to be revised in such a way that the intrinsic nature and purpose of its several parts, as also the connection between them, can be more clearly manifested, and that devout and active participation by the faithful can be more easily accomplished."[30] Most importantly, the Council recommended using the vernacular language of the region rather than Latin and restoring the cup to the laity at the discretion of the bishop. But other forms of participation were also recommended, including allowing the laity to "take part by means of acclamations, responses, psalmody, antiphons, and songs, as well as by actions, gestures, and bodily attitudes. And at the proper times all should observe a silence."[31] Further, the Council emphasized the importance of the homily or short sermon in helping lay people become more familiar with the Bible and its lessons.

As a result of this reenvisioning of liturgical services, priorities in church design also shifted significantly. No longer were the actions of the celebrant and servers to be self-contained; the congregants must be involved. Congregations now needed to be able to hear and see the proceedings in the chancel. The altars that had been distant from the congregation were replaced by tables, "provisional altars," positioned at the front edge of the chancel much nearer the laity. During the Eucharist service, celebrants stood behind this new altar, facing the congregation and speaking the liturgy in the language of the people. Seating for the laity was moved forward, closer to the altar, and was often curved somewhat to encourage a feeling of participation and community. In new churches, centralized plans became popular, as did plans that located congregational seating on three sides of the altar. All of these strategies had precedents both in a smattering of Catholic prototypes and in a wide range of Protestant churches.

As James White observes, Vatican II transformed the "house of God" to the "house of God's people."[32] In terms of access to social power, remodeled and new churches signaled a significant expansion of lay power. Now the liturgy was performed not only for their benefit but also for their participation. Now the seating was devised and the altar placed nearer so that each member of the congregation could see and hear the mass. Underlying these spatial elements was a reinterpretation of the Eucharist itself and the mandate that the laity share in both the bread and the wine during the Communion service. Thus it can be argued that the architectural changes that followed Vatican II stemmed more from the Council's acknowledgement of the centrality of the laity and its mandate to encourage their participation than from the specific liturgical changes it introduced.

Again, however, as with the Protestant elevation of lay power in the nineteenth century, this shift did not necessarily mean a diminishment of clerical power. Vatican II documents are adamant that the bishop is the head of the holy people and parish priests are the bishop's representatives in the field. Clergy did not yield power over the liturgy by encouraging lay participation, but rather invited the people into the celebration. Nevertheless, the Second Vatican Council encouraged clerical communication to expand in a number of ways, including through pastoral care and through ecumenical interaction. Transparency, not secrecy, would become the new mode of operation. Modern churches in which priests faced their flock directly across the altar exemplified this new attitude.

Los Angeles's Cathedral of Our Lady of the Angels, designed by Spanish architect José Rafael Moneo and completed in 2002, unites the modern aesthetic with the new spatial arrangements encouraged by Vatican II. The large oblong worship space, over three hundred feet long and ranging from eighty to a hundred feet high, is brightly lit by a large window above the chancel and clerestory embrasures in the nave (fig. 7.12). The space is oriented longitudinally, with the chancel located at the crossing. This spacious area, raised several steps above the main floor, is simply furnished with a large square table rather than an altar, located slightly off-center, and a freestanding tabernacle. Raked seating to the right accommodates the choir and chairs can be arranged in the chancel as needed for those involved in ceremonies. Ornamentation is spare. A parade of figures marches across tapestries on the south wall, but otherwise the rich marble of the walls and floor is bare. Overhead a web of iron bars is formed by the many chandeliers, but they, too, are simple in design. The room glows with golden light filtered through alabaster windows. Massive yet spare, the room, like its earlier modernist forbearers, draws attention to its space and is intended to encourage contemplation. The faithful bring their own thoughts to the space and find their own meaning in it and in the rituals performed in it.

But whereas some Catholics find these modernist spaces appropriate for and facilitative of spiritual contemplation and worship, others find the bare walls off-putting and plain, ordinary rather than extraordinary. Although these differences in perception are generally attributed to differing aesthetic preferences, we should not overlook the role of the effects of the power shifts that

FIGURE 7.12. Cathedral of Our Lady of the Angels, Los Angeles, 2002. Photo by
Marilyn Chiat, Ph.D.

initially gave rise to modernist church architecture in defining attitudes toward
architecture. Modern churches distribute social power between clergy and laity,
requiring the faithful to take much greater responsibility for their own religious
experience and understanding than in previous generations. The religious
experience that had previously been articulated and externalized through devotions to saints and ritual actions such as lighting candles has become more
internalized, through listening to the liturgy. Further, modern church architecture communicates and posits a far different understanding of supernatural
power than did earlier churches. Divine narratives inviting individual participation are rarely exhibited through images or statuary in modernist churches,
and the humanism of the Jesus story is eclipsed by the metaphoric ritual of the
Eucharist. In these ways, the presence of the divine becomes more abstract,
embodied no longer in a powerful, though distant, clergy nor in the presence of
saints or other visual references to the Jesus narrative.

Restorationist Efforts

Many Christians who considered the question of an appropriate setting for
worship in the post–World War II period looked even further back into history for prototypes of the ideal Christian church. Influenced by the spare

minimalism of the modernist movement, and with new information gleaned from archaeological sources, some congregations, both Protestant and Catholic, and architects assert that more simple forms and spare ornament better approximated the practices of early Christians and the churches of the second and third centuries.

Such efforts, called *restorationist* because they seek to "restore" the practices of earlier periods, have long been evident as theological movements. In the nineteenth century, several groups, including the Campbellites, or followers of Andrew Campbell, attempted to restructure their worship practice and polity, or church governance, along the lines of the early church. Their attempt was fueled by the belief that widespread adoption of the practices of the early church, what they considered the "true" church, would put an end to denominationalism and unify Christianity. Although this intended result did not materialize, it did not hamper their efforts to adopt what they saw as the more authentic practices of an earlier time.

In the mid-twentieth century, with new church buildings in demand by a growing suburban population in the United States and in Europe, architects joined congregations in once again looking to the ancient past for ways to create what they felt would be more authentic Christian churches. These groups, joining Protestants and Catholics, generally understood early Christian worship spaces to be simple, utilitarian assembly rooms, generally devoid of ornament, where the Word of God was preached. Thomas Merton, opining that it was absurd for modern congregations to try to get "a Gothic church out of a small budget," argued that it was far better to "put up something that would give glory to God and would be very simple and world also be in the tradition of our fathers."[33] Lutheran architect E. A. Sovik agreed, urging congregations to seek buildings of "full authenticity," directed outward to the broader community in an attitude of Christian service or servanthood rather than focused on the inward needs of the clergy, laity, or congregation itself. As a result, many new church buildings embraced not only the lack of ornament that modernism had already made popular but also a kind of modesty or understated character that reduced the space to the bare necessities. Further, they favored utilitarian spaces with movable seating that could accommodate a variety of activities from worship to classes and discussion sessions.[34]

Reprising the Auditorium Church

Changes in the mission and reach of evangelical Christians in the United States during the last half of the twentieth century also led to innovations in the design of modern churches. Through the summer of 1957, evangelical minister Billy Graham launched a series of revivals in the heart of New York City in Madison Square Garden. The Garden, generally used for sporting events and concerts, was perceived by many to be an odd choice for a religious revival, but it proved enormously successful, accommodating more than two million people over the course of three and one-half months. Graham's success demonstrated some significant changes underway within U.S. evangelicalism. First, his message was a moderate one that appealed to mainline as well as evangelical groups: convert and build a personal relationship Jesus.[35] Second, it tapped into renewed interest on the part of evangelicals in building their church membership through conversions. These elements united in the Church Growth Movement, which by the 1970s and 1980s began to spark an evangelical church building boom that would continue through the turn of the twenty-first century.

The church building type located at the center of this boom became known as the institutional megachurch, or, more commonly, the megachurch. The first of these megachurches, Willow Creek Community Church in South Barrington, Illinois, was designed with the needs of its target audience— unchurched families and individuals living in exurban Chicago—in mind. Its pastor, Bill Hybels, fresh out of seminary, surveyed local residents, asking for their opinions of churches and church services, and learned that many were not comfortable with traditional Christian buildings, imagery, and services. Feeling ill-informed and intimidated by the formalism of churches, they had either stopped attending church or had never begun.

In response, Hybels embraced antiformalism and antihistoricism as the functioning characteristics of Willow Creek. The new building would not look like a church: no Gothic towers or steeples, no vaulted nave. Instead, it would mimic the everyday office buildings of the exurbs, with a low profile and a surrounding campus. Inside, the building would minimize visual references to religion: no stained glass images or statuary. The worship room was an auditorium, an asymmetrical polygon with fan seating focused on a thrust stage.

Megachurches have become favored by denominations like the Southern Baptists that embrace the evangelizing mission in part because they satisfy their desire to bring large number of worshippers into a single space. Just as Billy Graham had filled Madison Square Garden and Promise Keepers, an evangelical men's group, would later fill sports stadiums throughout the United States, megachurches with seating capacities ranging from 2,000 to 8,000 would welcome huge groups every week.

Like the nineteenth-century auditorium churches, contemporary megachurches and smaller auditorium churches cater to the physical needs of congregations. As in the example of Wooddale Church in Edina, Minnesota, designed by architect Milo Thompson, seating is arranged in fans or banks of stadium like sections, all focused on the stage (fig. 7.13). From each seat in the house, individuals can easily see and hear the action taking place on the stage, assisted by the placement of several large video screens around the room and the use of microphones. The seats are comfortable and easily accessed from the large lobby area. Congregation members participate in services through hymn singing and watching the activities in the front. Depending upon the intentions of a church's leadership, authority onstage can be diffused among several participants or concentrated in the hands of one or two pastors. For charismatic church leaders, the stage setting provides an enormous boost to their power, focusing all attention on them while video screens multiply their visage many times throughout the room.

Antiformalism is a central component of megachurch worship and space, allowing, in fact requiring, individuals to take their own meanings from the performances and songs. The services include few or no liturgical elements but convey the message of accepting Jesus through storytelling, skits, and music. Video screens are used to project films, images, faith narratives, and testimonials, which in an earlier day may have been depicted in static stained glass

FIGURE 7.13. Interior, Wooddale Church, Eden Prairie, Minn., 1990. Milo Thompson, architect. Photo by William P. Halgren.

or other media. The use of video allows for ever-changing depictions, suggesting the divine narrative is never static but in continual flux.

As in earlier churches that adopted anti- and nonformalist techniques, the power of the clergy is downplayed in megachurches, yet still important. Rick Warren, for instance, pastor of the largest megachurch in the United States, Saddleback in Lake Forest, California, is noted for the casual Hawaiian shirts he wears during services rather than the formal collar of the ordained. Nevertheless, he and other successful megachurch ministers, delivering their messages from center stage and center screen in these impressive surroundings, wield a great deal of charismatic authority. Individual congregants also report experiencing significant personal or spiritual power during services, derived in part from their sense of participating in the fellowship of that gathered community of the faithful.[36] Within this gathered community, many report feeling close to Jesus, who is understood as a personal friend and savior deeply interested in the individual's life.

A similar closeness is the goal of services among congregations of the charismatic renewal movement and Pentecostals, both of which specifically invite the Holy Spirit to descend into the space and move individuals during services. The churches of these movements vary from simple, storefront rooms to megachurches, and most embrace the same antihistoricism and antiformalism of the megachurches.

The Reemergence of Historicism or the Rise of Postmodernism?

From the predominance of historicism to the triumph of modernism, the transformation in the architectural vocabularies of churches has been dramatic over the course of the nineteenth and twentieth centuries. Within the interiors of these churches, however, no single pattern of change is evident; instead, the negotiation between formalist and anti- or nonformalist elements is ongoing. Both Catholics and Protestants have experienced periods of liturgical revival, sometimes springing from, sometimes tempered by, concern for congregational participation. The modernist aesthetic has proven enormously flexible, adaptable to both formalism and nonformalism.

Nevertheless, by the late twentieth century, a new historicist movement was gaining momentum, particularly in the construction of Catholic churches. This new movement, centered at institutions such as the University of Notre Dame School of Architecture, championed classicism, and like previous architectural movements we have examined, it has advanced for both social and religious reasons. Generally sympathetic to the traditionalist position discussed in the introduction to this chapter, participants in this movement favor greater formalism than many modernist churches allow, including stronger distinctions between clergy and laity and great representation of clerical power. For these traditionalists, the replication and reinterpretation of Roman architecture in particular signals an appreciation for a traditional Rome-centered faith and leadership. Moreover, they encourage the use of visual means to direct attention to sacred stories and to convey information about them through iconography and representational art.

The meaning of such movements in the late twentieth and early twenty-first century is debated. In a period in which the very nature of "meaning" is widely contested and in which the political motivations and power plays underlying many architectural decisions have been widely parsed, the question of just what it means to "revive" a historical style is far from clear. For those of the postmodern camp, borrowing individual elements of historical styles is done playfully, without any intention of bringing along the historical meanings previously connected to the specific architectural features. Indeed, postmodernists have rejected the austere character of modern architecture and called for a hybrid architecture that creatively blend elements from all types of sources. Thus, in the 1990s, everything from shopping centers to churches began to sport such features as classical cornices and pedimented entries.

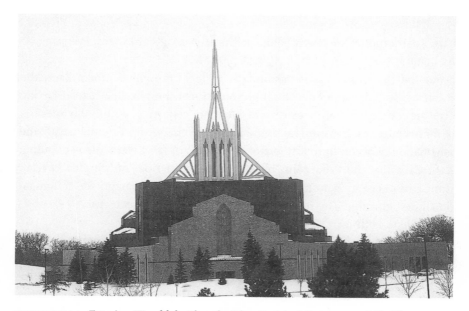

FIGURE 7.14. Exterior, Wooddale Church, Eden Prairie, Minn., 1990. Milo Thompson, architect. Photo by William P. Halgren.

Other designers, however, have borrowed or alluded to historical archi-tectural periods with the intention of conveying specific meanings about Christianity and demonstrating links between earlier periods and the present. The new Italianate churches of architect Duncan Stroik, for instance, inten-tionally connect their contemporary congregations to the earlier church. Simi-larly, the soaring central tower of Wooddale Church references Gothic spires, though in a very modern way (fig. 7.14). Such visual allusions and architectural borrowings go beyond simply being playful; they are attempts to make state-ments about Christianity itself. In this manner, then, contemporary Chris-tianity continues to wrestle with its relationship to the past.

8

Concluding Observations

Christian space is dynamic space. It is powerful space. The preceding chapters have demonstrated these two assertions repeatedly. They have also demonstrated that in order to understand the dynamism of Christian space, we must understand the function of power—divine, social, and personal—within it. But these categories are not mutually exclusive; they overlap and influence one another. Therefore, at the same time that we explore how linkages between the theological and the sociopolitical are articulated in the architecture of churches, we must acknowledge and investigate the personal.

Further, and most importantly, to understand power within churches, we must maintain a close eye on the *material* aspects of space *and* human experience. The material world is far from neutral; indeed, as we have seen, it is through physical spaces and material objects that many of the power relations we have witnessed are articulated and maintained. A rood screen or iconostasis reifies clergy-laity power relations at the same time that it articulates the theology of the incarnation and offers hope of salvation to the faithful. This material object, this piece of furniture, thus actively participates in articulating and maintaining an element of Christian creed, code, and cultus.

We have also seen the dynamism of religious space manifested in the diversity of Christian church types, ranging from small house churches to great cathedrals to auditoria. Linking all these diverse spaces is an effort to do one specific thing: to articulate some understanding of how God and humanity come together. By closely examining churches we can better understand the diversity of ideas and experiences that Christians hold with respect to this divine/human relationship.

There are caveats that we should keep in mind, however, as we continue to explore the meanings in and function of church buildings. First, although church spaces foster certain relationships and encourage certain behaviors, they do not necessarily require or *determine* those relationships and behaviors. People will be people. Both clergy and laity, as we have seen, have countered and resisted the normal patterns and activities encouraged by certain church spaces. Most obviously in this regard, we have seen the development of formalist practices in generally nonformalist space and vice versa. But we have also seen differences of opinion over appropriateness of ornament, design, and materials that demonstrate the willingness of individuals and groups to critique church spaces.

Second, buildings and spaces do not foster relationships and authorities in a vacuum. Numerous "outside" influences contribute to the defining of relationships between clergy and laity, between men and women, between members and nonmembers, between the faithful and the uninitiated, and so on. Decisions of church leadership, attitudes toward external issues, the media, even government contribute to the dynamics of relations among believers by lending greater or lesser influence to certain groups within a congregation or parish. The resulting relationships are then articulated and frequently naturalized—and sometimes resisted—by church buildings.

This brings us to a third caveat: buildings are not static. Congregations alter and remodel their buildings to address changing social or liturgical requirements, changing understandings of the worship and its role in the Christian life, changing technological advancements, changing trends and styles, and the like. Churches get torn down. New ones are built. Interiors are remodeled. Exteriors are altered. Within these processes of change all three categories of divine, social, and personal power have enormous bearing, but the latter—the question of how individuals have felt their own spiritual empowerment within the building—is often the unacknowledged foundation of many internal debates. For in the end, regardless of whether one is clergy or laity, female or male, believer or non-believer, insider or outsider, how one *experiences* a building is a very personal phenomenon.

Nevertheless, even the most personal spiritual meanings found in a church building exist within a complex web of social, cultural, and religious meanings and relationships, which are manifested in the fabric of the spaces and the material items brought to them. As a result, Christian churches and religious buildings of all sorts can provide students of religion a wealth of information about the beliefs and practices of a religious group as well as the relationships among individuals or groups within a particular religious community. Reading the relationships within the spaces and gaining an awareness of how religious spaces contribute to reifying and maintaining certain relationships and practices adds a new and important dimension to our understanding of religion and religious life.

Notes

NOTES TO CHAPTER 1

1. Mircea Eliade, *The Sacred and the Profane: The Nature of Religion,* trans. Willard R. Trask (New York: Harcourt Brace Jovanovich, 1959), 26.

2. Eliade, *Sacred and the Profane,* 32–47.

3. Jonathan Z. Smith, *To Take Place: Toward Theory in Ritual* (Chicago: University of Chicago Press, 1987), 76–95, 115–16.

4. Smith, *To Take Place,* 56–60.

5. Peter Richardson, *City and Sanctuary: Religion and Architecture in the Roman Near East* (London: SCM Press, 2002), 144–45.

6. David Chidester and Edward T. Linenthal, eds., *American Sacred Space* (Bloomington: Indiana University Press, 1995), 16–20.

7. Among the most popular Catholic pilgrimages is that to Santiago de Compostela in Spain, the home of the sepulcher and relics of the Apostle, St. James the Greater. Contemporary pilgrims walking one of the several *caminos* find the journey itself a powerful spiritual experience. Conversing with other pilgrims, or *peregrinos,* and walking contemplatively over a period of several days affects individuals in profound ways. The route itself, sacralized through repeated usage over centuries of time, illustrates the situational construction of sacred space.

8. For other methods for understanding Christian architecture, see Mark A. Torgerson, *An Architecture of Immanence: Architecture for Worship and Ministry Today* (Grand Rapids, Mich.: William B. Eerdmans Publishing Company, 2007), which examines the categories of immanence and transcendence within Christian space; Richard Kieckhefer, *Theology in Stone: Church Architecture from Byzantium to Berkeley* (New York: Oxford University Press, 2004), which offers helpful categories for examining how Christians

understand their own sacred places; Gretchen Buggeln, *Temples of Grace: The Material Transformation of Connecticut's Churches, 1790–1840* (Hanover: University Press of New England, 2003), which focuses on social and cultural themes embedded in church buildings during the period of the American Early Republic; Paul Eli Ivey, *Prayers in Stone: Christian Science Churches in the United States, 1894–1930* (Urbana: University of Illinois Press, 1999), which examines churches' interactions with civic meanings; Peter Williams, *Houses of God: Region, Religion, and Architecture in the United States* (Urbana: University of Illinois Press, 1997), which presents a regional analysis of religious buildings; and Marilyn J. Chiat, *America's Religious Architecture: Sacred Places for Every Community* (New York: J. Wiley & Sons, 1997), which examines religious buildings within the context of the ethnic groups that constructed them. The author's own *When Church Became Theater: The Transformation of Evangelical Architecture and Worship in Nineteenth-Century America* (New York: Oxford University Press, 2002) also focuses on the connections between the changing views of Protestant creed, code, and culture and the revolutionary new architecture of evangelical churches in the late nineteenth century.

NOTES TO CHAPTER 2

1. This text will use the designations Common Era (c.e.) and Before the Common Era (b.c.e.) to indicate years.

2. Michael White, *Building God's House in the Roman World: An Architectural Adaptation among Pagans, Jews, and Christians* (Baltimore: Johns Hopkins University Press, 1990), 39.

3. See Peter Richardson, *City and Sanctuary: Religion and Architecture in the Roman Near East* (London: SCM Press, 2002), 143–45.

4. Many Roman temples, for instance, do not contain longitudinal axes.

5. White, *Building God's House*, 47–48.

6. White, *Building God's House*, 64–67.

7. The question of the origins of Christian worship has occupied many scholars, many of whom have focused on synagogue practices as its source. Bradshaw counters this view somewhat, pointing out that Jewish practice was itself extremely diverse. He concludes that given the "pluriform nature of primitive Christianity," it is not likely that Christianity is based on a "single, uniform archetype" (37). Paul Bradshaw, *The Search for the Origins of Christian Worship: Sources and Methods for the Study of Early Liturgy* (New York: Oxford University Press, 1992).

8. White, *Building God's House*, 109.

9. Carolyn Osiek and David L. Balch, *Families in the New Testament World: Household and House Churches* (Louisville, Ky.: Westminster John Knox Press, 1997), 200–1.

10. On early Christian meanings of the Eucharist, see Gary Macy, *The Banquet's Wisdom: A Short History of the Theologies of the Lord's Supper*, 2nd ed. (Akron, Ohio: OSL Publications, 2005), 15–18. This book provides an excellent overview of the development of the Lord's Supper through the Reformation.

11. Osiek and Balch, *Families*, 200, 203–4. On the importance of food in contemporary Christian gatherings, see Andrew Brian McGowan, *Ascetic Eucharists: Food and Drink in Early Christian Ritual Meals* (Oxford: Clarendon, 1999); Veronika E. Grimm, *From Feasting to Fasting, the Evolution of a Sin: Attitudes to Food in Late Antiquity* (New York: Routledge, 1996); and Daniel Sack, *Whitebread Protestants: Food and Religion in American Culture* (New York: St. Martin's Press, 2000).

12. Gary Macy, *The Banquet's Wisdom*, 20–27, 32–34.

13. On liturgies of early Christian meetings, see Graydon Snyder, *Ante Pacem: Archaeological Evidence of Church Life before Constantine* (Macon, Ga.: Mercer, 1985), 83; White, *Building God's House*, 107–10; and several essays in *The Study of Liturgy*, ed. Cheslyn Jones, Geoffrey Wainwright, and Edward Yarnold (New York: Oxford University Press, 1978). Responding to assertions that Christians consistently met in the atria of Campanian-style villas, White points out that archeological evidence has revealed a variety of housing types in the Greco-Roman world, and that Christians were therefore not likely to have limited their gatherings to any particular house type.

14. See Elaine Pagels, *The Gnostic Gospels* (New York: Vintage Books, 1989 [1979]), 16, in which she discusses the Letter of Peter to Philip.

15. This restriction regarding the Mass is not to say that Catholics do not worship outdoors. Roman Catholics have celebrated a wide array of saints' days with processionals and outdoor activities, and services to bless fields during the spring; other outdoor blessings also have been quite common.

16. See Bradshaw, *Search for the Origins*, 30–40.

17. See Osiek and Balch, *Families*, 6–11.

18. Osiek and Balch, *Families*, 16, 34, 41.

19. Osiek and Balch, *Families*, 14.

20. Osiek and Balch, *Families*, 44–45.

21. Osiek and Balch, *Families*, 18.

22. It should be noted that the terms "Christian" and "Christianity" are anachronistic in this period, as the movement had not yet separated from Judaism. I use the terms, nevertheless, for convenience.

23. Whether a Tituli Prisca actually existed in not known.

24. Calvin J. Roetzel, *Paul: The Man and the Myth* (Columbia: University of South Carolina Press, 1998), 99; White, *Building God's House*, 105–6.

25. Osiek and Balch, *Families*, 208.

26. White, *Building God's House*, 110.

27. Osiek and Balch argue that the Christian communal meal was a modification of the Roman symposium, a communal meal characterized by eating food brought by the guests, a sacrifice to the gods, the removal of the tables once all had eaten, and toasting, conversation, debate, singing, and entertainment over abundant wine (*Families*, 193–201).

28. White, *Building God's House*, 3.

29. Richard Krautheimer, *Early Christian and Byzantine Architecture*, 4th ed. (London: Penguin Books, 1986), 24. The quotation from Acts is from the Revised Standard Version.

30. Krautheimer, *Early Christian and Byzantine Architecture*, 24. For an alternative interpretation, see Richard Sennett, *Flesh and Stone: The Body and the City in Western Civilization* (New York: Norton, 1994), 137. Sennett argues that seating in the triclinium demonstrated the equality of those gathered.

31. Krautheimer, *Early Christian and Byzantine Architecture*, 24; White, *Building God's House*, 103–10. White asserts that similar domestic meeting places were common among Roman religious groups, including Mithraists and Jews.

32. Snyder, *Ante Pacem*, 69; White, *Building God's House*, 120. White places the date of the renovation of the building in Dura-Europos into a domus ecclesiae between 240 and 41 C.E.

33. White points out that these buildings have been erroneously assumed to constitute a building type consciously replicated for Christian use. Instead, he argues that "of the cases known from archaeological remains no two are quite alike" (*Building God's House*, 24), precisely because of the diversity in Roman housing types. See also J. B. Ward-Perkins, *Studies in Roman and Early Christian Architecture* (London: Pindar Press, 1994), 457–59.

34. White argues that the adaptation of houses for religious use was particularly dependent upon local social situations and relationships (*Building God's House*, 107–9, 114–23).

35. White, *Building God's House*, 119–20. See also Snyder, *Ante Pacem*, 83, on the transformation of the agape meal into a symbolic liturgy.

36. The offertory consisting of a collection of alms referred to here should not be confused with the offertory as an element of the Mass in which the celebrant offers the bread and wine to God.

37. On the Christian building at Dura-Europos, see White, *Building God's House*, 120–23; Snyder, *Ante Pacem*, 68–71. The measurements and occupant figures are given by Snyder, *Building God's House*, 70.

38. To those who study religious spaces, finding the iconography of a previous occupying group within a religious building is not uncommon, for religious spaces are frequently bought and sold and remodeling may take some time, particularly if resources are sparse. In other cases, new groups purposely maintain an earlier groups' iconography as a gesture of respect or historical interest. Examples include Greater New Hope Baptist Church in Washington, D.C., and Pilgrim Baptist Church in Chicago. Both buildings were built as synagogues by Jewish congregations (Washington Hebrew Congregation and Kehilath Anshe Ma'ariv Temple, respectively) and were purchased by their respective Baptist congregations. Both retained Jewish symbols within their auditoriums, including a large Star of David in a center skylight in the former and in a frieze in the latter.

39. Snyder, *Ante Pacem*, 70.

40. It should be noted that other models of religious power existed during these early centuries. The followers of the Gnostic Valentius, for instance, believed that the power to serve as leaders rested within any initiated believer (including women) and so drew lots to select individuals to serve as bishop, priest, and prophet at each service. Pagels, *Gnostic Gospels*, 41.

41. White, *Building God's House*, 124. The tribunal was not exclusively reserved for clergy. Members of different orders within the church also occupied the tribunal, and accommodation for certain government officials is also mentioned in some texts. The tribunal, a site for leadership and authority, thus accommodated both religious and civil leaders. The author wishes to thank the anonymous reader of the manuscript for this information.

42. Krautheimer, *Early Christian and Byzantine Architecture*, 26.

43. Krautheimer, *Early Christian and Byzantine Architecture*, 26.

44. See Snyder, *Ante Pacem*, 71. For a complete inventory and description of the domus ecclesiae at Dura-Europos, see Carl H. Kraeling, *The Christian Building*, Part II of *The Excavations at Dura-Europos*, ed. C. Bradford Welles (New Haven: Dura-Europos Publications, 1967).

45. Cf. Erwin R. Goodenough, *Jewish Symbols in the Greco-Roman Period*, vol. 11, *Symbolism in the Dura Synagogue* (New York: Pantheon Books and the Bollinger Foundation, 1964), plates II and III; and C. Bradford Welles, *The Christian Building* (New Haven: Dura-Europos Publications, 1967), plate XXIV. For a full description of the Dura synagogue, see Erwin R. Goodenough, *Jewish Symbols in the Greco-Roman Period*, vol. 12, *Summary and Conclusion* (New York: Pantheon Books and the Bollinger Foundation, 1965), 158–83.

46. White, *Building God's House*, 121–22.

47. White, *Building God's House*, 122. It is interesting to note that the inclusion of dedicated dining facilities (dining rooms and kitchens) in Christian churches would not emerge until the late nineteenth century and even then was controversial. See Jeanne Halgren Kilde, *When Church Became Theater: The Transformation of Evangelical Architecture and Worship in Nineteenth-Century America* (New York: Oxford University Press, 2002), 161–63.

48. See Krautheimer, *Early Christian and Byzantine Architecture*, 28–29, 42–43; and White, *Building God's House*, 127–39.

49. White, *Building God's House*, 131, 137. See also Ward-Perkins, *Studies in Roman and Early Christian Architecture*, 458–62.

50. The Latin terms for these kinds of buildings (again, not to be considered a distinct, replicated building type as such) foster some confusion for those interested in the interior/exterior character of the buildings. Whereas the term *aula ecclesiae* or "hall of the church" places the interior (or plan) descriptor clearly in the adjectival position, the term *domus ecclesiae* or "house of the church" more ambiguously conflates interior and exterior, plan and envelope. As White emphasizes, however, both kinds of buildings featured domestic exteriors (*Building God's House*, 129).

51. Certainly the aula ecclesiae exterior distinguished itself in some fashion from the surrounding landscape. Although neighboring residents may well have known the location of domus ecclesiae by information carried word or mouth or by witnessing the comings and goings of worshippers, even a stranger to a neighborhood likely could have identified an aula ecclesiae immediately. Yet archeological evidence is apparently silent on the architectural cues that accomplished this.

52. Osiek and Balch, *Families*, 58–60.

53. Osiek and Balch, *Families*, 116–17.

54. See Ross Shepard Kraemer and Mary Rose D'Angelo, eds., *Women and Christian Origins* (New York: Oxford University Press, 1999).

55. Thomas F. Mathews, *The Early Churches of Constantinople: Architecture and Liturgy* (University Park: Pennsylvania State University Press, 1971), 12. Mathews, assessing the admittedly sparse evidence concerning the locations occupied by women and catechumens in Early Byzantine churches, finds some evidence that women were segregated from men. Although the data are not fully compelling, it also appears that in Byzantine churches galleries were sometimes reserved for women. By the Middle Byzantine period, however, women seem to have been relegated to the north aisles. There is greater evidence suggesting that catechumens were relegated to the galleries (117–33; see also Krautheimer, *Early Christian and Byzantine Architecture*, 43–45).

56. Snyder, *Ante Pacem*, 83.

57. On catacombs, see Snyder, *Ante Pacem*, 83–85; and Krautheimer, *Early Christian and Byzantine Architecture*, 30–31.

58. Krautheimer, *Early Christian and Byzantine Architecture*, 29–37; Ward-Perkins, *Studies in Roman and Early Christian Architecture*, 489–93, 500–2. Some archeological debate exists on just how dependent Christian martyria were on pagan precedents. Grabar's assertion that all martyria derive from Roman mausolea has been disputed. Although it is likely that these centralized-plan buildings were modeled at least to some extent on pagan mausolea because of their similar memorializing function, archaeological evidence has not fully proven a direction connection. White's thesis regarding the processes of adaptation of architectural spaces could likely be applied here. See "Imperial Mausolea and Their Possible Influence on Early Christian Central-Plan Buildings" in Ward-Perkins, *Studies in Roman and Early Christian Architecture*. See also Snyder, *Ante Pacem*, 115; and André Grabar, *Martyrium: Recherches sur le culte des reliques et l'art Chrétien antique*, 2 vols. (Paris: Collège de France), 1946. For Christians, who by the latter half of the fourth century searched for a plan for worship *not* based on pagan architectural forms, the fact that funeral rites were not considered in the realm of pagan religion (Krautheimer, *Early Christian and Byzantine Architecture*, 36) may have played a role in the adoption of central plans for some monumental churches.

59. On these early memorial churches, see Krautheimer, *Early Christian and Byzantine Architecture*, 73–75; the quotation is on page 75. See also Jonathan Z. Smith, *To Take Place: Toward Theory in Ritual* (Chicago: University of Chicago Press, 1987), 74–86. Krautheimer notes that of Constantine's martyria, only St. Peter's (initially a transept attached as a headpiece to a basilica) actually enclosed the shrine of a martyr (59); the rest memorialized hierophanies—appearances of Christ or other supernaturally infused events. Another important self-sufficient martyrium was the Church of the Holy Apostles (Apostoleion), built in the fourth century in Constantinople. This cross-shaped martyrium housed Constantine's sarcophagus for a time, situated at the center of a circle of twelve columns purported to represent the twelve apostles, symbolically including the emperor as the thirteenth. The sarcophagus was later moved, but the building was often copied (Krautheimer, 69–70).

60. Snyder, *Ante Pacem*, 83. This is not to say that clerical power did not extend to such spaces. Peter Brown holds that the episcopate supported the cult of the dead precisely because it was easier to control a dead martyr than a living holy person. See Peter Brown, *The Cult of the Saints: Its Rise and Function in Latin Christianity* (Chicago: University of Chicago Press, 1981).

61. Peter Brown, *Cult of the Saints*, 11. Brown is quoting *Barsanuphe et Jean: Correspondence 433*, trans. L. Regnault and P. Lamaire (Solesmes: Abbaye de Solesmes, 1971), 297–98.

NOTES TO CHAPTER 3

1. This is not to say that Christianity was adopted as the official religion of the Empire, but rather that it was approved as a legally existing religion alongside many others.

2. Deno John Geanakoplos, "Church Building and 'Caesaropapism,' A.D. 312–565," *Greek, Roman and Byzantine Studies* 7 (Summer 1966): 167–86. The quotation appears on p. 167. See also Gregory T. Armstrong, "Imperial Church Building and Church-State Relations, A.D. 313–363," *Church History* 36 (March 1967): 3–17.

3. Jonathan Z. Smith, *To Take Place: Toward Theory in Ritual* (Chicago: University of Chicago Press, 1987), 75; Richard Krautheimer, *Early Christian and Byzantine Architecture*, 4th ed. (London: Penguin Books, 1986), 39–41, 46–48. See also Richard Krautheimer, "The Constantinia Basilica," *Dumbarton Oaks Papers* 21 (1967): 117–40.

4. Smith, *To Take Place*, 75–76, drawing on Krautheimer, *Early Christian and Byzantine Architecture* and "Constantinian Basilica"; J. B. Ward-Perkins, "Constantine and the Original of the Christian Basilica," *Papers of the British School at Rome* 22 (1954): 69–90; and M. H. Shepherd, Jr., "The Earliest Christian Basilicas," *Yearbook of Liturgical Studies* 7 (1966): 73–86.

5. W. Telfer, "Constantine's Holy Land Plan," in *Studia Patristica*, eds. Kurt Aland and F. L. Cross, vol. 1 (Berlin: Akademie-Verlag 1957), 697.

6. Scholars continue to debate whether this was the actual site of Jesus's tomb. Many, including Smith, argue that it is unlikely that memory of the exact site would have been retained three centuries after the event. Others, including Biddle, argue that preserving history through oral means was an important skill among people who were mostly illiterate and that thus it is likely that people did maintain a memory of the holy location. Moreover, Biddle argues that it is also quite possible that graffiti carved on the tomb by many early pilgrims to the site would have indicated to Constantine that he had found the correct location. See Smith, *To Take Place*, 78–83; and Martin Biddle, "The History of the Church of the Holy Sepulchre," in Martin Biddle, et al, *The Church of the Holy Sepulchre* (New York: Rizzoli, 2000), 52–55.

7. This argument is made by Gregory T. Armstrong, "Imperial Church Building in the Holy Land in the Fourth Century," *The Biblical Archaeologist* 30 (September 1967): 97.

8. Peter Richardson, *City and Sanctuary: Religion and Architecture in the Roman Near East* (London: SCM Press, 2002), 124.

9. For an overview of Gnosticism, orthodoxy, and the politics of Christology, see Elaine Pagels, *The Gnostic Gospels* (New York: Vintage Books, 1979), 3–27; and Calvin Roetzel, "Paul in the Second Century," *The Cambridge Companion to St. Paul,* ed. James D. G. Dunn, 227–41 (Cambridge: Cambidge University Press, 2003). On Arianism, see R. P. C. Hanson, *The Search for the Christian Doctrine of God: The Arian Controversy, 318–381* (Edinburgh: T. & T. Clark, 1988), 5–18; on Constantine, the Council of Nicea, and the Nicene Creed, see Hanson, 159–70.

10. The relevant portion of the Nicene Creed reads as follows: "I believe . . . in one Lord Jesus Christ, the only-begotten Son of God, Begotten of his Father before all worlds, God of God, Light of Light, Very God of very God, Begotten, not made, Being of one substance with the Father . . . ."

11. The term *hierophany* was coined by Mircea Eliade.

12. In yet another alternative story, Krautheimer relates that of a Roman woman, Pomoenia, who erected a building known as the Imbomon on the Mount of Olives "to commemorate the site from which Christ rose of Heaven." Krautheimer, *Early Christian and Byzantine Architecture* (75). Richardson discusses the changing fabric of Jerusalem and the impact of excessive church building in the fourth century in *City and Sanctuary*, 153–54.

13. Plans in Warren Sanderson, *Early Christian Buildings, 300–600* (Champlain, NY: Astrion, 1993), 443.

14. Pudenziana and Prassede, daughters of the Roman senator Pudens, were baptized by Peter during his stay in their father's home.

15. On the many legends that passed into "histories" of Constantine, see Sam Lieu, "Constantine Byzantinus: The Anonymous *Life of Constantine"* in *From Constantine to Julian: Pagan and Byzantine Views,* eds. Samuel N. C. Lieu and Dominic Montserrat (New York: Routledge, 1996), 101–6.

16. Krautheimer, "The Constantinian Basilica," 122. Ward-Perkins traces the evolving use of the term *basilica* in his 1954 essay "Constantine and the Origins of the Christian Basilica," reprinted in his *Studies in Roman and Early Christian Architecture* (447–68). Demonstrating the flexibility of the term, Ward-Perkins points out that even the circular San Vitale at Ravenna, a centrally planned building, was referred to as a basilica (456). See also Krautheimer, *Early Christian and Byzantine Architecture, 41–43.*

17. Krautheimer, "The Constantinian Basilica," 129, and *Early Christian and Byzantine Architecture, 41–43.* See also Smith, *To Take Place,* 75.

18. Krautheimer, "The Constantinian Basilica," 123.

19. By the early medieval period, rules for this approach would be instituted, particularly as the display of a cross or crucifix became common in churches, which also helped mark the significance of the chancel. To make the sign of the cross, to kneel, to prostrate one's self during approach, all took on ritual significance, expressing devotion and focusing the worshipper's attention during the journey toward the altar.

20. The processional description here follows Thomas Mathews, *The Early Churches of Constantinople: Architecture and Liturgy* (University Park: Pennsylvania State University Press, 1971), 178–79. Mainstone's description of Byzantine practices

includes some variations, including his claim that the Gospel carried by a deacon would precede all into the church. See Rowland J. Mainstone, *Hagia Sophia: Architecture, Structure and Liturgy of Justinian's Great Church* (New York: Thames and Hudson, 1988), 227.

21. In some regions, it seems to have been customary to exclude lay worshippers from the nave, relegating them to the aisles only.

22. For a discussion of the sometimes competing, sometimes complementary imperial and religious meaning systems, see Smith, *To Take Place*, 80–81.

23. Mainstone argues that in Hagia Sophia, the emperor's loge was likely shielded from public view by a screen. See his *Hagia Sophia*, 225–26.

24. On tensions between clerical and imperial power, see Smith, *To Take Place*, 47–65.

25. Mathews, *Early Churches of Constantinople*, 117–33; Krautheimer, *Early Christian and Byzantine Architecture*, 39–40; Mainstone, *Hagia Sophia*, 226–27. The catechumenate gradually dissolved as mass conversion to Christianity took place.

26. Krautheimer, *Early Christian and Byzantine Architecture*, 40.

27. Ibid.

28. On the hierarchy-naturalizing process within religious space, see Smith, *To Take Place*, 47–73.

29. In neither Jewish nor Roman temples were laity allowed to enter the main worship areas.

30. Mathews, *Early Churches*, 177.

31. Archaeological details of the original building are sketchy. For a full analysis of what remains and what archaeologists have reconstructed from those remains, see Krautheimer, *Early Christian and Byzantine Architecture*, 60–63.

32. See Krautheimer, *Early Christian and Byzantine Architecture*, 32–36, 51.

33. Mainstone, *Hagia Sophia*, 37.

34. For an excellent description and analysis of this space, see Marvin Trachtenberg and Isabelle Hyman, *Architecture: From Prehistory to Postmodernity*, 2nd ed. (New York: Harry N. Abrams, 1986), 173–75. See also Mainstone, *Hagia Sophia*, 37.

35. Procopius I, 54–61. As quoted in Mainstone, *Hagia Sophia*, 10. See also Robert S. Nelson, *Hagia Sophia, 1850–1950: Holy Wisdom, Modern Monument* (Chicago: University of Chicago Press, 2004), 1–28.

36. As quoted in Mainstone, *Hagia Sophia*, 10

37. Trachtenberg and Hyman, *Architecture*, 180.

38. Trachtenberg and Hyman, *Architecture*, 175–76.

39. For examples, see Magnus Backes and Regine Dölling, *Art of the Dark Ages* (New York: Harry N. Abrams, 1969), 92–94.

40. On the Byzantine experimentation, see Trachtenberg and Hyman, *Architecture*, 179–83.

41. On the growth of saints' cults, see Peter Brown, *The Cult of the Saints: Its Rise and Function in Latin Christianity* (Chicago: University of Chicago Press, 1981).

42. On Orthodox liturgy and churches, see John Bines, *An Introduction to the Christian Orthodox Churches* (Cambridge, England: Cambridge University Press,

2002), 41–59; Hans-Joachim Schulz, *The Byzantine Liturgy: Symbolic Structure and Faith Expression*, trans. Matthew J. O'Connell (New York: Pueblo Publishing Company, 1986 [1980]); and J. M. Hussey, *The Orthodox Church in the Byzantine Empire* (Oxford: Clarendon Press, 1986).

NOTES TO CHAPTER 4

1. *Romanesque*, like *Gothic*, is a term coined in the eighteenth century to describe the architecture of the historical period.

2. F. H. Crossley, *The English Abbey* (London: B.T. Batsford, Ltd., 1962), 15.

3. If the abbey contained a cathedral and bishop's chair, the term *prior* was substituted for *abbot* (leaving the bishop in the position of abbot).

4. On the Abbey of Montecassino, see http://www.officine.it/montecassino/ storia_e/abbazia.htm.

5. Gary Macy, *The Banquet's Wisdom: A Short History of the Theologies of the Lord's Supper* (New York: Paulist Press, 1992), 93.

6. Rosamund McKitterick, *The Frankish Church and the Carolingian Reforms: 789–895* (London, 1977), 154. For an excellent overview of changing theological understandings of liturgy and the Mass, see Macy, *The Banquet's Wisdom*.

7. Macy, *The Banquet's Wisdom*, 74.

8. Although the term *cathedral* technically means a church designated as the home of a bishop (and thus contains his throne or *cathedra*, usually placed next to the high altar), it is frequently used to designate any large medieval church. I use the term *great church* to avoid this usage problem.

9. Otto von Simson, *The Gothic Cathedral: Origins of Gothic Architecture and Medieval Concept of Order*, 3rd ed. (Princeton: Princeton University Press, 1988), 8; James Snyder, *Medieval Art: Painting, Sculpture, Architecture, 4th–14th Century* (New York: H. N. Abrams, Inc., 1989), 40; Christopher Wilson, *The Gothic Cathedral: The Architecture of the Great Church, 1130–1530* (New York: Thames and Hudson, 1990), 8; Paul Frankl, *Gothic Architecture* (Baltimore: Penguin Books, 1962), 232–35.

10. Georges Duby, *The Age of Cathedrals: Art and Society, 980–1420*, trans. Eleanor Leveiux and Barbara Thompson (Chicago: University of Chicago Press, 1981), 100–1, quoting from Suger.

11. Wilson, *Gothic Cathedral*, 10. On the manipulation of light as a trope for divine power, see von Simson, *Gothic Cathedral*, 50–55, and Duby, *Age of Cathedrals*, 97–135.

12. On the use of the cross as a symbol during the early Christian period, see Graydon F. Snyder, *Ante Pacem: Archaeological Evidence of Church Life Before Constantine* (Macon, Ga.: Mercer University Press, 1985), 26–29.

13. The term *rood* comes from the Anglo-Saxon term *rod* or *rode*, meaning *cross*. The adjective was added to many elements in the medieval church, including the rood arch, the arch separating the chancel from the nave. The online *Catholic Encyclopedia* has an excellent entry for *rood screen*, http://www.newadvent.org/cathen/ 13181a.htm (accessed June 16, 2003).

14. An oil painting by the Master of St. Giles of *The Mass of Saint Giles* (c. 1500), housed in the London National Gallery, depicts the Saint-Denis sanctuary, complete with curtains.

15. Eamon Duffy, *The Stripping of the Altars: Traditional Religion in England, c. 1400–c. 1580* (New Haven: Yale University Press, 1992), 91.

16. Macy, *The Banquet's Wisdom*, 158–59.

17. Macy, *The Banquet's Wisdom*, 91–92.

18. Macy, *The Banquet's Wisdom*, 94.

19. Most medieval Christians took communion only once a year, on Easter Sunday. Duffy argues that during some services, the priest would offer the plate on which the Host lay and the lip of the chalice to congregants to kiss as a substitute for communion, and at the end of some masses, a loaf of bread was cut up and distributed, again, as a communion substitute (Duffy, *Stripping of the Altars*, 124–25). On the development of the medieval Mass, see Macy, *The Banquet's Wisdom*, 84–95; Joseph A. Jungmann, *The Mass of the Roman Rite: Its Origins and Development*, rev. ed. Charles K. Riepe, trans. Francis A. Brunner (London: Burns and Oates, 1959), 81–96; and Francois Amiot, *History of the Mass* (New York: Hawthorne Books, 1959).

20. Duffy, *Stripping of the Altars*, 111.

21. The phrase is Jungmann's, *Mass of the Roman Rite*, 62.

22. Duffy, *Stripping of the Altars*, 112. In those churches in which a veil was used to conceal the altar, it was lifted as the Host was lifted.

23. On the meaning of viewing the elevated Host, see Jungmann, *Mass of the Roman Rite*, 90–91, and Macy, *Banquet's Wisdom*, 84–92.

24. Pamela Sheingorn, " 'No Sepulchre on Good Friday': The Impact of the Reformation on the Easter Rites in England," in *Iconoclasm vs. Art and Drama*, eds. Clifford Davidson and Ann Eljenholm Nichols (Kalamazoo, Mich.: Medieval Institute Publications, Western Michigan University, 1989), 145–63, particularly 146. See also Pamela Sheingorn, *The Easter Sepulchre in England* (Kalamazoo, Mich.: Medieval Institute Publications, 1977).

25. Duffy, *Stripping of the Altars*, 91–130, particularly 109–10.

26. William Anderson and Clive Hicks, *The Rise of the Gothic* (Salem, N.H.: Salem House, 1985), 167.

27. The holy search is, of course, apparent in many medieval forms, including the search for the grail.

28. Duby explains that "in twelfth-century France, it was still considered a mortal sin to make a profit through trading" and that spending profits on ecclesiastical items replaced the giving of alms during the period. Kings gave most lavishly of all, but other landowners, tradesmen, and guilds were also willing to give contributions of money and labor to the church, which might otherwise have gone to the poor. Duby, *Age of Cathedrals*, 109–12.

29. Paul Binsky, *Westminster Abbey and the Plantagenet: Kingship and the Representation of Power, 1200–1400* (New Haven: Yale University Press, 1995), 5.

30. Frankl, *Gothic Architecture*, 227.

31. On patronage and use of side altars, see Duffy, *Stripping of the Altars*, 112–114. In English great churches, altars in the nave were hidden during use by parclose screens. See G. W. O. Addleshaw and Frederick Etchells, *The Architectural Setting of Anglican Worship* (London: Faber and Faber, 1948), 17–18. In England, chantry societies developed, charged with the decoration of the main building, though clergy retained control over the sanctuary. This situation not only enhanced competition but also led to mixtures of divergent tastes. The author thanks Dr. Michael Driscoll for bringing this information to her attention.

32. Separating clergy from laity, Duffy states that laity "controlled, often indeed owned these altars" (*Stripping of the Altars*, 114). I would argue that what is most clear is that social power, whether wielded by clergy or laity, informs these altars. Such power did allow poorer congregants access to the Mass, however, providing locations for innumerable "low" masses, or simplified masses said only by the priest aided by a server, during the week (112).

33. Wilson, *Gothic Cathedral*, 223.

34. Albert Storme, *The Way of the Cross: A Historical Sketch*, trans. 2nd rev. ed. Kieran Dunlop (Jerusalem: Franciscan Printing Press, 1976), 80.

35. Note the similarities between this mid-twelfth-century portal and the sanctuary painting in the Church of St. Pudenziana in Rome (Chapter 3), which was built around 400.

36. Moreover, murals depicting Christ in majesty with his heavenly court encouraged worshippers toward a specifically otherworldly understanding of divinity. On the heuristic function of church murals, see Snyder, *Medieval Art*, 48; von Simson, *Gothic Cathedral*, 8; Wilson, *Gothic Cathedral*, 9.

37. On Christian pilgrimage, see David Hunt, "Space and Time Transcended: The Beginnings of Christian Pilgrimage," in *The Sense of the Sacramental: Movement and Measure in Art and Music, Place and Time*, eds. David Brown and Ann Loades (London: Society for Promoting Christian Knowledge, 1995), 59–77. On the early pilgrimage through Jerusalem, see Storme, *Way of the Cross*.

38. On San Clemente, see Snyder, *Medieval Art*, 317–19. Of course, worshippers were forbidden entry into the chancel and thus could not "climb the tree" completely.

39. Abbot Suger, who directed the construction of St. Denis, selected its inscriptions. Wilson, *Gothic Cathedral*, 33.

40. Here I am indebted to Richard Schneider, "The Building as Text(s): Why Did Suger Mark His Church with Inscriptions?" Paper presented at meeting of American Society for Church History, Oberlin, Ohio, March 25, 1994. On spiritual pilgrimage and the Stations of the Cross, see Storme, *Way of the Cross*; see also Herbert Thurston, *The Stations of the Cross: An Account of Their History and Devotional Purpose* (New York: Benziger Bros. and London: Burns and Oates, 1906). Another manifestation of the actor-worshipper came with the construction of the labyrinth on the floor of Chartres Cathedral in the thirteenth century. See Anne Prache, *Chartres Cathedral: Image of the Heavenly Jerusalem*, trans. Janice Abbott (Paris: Caisse Nationale des Monuments Historiques et des Sites, 1993), 17, 76–77.

41. Historians cite John Van Paeschen's (John Pascha's) popular book *The Spiritual Pilgrimage of Hierusalem, containing three hundred sixtie five dayes Jorney,* published in 1563 (English translation 1630), as best known among the earliest attempts to formalize several "stations." See Storme, *Way of the Cross,* 119–24, and Thurston, *Stations of the Cross,* 79–95. On labyrinths, see Prache, *Chartres Cathedral,* 76–77.

42. Eva Valebrokk and Thomas Theiis-Evensen, *Norway's Stave Churches: Architecture, History and Legends,* trans. Ann Clay Zwick (n.p.: Boksenteret, n.d.), 10–11.

NOTES TO CHAPTER 5

1. Howard Clark Kee et al., *Christianity: A Social and Cultural History,* 2nd ed. (Upper Saddle River, N.J.: Prentice Hall, 1998), 255. For an excellent study of the meaning and role of death in medieval Christianity, see Eamon Duffy, *The Stripping of the Altars: Traditional Religion in England, 1400–1580,* 2nd ed. (New Haven, Conn.: Yale University Press, 2005), 301–37.

2. On purgatory, see Duffy, *Stripping of the Altars,* 338–54; and Jacques Le Goff, *The Birth of Purgatory,* trans. Arthur Goldhammer (Chicago: University of Chicago Press, 1984).

3. On these chantries, see http://www.stgeorges-windsor.org/tour/tour_north.asp.

4. On growing lay influence, see R. N. Swanson, "The Pre-Reformation Church," in *The Reformation World,* ed. Andrew Pettegree (London: Routledge, 2000), 15–16.

5. David Chidester, *Christianity: A Global History* (San Francisco: HarperSanFranciso, 2000), 298. On the classical revival of the Renaissance, see pp. 293–301.

6. The Italian classicists of this period operated on incomplete or incorrect information about the ancient world. In many cases, what they understood as ancient was simply a few hundred years old. See Marvin Trachtenberg and Isabella Hyman, *Architecture: From Prehistory to Postmodernity,* 2nd ed. (New York: Harry N. Abrams, 2002), 283–84.

7. L. B. Alberti, *Ten Books on Architecture,* English ed. (London, 1755; reprint London, 1955), 136. As quoted in Christian Norberg-Schulz, *Baroque Architecture* (New York: Harry N. Abrams, 1971), 13.

8. Trachtenberg and Hyman, *Architecture,* 292.

9. On the adoption of classical forms during the fifteenth century, see Vernon Hyde Minor, *Baroque and Rococo Art and Culture* (New York: Harry N. Abrams, 1999), 75–90.

10. Trachtenberg and Hyman, *Architecture,* 296.

11. See Nathan D. Mitchell, "Reforms, Protestant and Catholic," in *The Oxford History of Christian Worship,* eds. Geoffrey Wainwright and Karen B. Westerfield Tucker (New York: Oxford University Press, 2006), 342; James F. White, *Roman Catholic Worship: Trent to Today,* 2nd. ed. (Collegeville, Minn.: Liturgical Press, 2003), 8, 14–15.

12. See Gary Macy, *The Banquet's Wisdom: A Short History of the Theologies of the Lord's Supper*, 2nd ed. (Akron, Ohio: OSL Publications, 2005), 219–26.

13. Mitchell, "Reforms," 335.

14. White, *Roman Catholic Worship*, 12.

15. White, *Roman Catholic Worship*, 15.

16. White, *Roman Catholic Worship*, 15.

17. White, *Roman Catholic Worship*, 4–5, quoting Borromeo as quoted in Evelyn Carole Voelker, "Charles Borromeo's *Instructiones Fabricae et Supellectilis Ecclesiasticae, 1577:* A Translation with Commentary and Analysis," (Ph.D. diss., Syracuse University, 1977), 297.

18. White, *Roman Catholic Worship*, 5.

19. Macy, *The Banquet's Wisdom*, 242.

20. Mitchell, "Reforms," 343.

21. Minor, *Baroque and Rococo Art and Culture*, 78, quoting Voelker, "Charles Borromeo's *Instructiones*," 51–2, 63.

22. For an excellent discussion of Italian Baroque churches—cruciform, centrally planned, and elongated—see Christian Norberg-Schulz, *Baroque Architecture* (New York: Rizzoli, 1986), 22–23, 105–82.

23. Minor, *Baroque and Rococo Art and Culture*, 76.

24. Norberg-Schultz, *Baroque Architecture*, 105.

25. See Sarah McPhee, *Bernini and the Bell Towers: Architecture and Politics at the Vatican* (New Haven, Conn.: Yale University Press, 2002).

26. Norberg-Schultz, *Baroque Architecture*, 13.

27. White, *Roman Catholic Worship*, 20–21.

28. Norberg-Schultz, *Baroque Architecture*, 174.

29. Excellent descriptions and illustrations appear in Trachtenberg and Hyman, *Architecture*, 317–17, 327–28.

30. Norberg-Schultz, *Baroque Architecture*, 13.

31. James McEvoy, "The Catholic Eye, The Protestant Ear, and the Age of the Baroque," *Neue Zeitschrift für Systematische Theologie und Religionsphilosophie*, 26 (1984), 182–83.

32. Andrea Palladio, *I Quattro libri dell'Architecttura* (Venice, 1570), English edition (London: Isaac Ware, 1738), n.p. as quoted in Norberg-Schulz *Baroque Architecture*, 13.

33. Norberg-Schulz, *Baroque Architecture*, 13.

34. McEvoy, "Catholic Eye," 180–82.

35. On church music during the Mass, from Gregorian chant to post-Tridentine liturgical music, see Josef Jungmann, *The Mass of the Roman Rite*, trans. F. A. Brunner, 2 vols. (New York: Benziger, 1955), 1:145–50.

36. James McEvoy, "Catholic Eye," 177–94. The quotation appears on page 179.

37. Scholars have questioned whether Luther actually did nail his list to the cathedral door. Luther's contemporary Melanchthon suggests he did not. See Albrecht Beutel, "Luther's Life," trans. Katarina Gustavs, in *The Cambridge Companion to Martin Luther*, ed. Donald K. McKim (Cambridge, Cambridge University Press, 2003),

8–9. See also Dairmaid MacCulloch, *The Reformation* (New York: Viking, 2003), 119. Among those who argue that he most likely did nail the list to the door is Carl Truman, who claims that because posting ideas for debate on the church door was common practice, Luther may well have done so, but the act "indicated no real significance in and of itself." See his "Luther and the Reformation in Germany," in *The Reformation World* (London: Routledge, 2000), 80. In any event, there is no doubt that the image of Luther doing this has carried immense symbolic significance for Protestants for centuries.

38. Martin Luther, *D. Martin Luthers Werke: Kritische Gesamtausgaber [Schriften]* (Weimar, Germany: H. Böhlau, 1883–1993), 51:517. As quoted in Fred W. Meuser, "Luther as Preacher of the Word of God," in *The Cambridge Companion to Martin Luther*, ed. Donald K. McKim (Cambridge: Cambridge University Press, 2003), 136.

39. Meuser, "Luther as Preacher," 136.

40. For a more traditional interpretation of this building, see Andrew Spicer, "Architecture," in *The Reformation World*, ed. by Andrew Pettegree (London: Routledge, 2000), 509. Spicer asserts that the pulpit does in fact dominate this room because it is more elaborately ornamented than the altar in the east end. I disagree with this interpretation on the basis that the spatial dynamics counter the mid-nave focus, forcing the attention of the visitor to the east end.

41. Macy, *The Banquet's Wisdom*, 206–7.

42. K. E. O. Fritsch, *Der Kirchenbau des Protestismus von der Reformation bis zur Gegenwart/Herausgegeben von der Vereinigung Berliner Architekten* (Berlin: Ernst Toeche, 1893), 34–35. This arrangement echoed that of the much earlier Sainte-Chapelle in Paris.

43. Two excellent works on early Calvinist churches are Hélène Guicharnaud, "An Introduction to the Architecture of Protestant Temples Constructed in France before the Revocation of the Edict of Nantes," and Raymond A. Mentzer, Jr., "The Reformed Churches of France and the Visual Arts," both in *Seeing Beyond the Word: Visual Arts and the Calvinist Tradition*, ed. Paul Corby Finney (Grand Rapids, Mich.: William B. Eerdmans, 1999). The following discussion draws substantially upon these essays.

44. Mentzer, "Reformed Churches," 205, quoting G. W. O. Addleshaw and Frederick Etchells, *The Architectural Setting of Anglican Worship* (London: Faber and Faber, 1948), 245, quoting Martin Bucer, *Sripta Anglicana fere omnia . . . . Collecta . . .* (Basel, 1577), 457.

45. See Anthony Blunt, *Art and Architecture in France, 1500 to 1700* (New York: Penguin Books, 1973), 13–20.

46. Blunt, *Art and Architecture*, 73.

47. On Anet chapel, see Blunt, *Art and Architecture*, 89–91.

48. On other forms of bodily discipline emerging during the period, see Michel Foucault, *Discipline and Punish: The Birth of the Prison*, trans. Alan Sheridan (New York: Vintage, 1979). On audiences as corporate bodies, see Rudolf Arnheim, *The Dynamics of Architectural Form* (Berkeley: University of California Press, 1977), 269.

49. On Calvinist ornamentation, see several articles in *Seeing Beyond the Word: Visual Arts and the Calvinist Tradition,* ed. Paul Corby Finney (Grand Rapids, Mich.: William B. Eerdmans, 1999).

50. Spicer, "Architecture," 515.

51. Mentzer, "Reformed Churches," 213–14.

52. Helmar Junghans, "Luther's Wittenberg," trans. Katharina Gustavs, in *The Cambridge Companion to Martin Luther,* 25.

53. Junghans, "Luther's Wittenberg," 29; Joseph Leo Koerner, *The Reformation of the Image* (Chicago: University of Chicago Press, 2004), 75–76.

54. See Stanford E. Lehmberg, *The Reformation of Cathedrals: Cathedrals in English Society, 1485–1603* (Princeton, N.J.: Princeton University Press, 1988), 2, 38–66.

55. On Anglican worship, see Horton Davies, *Worship and Theology in England: From Cranmer to Baxter and Fox, 1534–1690* (Grand Rapids, Mich.: William B. Eerdmans, 1996; rpt. 1970), 165–73.

NOTES TO CHAPTER 6

1. On St. Paul's, see Ralph Dutton, *The Age of Wren* (London: B. T. Batsford, Ltd., 1951), 31–35; Kerry Downes, *The Architecture of Wren,* 2nd ed. (n.p.: Redhedge, 1988 [Granada, 1982]), 51–67.

2. See Lydia M. Soo, *Wren's "Tracts" on Architecture and Other Writings* (Cambridge: Cambridge University Press, 1998), 4, 135.

3. An ardent anti-Catholic, Compton would become known for his efforts to bring Puritans back into the Church of England.

4. Soo, *Wren's "Tracts,"* 109.

5. Soo, *Wren's "Tracts,"* 274n8, quoting the *Journal Book of the Royal Society,* Royal Society, London, 7 (June 18, 1688). See also Penelope Gouk, "The Role of Acoustics and Music Theory in the Scientific Work of Robert Hooke," *Annals of Science* 37 (1980): 573–605.

6. Plans of several of the London churches appear in Downes, *Architecture of Wren,* 58–59. Illustrations and photographs of most of the buildings are available in Colin Amery, *Wren's London* (Luton, England: Lennard Publishing, 1988). See also Margaret Whinney, *Wren* (New York: Thames and Hudson, 1998 [London, 1971]).

7. Wren also created a new plan for the City of London, which imposed a rational, pattern of wheel hubs and grids on the previous tangle of medieval roads and passageways. The plan, however, was never implemented. See Amery, *Wren's London,* 6–7, 156–59.

8. Gospel accounts of Jesus himself set the prototype for outdoor preaching. Outdoor preaching was not uncommon in the medieval period, though it was looked down upon as not sanctioned by the church. Worship, in contrast, was restricted to indoor observance.

9. John Wesley, *The Journal of the Rev. John Wesley, A.M.,* ed. Nehemiah Curnock (London: Culley, 1909–1916), 5:187.

10. Benjamin Franklin, *The Autobiography of Benjamin Franklin*, eds. Leonard W. Labaree, Ralph L. Ketcham, Helen C. Boatfield, and Helene H. Fineman (New Haven, Conn.: Yale University Press, 1964), 179. The editors of the text point out that Franklin moves back about 500 feet from the courthouse steps, thus making his estimate faulty.

11. Rudolph Arnheim, *The Dynamics of Architectural Form* (Berkeley: University of California Press, 1977), 269.

12. Excellent works on evangelicalism include Nathan O. Hatch, *The Democratization of American Christianity* (New Haven, Conn.: Yale University Press, 1989); Charles Hambrick-Stowe, *Charles G. Finney and the Spirit of American Evangelicalism* (Grand Rapids, Mich.: Eerdmans, 1996); George M. Marsden, *Understanding Fundamentalism and Evangelicalism* (Grand Rapids, Mich.: Eerdmans, 1991).

13. On camp meetings, see Charles A. Johnson, *The Frontier Camp Meeting: Religion's Harvest Time* (Dallas: Southern Methodist University Press, 1955); and Steven D. Cooley, "Manna and the Manual: Sacramental and Instrumental Constructions of the Victorian Methodist Camp Meeting during the Mid-Nineteenth Century," *Religion and American Culture: A Journal of Interpretation* 6 (Summer 1996): 131–60.

14. See Jeanne Halgren Kilde, *When Church Became Theater: The Transformation of Evangelical Architecture and Worship in Nineteenth-Century America* (New York: Oxford University Press, 2002), 42–55.

15. On auditorium churches, see Kilde, *When Church Became Theater*, 112–96.

NOTES TO CHAPTER 7

1. See Michael Rose, *Ugly as Sin: Why They Changed Our Churches from Sacred Places to Meeting Spaces and How We Can Change Them Back Again* (Omaha, Neb.: Sophia Institute Press, 2001); and Steven J. Schloeder, *Architecture in Communion: Implementing the Second Vatican Council through Liturgy and Architecture* (San Francisco: Ignatius Press), 1998.

2. Thomas Merton, *The Sign of Jonas* (New York: Harcourt, Brace and Company, 1953), 77. This quotation appears on plaque near the Roofless Church in New Harmony, Indiana. The author is grateful to Dr. Paul M. Pearson and Mark C. Meade, CA, at the Thomas Merton Center at Bellarmine University for tracking down this citation.

3. Phoebe B. Stanton, *The Gothic Revival and American Church Architecture: An Episode in Taste, 1840–1856* (Baltimore: Johns Hopkins University Press, 1968), xxi.

4. Richard Kieckhefer points out that the revival of architectural styles has roots as early as the fifth century when church builders under Pope Sixtus III adopted pre-Constantinian basilicas. Richard Kieckhefer, *Theology in Stone: Church Architecture from Byzantium to Berkeley* (New York: Oxford University Press, 2004), 296–97.

5. See Jeanne Halgren Kilde, *When Church Became Theater: Evangelical Architecture and Worship in Nineteenth-Century America* (New York: Oxford University Press, 2002), 56–76.

6. See Jeanne Halgren Kilde, "Church Architecture and the Second Great Awakening: Revivalism, Space, and Politics," *New Perspectives on North American Revivalism,* ed. Michael J. McClymond (Baltimore: Johns Hopkins University Press, 2004), 84–108.

7. On Modernism, see Marvin Trachtenberg and Isabelle Hyman, *Architecture: From Prehistory to Postmodernity,* 2nd ed. (Upper Saddle, N.J.: Prentice-Hall, 2002), 465–66.

8. Some early Roman churches included two ambos, one for the reading of the Epistle and one for the reading of the Gospel.

9. On the liturgical movement of this period and the split chancel church, see David Ralph Bains, "The Liturgical Impulse in Mid-Twentieth-Century American Mainline Protestantism" (Ph.D. diss., Harvard University, 1999).

10. James F. White, *Roman Catholic Worship: Trent to Today,* 2nd ed. (Collegeville, Minn.: Liturgical Press, 2003), 81, quoting R. Kevin Seasoltz, *The New Liturgy: A Documentation, 1903–1965* (New York: Herder and Herder, 1966), 4.

11. White, *Roman Catholic Worship,* 81, quoting Seasoltz, *The New Liturgy,* 13.

12. André Haquin, "The Liturgical Movement and Catholic Ritual Revision," *The Oxford History of Christian Worship,* eds. Geoffrey Wainwright and Karen B. Westerfield Tucker (New York: Oxford University Press, 2006), 699.

13. See White, *Roman Catholic Worship,* 82.

14. See Saint John's Abbey, "History of Worship," http://www.saintjohnsabbey .org/worship/worship/page1.htm, accessed June 16, 2007.

15. Haquin, "Liturgical Movement," 702.

16. White, *Roman Catholic Worship,* 83.

17. White, *Roman Catholic Worship,* 85.

18. See Marvin Trachtenberg and Isabelle Hyman, *Architecture from Prehistory to Postmodernity,* 2nd ed. (Upper Saddle River, N.J.: Prentice-Hall, 2002), 488.

19. On the original plan of Sagrada Família, see *Gaudí and Art Nouveau in Catalonia,* http://www.gaudiallgaudi.com/AA012.htm.

20. Brainy Quote, http://www.brainyquote.com/quotes/quotes/a/antoniogau 291541.html (accessed January 28, 2008).

21. Hegel, *Philosophy of Art.* As quoted in Peter Collins, *Changing Ideals in Modern Architecture, 1750–1950,* 2nd ed. (Montreal: McGill-Queens University Press, 1998), 286.

22. On Jones, see Jeanne Halgren Kilde, *When Church Became Theater: Evangelical Architecture and Worship in Nineteenth-Century America* (New York: Oxford University Press, 2002), 141; and Joseph Siry, "Frank Lloyd Wright's Unity Temple and Architecture for Liberal Religion in Chicago, 1885–1909, *Art Bulletin* 73 (June 1991): 257–59.

23. This is not to say that spaces determine action or behavior, though some have argued that they do.

24. This strategy, which moves beyond the modernist rejection of sociohistorical meaning, has earned the building attention as one of the first postmodern buildings.

See Charles Jencks, *Le Corbusier and the Continual Revolution in Architecture* (New York: The Monacelli Press, 2000), 262–75.

25. Jencks, *Le Corbusier*, 261, 265.

26. Jonathan Z. Smith, *To Take Place: Toward Theory in Ritual* (Chicago: University of Chicago Press, 1987), 103.

27. On Schwarz, see Kieckhefer, *Theology in Stone*, 232–48, and Schloeder, *Architecture in Communion*, 234–38.

28. Victoria M. Young, in particular, makes this argument in her analysis of the Abbey Church of Saint John's. See "St. John's Abbey Church, Collegeville, Minnesota (1953–1961): The Benedictines and Marcel Breuer Search for the Sacred," Ph.D. diss., University of Virginia, 2003.

29. Walter M. Abbott, ed. *Documents of Vatican II* (New York: Guild Press, 1966), 152.

30. Abbott, *Document of Vatican II*, 155.

31. Abbott, *Document of Vatican II*, 148.

32. White, *Roman Catholic Worship*, 124.

33. Merton, *Sign of Jonas*, 86–87.

34. E. A. Sovik, *Architecture for Worship* (Minneapolis: Augsburg Publishing House, 1973), 39.

35. On Graham, see Jon Butler, "Religion in New York City: Faith that Could Not Be," *U.S. Catholic Historian* 2 (Spring 2004), 51–61.

36. For instance, see Beth Hawkins, "Getting Rich with God," *(Twin Cities) City Pages*, Dec. 13, 2006. For a more complete analysis of megachurch spaces, see Jeanne Halgren Kilde, "Reading Megachurches: Investigating the Religious and Cultural Work of Church Architecture," in *American Sanctuary: Understanding Sacred Spaces*, ed. Louis P. Nelson, 225–49 (Bloomington: Indiana University Press, 2006).

Glossary of Architectural Terms

abbey A monastery or convent supervised by an abbot or abbess, or a church that is part of a monastery or convent.

aisle Part of the main room of a church, demarked laterally from the nave by a colonnade or row of columns.

altarpiece A carving, painting, or other artwork that is placed on the wall above and behind the altar.

ambo In the Constantinian and Byzantine periods, a pulpit or raised stand located in the front of a church from which scripture was read and homilies delivered during services.

ambulatory A semicircular walkway enclosing the sanctuary apse, which provides access to chapels radiating from the apse.

amphitheater An oval, round, or semicircular theater structure having rows of raked seats rising from a central open space at the center.

apse A domed, semicircular space projecting from the side of a church, usually housing a chapel.

arch A structural or supporting element in buildings. Roman arch: an arch that is rounded or semicircular at the top. Gothic arch: an arch that comes to a point at the top.

architrave In classical architecture, the lowest of the three main parts of an entablature, which rests directly on the columns.

atrium   An inner court of a building or house, open to the sky or covered with skylights. The inner, open-air court of a Roman house.

auditorium plan   A church plan of square, oblong, or round shape, in which the seating curves around the pulpit area (usually a pulpit platform) and slopes from the back of the room down to the pulpit.

aula ecclesiae   An early Christian meeting space (ecclesia) consisting of a rectangular room or hall (aula).

aumbry (also ambry)   A cupboard or niche in the front of the church used for the safekeeping of vessels, particularly those containing the consecrated Host and wine of the Eucharist service.

axis   A straight line or path from the entry of a longitudinal plan church to the chancel.

baldacchino (also baldachin)   A canopy of marble, stone, wood, or fabric placed over an altar, throne, or other sacred or important site.

balustrade   A series of short posts or balusters supporting a rail, used in churches in the front of galleries and as altar rails. See also *parapet*.

baptistery   A room in which baptisms are performed.

basilica   A Roman public meeting hall, rectangular in plan, featuring a narthex or entry area, a nave with two or more side aisles defined by rows of columns, and terminating in an apse. In the Constantinian period, this spatial plan was widely adopted for Christian architecture.

bema   A raised area at the front of a church or other public meeting room, reserved for dignitaries. In churches, the sanctuary.

battered wall (batter)   An inclined face of a wall.

cathedral   A church that houses the throne of the bishop, called the cathedra.

centralized plan   A symmetrical spatial plan in which, generally, all sides radiate equally from a central point. For instance, a square or circular plan. Symmetrical plans such as the Greek cross are also considered centralized though they not radiate equally in all directions.

chancel   The sanctuary of a church, extending from the raised or otherwise demarcated separation from the nave through the choir (if present) and to the front wall of the church, usually located in an apse.

chantry   A building or chapel dedicated to the performance of masses for the souls of the dead. The term is also used for the endowment to cover the expenses of such masses.

choir   The area of a church reserved for the seating of singers who perform during services. Part of the chancel in medieval churches.

ciborium   A vaulted canopy placed over an altar (a baldacchino) or a covered receptacle for the consecrated Host.

clerestory   The upper walls of the nave, transepts, and choir, which is usually pierced by windows.

cloister   A covered walkway with an open colonnade on one side, running along the outer wall of a building and connecting an abbey church with other parts of the monastery.

colonnade   A row of columns supporting an entablature, arches, gallery, or roof.

columb   A niche in the wall in the front of the church for the safekeeping of vessels containing the consecrated Host and wine of the Eucharist service. An aumbry.

crossing   The point in a church plan at which the transept intersects the nave.

cruciform   In the shape of a cross.

dado   The lower portion of a wall.

dais   A raised platform in the front of a meeting room for dignitaries.

domus ecclesiae   An early Christian meeting space within a residential setting, often within a house; literally, the "house church" or "house assembly."

drum   A round vertical wall supporting a dome.

embrasure   A recess for a window, usually splayed on the inside.

entablature   In classical architecture, the horizontal rail, consisting of three levels, that is supported by columns.

envelope   The outer walls or shell of a building.

exedra   A semicircular recess or projection from the side of a building, containing a seat.

ferroconcrete   Concrete reinforced with iron bars, the precursor to steel-reinforced concrete.

fresco   An artistic technique of painting on wet or moist plaster using water-soluble pigment.

gallery   A balcony, supported by arches or columns and providing seating.

Greek cross plan   A spatial plan in the shape of a cross with four arms of equal length.

Holy Door   In Byzantine churches, the center door through the iconostasis leading into the sanctuary.

iconostasis   In Byzantine churches, a segmented screen several feet high, separating the sanctuary from the nave and pierced by three doors. Icons of saints appear in each niche within the iconostasis.

lancet window   In Gothic architecture, long, narrow windows pointed at the top like a spear.

Latin cross plan   A spatial plan in the form of a cross with a long arm intersected near to top by a shorter transept.

loge   In the early church, a dais located to the right side of the sanctuary and reserved for the emperor and political dignitaries.

loggia   An open-sided gallery or arcade along a building.

martyrium   A building used to house the remains of the honored dead and in which ceremonies in honor of those individuals are performed.

meetinghouse   A building used by sixteenth- and seventeenth-century Puritans and other groups for public assemblies and religious services. A physically austere building used for worship.

mosaic   An artistic technique using small pieces of colored glass or stone to create an image.

naos   In a Greek temple, the innermost area, enclosed by walls, in which the statue of the god stood.

narthex   A portico or vestibule at the entry of a church, usually separated from the nave by a rail or screen.

nave   In a basilica, the center aisle extending from the narthex to the sanctuary or chancel. More generally, the center aisle and congregational space of an oblong church.

niche   A recess in a wall or pier, usually housing a statue or urn.

oculus   A circular opening in the top of a dome or in a wall.

parapet   A low wall placed to protect people from falling over a sudden drop-off. The low front wall of a gallery.

pediment   A low-pitched gable resting on an entablature above a portico.

pendentives   A triangular support connecting the corner of two adjacent walls or arches with the drum of a dome.

peristyle   A series of columns surrounding a building or open court.

portico   A roofed porch, usually at the entry to a building.

post-and-lintel   A supporting structure consisting of two vertical "posts" supporting a horizontal rail or "lintel."

preaching hall   A church type popularized in the eighteenth century, consisting of a longitudinally oriented, rectangular or oblong space, with a pulpit at one end, and often including galleries.

pulpit platform   In nineteenth-century churches, a bema raised several feet above the main floor, housing a central pulpit and seating for several dignitaries and for the choir.

refectory   A dining hall.

reredos   The wall or screen behind an altar, often highly ornamented with niches and statuary.

rood   Literally "cross" in Saxon. Rood beam: a large wooden beam surmounted by a cross over the crossing in a medieval church. Rood screen: a high screen separating the sanctuary from the nave in a medieval church.

rotunda   The circular area in a church beneath the dome.

sacristy   A room used for the storage of vessels, vestments, and other sacred objects. A vestry.

sanctuary   The space in the church around the altar. More generally, a room in which religious services are held.

scriptorium   A room in a monastery used for the copying, writing, or illuminating of manuscripts.

solea   In the early Byzantine church, the raised pathway lined by parapets, between the ambo and the bema.

synthronon   In Roman buildings and early churches, a semicircle of tiered seats or benches lining the wall of the apse.

tabernacle   A canopied receptacle placed on the altar and containing the consecrated host and wine of the Eucharist. A building or temporary structure for religious services.

transept   The traverse arms of a cross-shaped plan. A transept crossing partway down the main space forms a Latin cross space. A transept located at the top end of the main space to form a T is called a "headed transept."

tribunal   A dais.

triclinium   The dining room in a Roman house.

tympanum   The semicircular area over a doorway, between the lintel and an arch above.

vault   An arched ceiling or roof. Barrel vaults use round arches, whereas pointed or Gothic arches are used to create a variety of vaults, such as rib and fan vaults.

vestry   A room in a church used for the storage of religious vestments and sacred objects and where the clergy don vestments prior to services.

vestibule   A small entry room or passage between rooms.

voussoir   A wedge-shaped stone or brick forming the top of an arch.

Index

Salvatoris, Basilica, 40, 41
Sancroft, William, 137
sanctuary, 56, 50–51, 72, 73–74, 177
   screening of, 49, 213n22
   See also altar; chancel
San Sorvino, Abbey of, Pisa, Italy, 95
Santa Maria della Consolazione, Todi, Italy,
   101–2
Santa Maria delle Carceri, Pronto, Italy,
   96
Santa Maria delle Grazie, Milan, 109
Santiago de Compostela, Spain, 84, 203n7
San Vitale, Ravenna, Italy, 210n16
sarcophagus, 36, 208n59
Savonarola, Girolamo, 111
Schloeder, Steven, J., 161
Schneider, Richard, 85
Schwartz, Rudolf, 187
seating in churches, 118–19, 140, 149–51
   arrangements, 183, 187, 189, 194
   as a congregation, 122
   egalitarianism in, 178–79
   by gender, 27, 51, 119, 125, 208n55
   hierarchical organization of, 120
   See also pews
Second Vatican Council, 188–90
Serlio, Sabastiano, 121
Shakers, 153
Sheldonian Theater, Oxford, England, 135
Sienna, Cathedral of, 95
Smith, Jonathan Z., 6–7, 8, 9, 29, 46, 185
Snyder, Graydon, 34
Soo, Lydia, 137, 139
Sovik, Edward A., 192
space, awareness of, 177–79, 181, 183–85
Spicer, Andrew, 124
stained glass, 66, 69, 163, 171, 177, 181,
   194
Stanton, Phoebe, 165
Stations of the Cross, 86, 185
stave churches, 86–88
steeples, 62–63, 140, 193
Stettin Castle (Schloss Stettin), Moravian
   Silesia, Czech Republic, 120
Storme, Albert, 81
Stroik, Duncan, 197
Suger, Abbot, 69
Sunday schools, 158
synagogues, 15, 28, 207n45
synthronon, 48, 49, 72, 176

tabernacle, 77
temples, 37, 211n29
   divine power in, 14–15
   Greek, 5
   Hindu, 5
   Jewish, 5, 7–8, 9, 14–15
   preparation for entering, 8
   Protestant, 120–25
Ten Commandments, 123
Tertullian, 24, 43
Tetzel, Johann, 111–12
theaters, 135, 150
Thomas à Becket, Saint, shrine of,
   Canterbury, England, 84
Thompson, Milo, 194
Tintern Abbey, Monmouthshire, Wales, 127
Trachtenberg, Marvin, 97
Tree of Life, 85
Trent, Council of, 64, 98, 99–102, 107, 110,
   121, 128, 169
tribunal, 31, 207n41
   See also bema; dais
triclinium, 19–24, 30, 37
Trinity, 5, 67
Trinity Episcopal Church, New Haven,
   Conn., 164
Troas, 22

Unitarians, 95, 178
Unity Temple, Oak Park, Ill., 178–81
Upjohn, Richard, 165

vestments, 74, 133
Vézelay Abbey, Bourgogne, France, 84
Via Dolorosa, Jerusalem, 84, 86
Vitruvius, 20, 95, 102

Waltham Abbey Church, Essex, England,
   127
Washington Hebrew Congregation,
   Washington, D.C., 206n38
Wesley Chapel, London, 148
Wesley, John, 146, 151
   at Gwennap Pit, 147
Westminster Abbey, London, 79, 80
Westminster Presbyterian Church,
   Minneapolis, Minn., 156–57
Whitby Abbey, Yorkshire, England, 127
Whitefield, George, 146, 147–48, 151
Whitefield's Tabernacle, London, 148